# Charting the Course of Psalms Research

# Charting the Course of Psalms Research

Erhard S. Gerstenberger

Edited by
K. C. Hanson

James Clarke & Co.

James Clarke & Co.
P.O. Box 60
Cambridge
CB1 2NT
United Kingdom

www.jamesclarke.co
publishing@jamesclarke.co

Paperback ISBN: 978 0 227 18001 3
PDF ISBN: 978 0 227 18002 0

*British Library Cataloguing in Publication Data*
A record is available from the British Library

First published by Cascade Books, 2022

This edition published by James Clarke & Co., 2024,
by arrangement with Wipf and Stock Publishers

Copyright © Erhard S. Gerstenberger, 2022

All rights reserved. No part of this edition may be reproduced, stored electronically or in any retrieval system, or transmitted in any form or by any means, electronic, mechanical, photocopying, recording, or otherwise, without prior written permission from the Publisher (permissions@jamesclarke.co).

This collection of Psalm studies written over a period of about sixty years is dedicated to all, students, friends, colleages at Yale Divinity school, the parish of Essen-Frohnhausen, the Escola Superior de Teologia, São Leopoldo, Brazil, the theological faculties of Giessen and Marburg. In particular, however, I am thinking of three good friends, who sometimes sternly rejected one or the other of my conclusions: Erich Zenger, Klaus Seybold, and Patrick D. Miller.

# Contents

*Editor's Foreword by K. C. Hanson* | ix
*Preface* | xi
*Acknowledgments* | xv
*List of Abbreviations* | xvii

1 The Lyrical Literature | 1
2 The Psalms in Form-Critical Perspective | 31
3 The Psalms: Genres, Life-Situations, and Theologies—Towards a Hermeneutics of Social Stratification | 74
4 Theologies in the Book of Psalms | 87
5 Modes of Communication with the Divine in the Hebrew Psalter | 107
6 The Psalms and Ritual Praxis | 127
7 Non-Temple Psalms: Their Cultic Setting Revisited | 143
8 The Psalter as Book and as Collection | 156

*Bibliography* | 167
*Author Index* | 189
*Scripture Index* | 195

Contents

# Editor's Foreword

THIS VOLUME IS THE first of three essay collections on the book of Psalms by Erhard S. Gerstenberger. It draws together those essays that focus on the big-picture issues for biblical interpreters.

Gerstenberger is not simply an experienced exegete of the Psalms—he is a trailblazer and leader in the field. It is helpful to put his interpretive work in the context of some of his major publications. Since the publication of his *Habilitationschrift* in 1980, *Der bittende Mensch: Bittritual und Klagelied des Einzelnen im Alten Testament* (The Petitioning Person: Petition Ritual and Complaint Song of the Individual in the Old Testament) Neukirchener Verlag (reprint, Wipf and Stock, 2009), he has been recognized as someone who both builds on the exegetical tradition and also forges new paths. In that volume, he creatively uses not only form criticism and tradition history, but anthropology, communication theory, and ritual studies in an integrated way, and throughout with a view to an in-depth analysis of the comparative ancient Near Eastern texts. This broad-ranging approach is seen in the essays of this volume as well.

This path led Gerstenberger to write his two-volume commentary on the Psalms for the series The Forms of the Old Testament Literature (Eerdmans): *Psalms, Part 1: With an Introduction to Cultic Poetry* (1988), and *Psalms, Part 2, and Lamentations* (2001). These volumes demonstrate on a text-by-text basis his sensitivity to the genres, the settings, the theologies, and the tradition history, expanding our vision throughout. Especially noteworthy in those volumes is his sensitivity to how the historical experiences in the Babylonian exile and the post-exilic Persian era shifted the frame of reference for many psalms as community worship and synagogal services emerged. And related in this respect is his *Israel in der Perserzeit: 5. und 4. Jahrhundert v. Chr.*, in the series Biblische Enzyklopädie (Kohlhammer, 2005), translated as *Israel in the Persian Period: The Fifth and Fourth Centuries B.C.E.*, in the series Biblical Encyclopedia (Society of Biblical Literature, 2011).

Another major work is his *Theologien im Alten Testament* (Kohlhammer, 2001), which was published in English as *Theologies in the Old Testament* (Fortress, 2002). This is relevant here because it addresses the major settings of religious experience and ritual practice in the family, the village, the tribe, and the kingdom. Here Gerstenberger brings to the fore how situational religious experience and practice are enacted. This, of course, impinges on how he addresses the issue of setting for the Psalms in particular.

The first two essays in the present collection are reviews of the secondary literature—the first on all of the "lyrical literature" in the Old Testament, and the second on the history of interpretation of the book of Psalms from a form-critical perspective. While these sorts of reviews might not interest some readers, anyone who wants to develop a clear sense for both the gains of exegetical research as well as some of the dead-end avenues will find them engaging and illuminating. While research has proceeded since these essays first appeared, they remain relevant and helpful touchstones in charting the course of where we have been and where we can go.

The rest of the essays explore the varieties of social settings of the Psalms, the connection between social setting and theology, communication theory, the relationship between psalms and ritual practice, the relationship between so-called wisdom psalms and cult, and the interpretive approach to the book of Psalms in its final form.

It is also relevant to note that just as Gerstenberger continues to pursue his interpretation of the biblical psalms, he has also pursued his longstanding interest in the Mesopotamian tradition. In 2014, in his retirement, he completed another doctoral degree in Sumerian at the University of Marburg, where he taught for so many years. In 2018 it was published as *Theologie des Lobens in sumerischen Hymnen: Zur Ideengeschichte der Eulogie* (Theology of Praise in Sumerian Hymns: On the History of Ideas of the Eulogy) in the series Orientalische Religionen in der Antike: Ägypten, Israel, Alter Orient from Mohr Siebeck.

As editor, I organized each of the volumes, and I edited them primarily in standardizing the format and notes as well as creating the comprehensive bibliography and indexes. I have also added to the notes and bibliography the recent English translations of two important works: Gunkel and Begrich, *Introduction to Psalms* (1998; reprint 2002), and Mowinckel, *Psalm Studies* (2014). I also translated chapters six and eight, with the author's helpful guidance.

K. C. Hanson

August 19, 2022

# Preface

THE OLD TESTAMENT PSALTER comprises an amazing variety of poems. Their common denominator seems to be a thoroughly spiritual and mostly liturgical perspective on life, world, and Deity, as may be suggested already by their poetical forms. This means: The Psalms are definitely not doctrinal treatises or theological pamphlets. Rather they modulate the deepest feelings of individuals or communities, even if they have to be performed in calculated ceremonies by trained experts. The Psalter is surely the richest "book" (is it really a book?) of the Hebrew Scriptures, in terms of personal commitment, spirituality, openness to the Divine. And it has been commented upon, translated, and retold—as well as having instigated new kinds of psalmic literature through the centuries, which fill libraries.

My own preoccupation with Old Testament psalms grew out of a prior immersion into legal traditions of ancient Israel. It was Hans Walter Wolff who suggested that I investigate "apodictic law" in the wake of Albrecht Alt's thesis of its being unique in the Bible. Martin Noth accepted my critical study in 1960 as a doctoral dissertation, *Wesen und Herkunft des "Apodiktischen Rechts"* (The Nature and Origin of "Apodictic Law," published in 1965 by Neukirchener Verlag; reprint, Wipf and Stock, 2009). Further research especially in cultic regulations stimulated questions pertaining to ceremonial and oral performances, e.g., around sacrifices. The invitation of Rolf Knierim and Gene Tucker to join The Forms of Old Testament Literature commentary team was a strong motivation to fully delve into the study of the Psalms. I worked on this project for many years; the first volume appeared in 1988, the second in 2001 (both published by Eerdmans), and there are no German originals. Also, my habilitation work, again due to a suggestion of Hans Walter Wolff, concentrated on the most frequent genre of Old Testament psalms, the "complaints of the individual," published as *Der bittende Mensch* in 1980 by Neukirchener Verlag (reprint, Wipf and Stock, 2009).

Through all these years of research in the Psalter my conviction that psalmic poetry grew out of diverse and real life-situations kept growing. Not in the sense that each individual text represented a spontaneous utterance captured by chance by an attentive scribe. Artistic language, imagery, style, contents, and intention proved most of the poems to have flown out of the experience of experts in their fields. Neither would the real-life label diminish the importance of literary fixation of extant psalms and their possible use as reading material in literate societies. But the original and enduring *Sitz im Leben* of the psalms were various performative acts around individuals or social groups and their life-concerns, such as physical and spiritual needs, experienced help and gifts from deities, educative meditations, etc. The psalms thus reflect the wide variety of existential life-experiences in relation to God and the world, the basics of human being. If they are sometimes polemical against "other gods" or foes and enemies, they are also wide open to foreign influences, experiences of empathy, and desire for peace.

From an interreligious perspective it is small wonder that psalmic poetry is well-known and much used in many other cultures, both ancient and modern. The vast corpus of Sumero-Akkadian literature also contains numerous collections of psalm-genres, which quite often indicate exact descriptions of their performative, ritual use and the performer who would stage the concomitant ceremony. This material always, with its discovery, challenged Old Testament researchers to draw comparisons with ancient Israelite texts and cautiously draw conclusions for the practical use of the latter ones in their different but analogous situations. Traditional societies even today often cling to age-old rituals employing psalm-poetry, which have sprung up as conscious revivifications of ancient ceremonies, for example of the shamanistic type. All this should make us aware of the extraordinary power of performed poetry. I do not hesitate to include modern pop-music, which quite frequently has a cultic character, taking on functions similar to psalmic poetry of ancient times. We may even point out the present-day relationship between written and sung or performed presentations today being in line with ancient customs: written texts are not ends in themselves but underline or assist the orally presented main form of a given psalm or song.

The collection of some of my studies on the Old Testament Psalms, kindly prepared by my friend K. C. Hanson, clearly shows the immense value of this influential, many times acutely important poetry within all Jewish and Christian communities and far beyond their boundaries. There is much to be done for really understanding these precious texts, and even a long life is much too short to achieve such a goal.

Erhard S. Gerstenberger

# Acknowledgments

ABOUT SIXTY YEARS OF Psalm research, and a final edition of some twenty-four essays in three volumes certainly requires the brains and hands of many people. The author of texts is but the point of crystallization. From beginning to the end, there are many contributors to the finished work (note dedication!). At the end, this collection would not have been possible at all without the vision, energy, and continuous effort of my friend K.C. Hanson, who not only translated two essays (ch. 6 and 8) from the original German, but did all the editing work, including a delightful thematic composition of the widely dispersed articles bringing to light their inner affinity. Furthermore, I want to mention the skillful hands of Wipf and Stock's technicians and artists, notably Calvin Jaffarian, Jonathan Hill, and in the business sector Jason Robek. To all these architects of the present and coming volumes, my heartfelt thanks. A special word of gratitude must go to the generous first publishers of the selected essays who granted license for reprinting.

The author and publisher gratefully acknowledge the earlier publications of these essays and permission from the original publishers.

Chapter 1: "The Lyrical Literature" first appeared in *The Hebrew Bible and Its Modern Interpreters*, edited by Douglas A. Knight and Gene M. Tucker, 409–44. Philadelphia: Fortress, 1985.

Chapter 2: "The Psalms in Form-Critical Perspective" first appeared as "The Psalms," in *Old Testament Form Criticism*, edited by John H. Hayes, 179–223. Trinity University Monograph Series in Religion 2. San Antonio: Trinity University Press, 1974.

Chapter 3: "The Psalms: Genres, Life-Situations, and Theologies—Towards a Hermeneutics of Social Stratification" first appeared in *Diachronic and Synchronic: Reading the Psalms in Real Time. Proceedings of the Baylor Symposium on the Book of Psalms*, edited by Joel S. Burnett et al., 81–92. LHBOTS 488. London: T. & T. Clark, 2007.

Chapter 4: "Theologies in the Book of Psalms" first appeared in *The Book of Psalms: Composition and Reception*, edited by Peter W. Flint and Patrick D. Miller Jr., 603–25. VTSup 99. Leiden: Brill, 2005.

Chapter 5: "Modes of Communication with the Divine in the Hebrew Psalter" first appeared in *Mediating between Heaven and Earth: Communication with the Divine in the Ancient Near East*, edited by C. L. Crouch et al., 93–113. LHBOTS 566. London: T. & T. Clark, 2012.

Chapter 6: "The Psalms and Ritual Practice" first appeared as "Psalmen und Ritualpraxis." In *Ritual und Poesie: Formen und Orte religiöser Dichtung im Alten Orient, im Judentum und im Christentum*, edited by Erich Zenger, 73–90. Herders biblischen Studien 36. Freiburg: Herder, 2003.

Chapter 7: "Non-Temple Psalms: Their Cultic Setting Revisited" first appeared in *The Oxford Handbook of the Psalms*, edited by William P. Brown, 338–49. Oxford Handbooks. Oxford: Oxford University Press, 2014.

Chapter 8: "The Psalter as Book and as Collection" first appeared as "Der Psalter als Buch und als Sammlung," in *Neue Wege der Psalmenforschung: Für Walter Beyerlin*, edited by Klaus Seybold and Erich Zenger, 3–13. 2nd ed. Herders biblische Studien 1. Freiburg: Herder 1994.

# Abbreviations

| | |
|---|---|
| AB | Anchor Bible |
| ANET | James B. Pritchard, ed., *Ancient Near Eastern Texts Relating to the Old Testament*, 3rd ed. Princeton: Princeton University Press, 1969 |
| ANVAO | Avhandlinger utg. av det Norske videnskaps-akademi i Oslo |
| AOAT | Alter Orient und Altes Testament |
| *Bib* | *Biblica* |
| BKAT | Biblischer Kommentar: Altes Testament |
| BWANT | Beiträge zur Wissenschaft vom Alten und Neuen Testament |
| BZAW | Beihefte zur Zeitschrift für die alttestamentliche Wissenschaft |
| *CBQ* | *Catholic Biblical Quarterly* |
| FOTL | The Forms of the Old Testament Literature |
| FRLANT | Forschungen zur Religion und Literatur des Alten und Neuen Testaments |
| HKAT | Handkommentar zum Alten Testament |
| HKATErg | Handkommentar zum Alten Testament, Ergänzungsband |
| *HTR* | *Harvard Theological Review* |
| *HUCA* | *Hebrew Union College Annual* |
| *IDB* | *Interpreter's Dictionary of the Bible.* Edited by George Arthur Buttrick. 4 vols. Nashville: Abingdon, 1962 |
| *JBL* | *Journal of Biblical Literature* |
| JSOT | Journal for the Study of the Old Testament |
| JSOTSup | Journal for the Study of the Old Testament Supplement Series |

| | |
|---|---|
| *JSS* | *Journal of Semitic Studies* |
| LAI | Library of Ancient Israel |
| LHBOTS | Library of Hebrew Bible / Old Testament Studies |
| LXX | Septuagint |
| MT | Masoretic text |
| OBO | Orbis biblicus et orientalis |
| *RB* | *Revue biblique* |
| SBLDS | Society of Biblical Literature Dissertation Series |
| SBS | Stuttgarter Bibelstudien |
| TB | Theologische Bücherei |
| *TDOT* | *Theological Dictionary of the Old Testament.* Edited by G. Johannes Botterweck, Helmer Ringgren, and Heinz-Josef Fabray. 17 vols. Translated by David E. Green et al. Grand Rapids: Eerdmans, 1974–2021 |
| *TRu* | *Theologische Rundschau* |
| *TWAT* | *Theologische Wörterbuch zum Alten Testament.* Edited by G. Johannes Botterweck, Helmer Ringgren and Heinz-Josef Fabray. 10 vols. Stuttgart: Kohlhammer, 1973–2015 |
| *VT* | *Vetus Testamentum* |
| VTSup | Vetus Testamentum Supplements |
| *VuF* | *Verkündigung und Forschung* |
| WMANT | Wissenschaftliche Monographien zum Alten und Neuen Testament |
| ZAW | *Zeitschrift für die alttestamentliche Wissenschaft* |
| ZTK | *Zeitschrift für Theologie und Kirche* |

# 1

# The Lyrical Literature

## Lyrics in the Hebrew Scriptures

IS IT APPROPRIATE TO employ a Greek term to identify a complex body of literature in the Hebrew scriptures? Lyric/lyrical is derived from "lyre" or "harp," and for many it brings to mind images of romantic individualism and sentimentality. However, that part of the Hebrew scriptures under discussion here is all but void of such romanticizing features. Lyrics in this case, even though implying poetry set to music and accompanied by stringed and other instruments, designates compositions deeply rooted in the life and work, war and cult of the Israelite people. No matter how varied such "lyrical" manifestations may appear, they have in common just this social, festive, and ritual dimension. Thus, if the Greek concept is understood in this extended sense, it can legitimately be applied to this body of Hebrew materials.

The lyrical literature of the Hebrew scriptures is found primarily in the books of Psalms, Lamentations, and the Song of Songs. It is generally recognized, however, that lyrical materials have also been combined with other literary genres in the Hebrew Bible—most notably with narrative, prophecy, and wisdom. Thus, Judges 5 (victory song), Isaiah 12 (thanksgiving hymn), and Job 30 (personal lament), although representing different categories of lyrical literature, are illustrative of the way in which this type of material has been incorporated into a number of different literary contexts. In addition, poetic oratory has influenced the style of a number of other genres in the Hebrew scriptures, although we cannot disregard the differences between the poetic styles of prophecy and wisdom, epic and lyric. However, in spite of obvious points of contact and interrelationship with other literary genres, we must remember that the lyrical materials of the Hebrew Bible constitute a separate body of literature that is distinguishable by particular characteristics. The distinctive linguistic structure of the lyrical literature, its musical qualities, and its ritualistic setting, all serve to identify it as a separate literary genre and consequently call for a method of analysis responsive to the particular characteristics and needs of the Hebrew poetic materials. In addition to providing a general knowledge of the content and form of the Hebrew lyrical literature, the study of this material is significant in view of its influence on our own culture and faith. The Psalms have inspired liturgy, songs, and prayer in both the Jewish and Christian communities. The theological affirmations of this literature have profoundly molded the thinking of many religious figures in the past and continue to play a vital role in modern theological movements, especially in the Third World.[1] Moreover, the ongoing spiritual power of Israel's poetry transcends its spiritual communities; its influence is discernible not only in the religious sphere but also in modern literature, poetry, and art.[2]

Research since 1945 on Israel's lyrical material reflects this widespread influence. Studies with a direct bearing on lyrical literature range from archaeological reports to essays deeply rooted in philosophy and theology, from anthropological observations to historical and literary scrutinies. The great variety of methods and perspectives represented by these studies, as well as the sheer mass of relevant publications, prohibits extensive discussion of all items. The aim of this study, then, is to provide an overview of the research done on the lyrical material of the Hebrew Bible since 1945 and to serve as an introduction to the most significant issues and findings of that research.

## Text Criticism

The foundation of any exegetical endeavor is the painstaking work of recovering the oldest possible wording of the text. Unfortunately, because of its very nature and its widespread use throughout its history, the lyrical material in the Hebrew Bible has suffered considerable alteration and corruption. As a result, on almost every page the text poses more problems than the interpreter may be able to solve. In two new areas of research, the Dead Sea Scrolls and the Ugaritic materials, scholars are attempting to deal with these problems. By looking at their work, we can gain a representative picture of the state of modern text criticism of the lyrical literature.

When the discovery of the Dead Sea Scrolls was announced in 1947, hope was immediately kindled in the scholarly world that this could advance

---

1. See Cardenal, *Zerschneide*.
2. See Kurz, *Psalmen*.

the knowledge of archaic forms of Hebrew writings. However, the edition of the Qumran Psalms scroll[3] and its comparison with the Masoretic text (MT)[4] showed a surprising degree of agreement between these manuscripts, which originated centuries apart. While the Qumran community took great liberty in arranging the psalms and even in including noncanonical psalms, textual variants are at a minimum. Apart from the Psalms scroll, virtually no canonical material of the lyrical type has been found. The only other lyrical texts discovered at Qumran are *Hodayot*. These thanksgiving songs, however, represent a later stage of psalmody and allow for inference back to the MT only in exceptional cases.[5]

The materials found at Ugarit proved to be an extraordinary stimulus to text-critical work. Excavation began at Ugarit in 1929 and in subsequent years yielded hundreds of tablets containing poetic texts. Analysis of these texts revealed that the Ugaritic language was closely related to Hebrew and that Ugaritic poetic style was quite similar to that of Israelite poetry. Consequently, numerous scholars began to draw on this newly recovered vocabulary and poetic structure in order to solve textual enigmas in the MT, and many emendations and new meanings of difficult terms and passages in the Hebrew scriptures were proposed. The use of Ugaritic materials thus touches not only the establishment of the text but matters of philology as well. A host of specialist from any countries dedicated themselves to this study of the Ugaritic literature: C. Virolleaud, C. H. Gordon, J. Gray, G. R. Driver, R. Dussaud, W. F. Albright, F. M. Cross, M. H. Pope, O. Loretz, L. R. Fisher, J. C. de Moor, A. S. Kapelrud, H. Gese, U. Cassuto, S. E. Loewenstamm, L. Delekat, and many others.

However, none of these scholars has been more prolific than Mitchell Dahood, who has published numerous articles as well as a three-volume commentary on Psalms. Throughout his studies the working premise is that analogies established between the Ugaritic and Hebrew literature warrant direct inference from Ugaritic to Hebrew poetry and vocabulary; consequently, Dahood is largely concerned to emend the Hebrew text on the basis of Ugaritic parallels. To cite but one example: Ps 22:30 reads in Dahood's translation:

> Indeed to him shall bow down
>     All those who sleep in the nether world;

---

3. Sanders, *Dead Sea Psalms Scroll*.
4. Sanders, "Variorum"; Bardtke, *Liber Psalmorum*; Homan, "Comparative Study."
5. See Sukenik, *Dead Sea Scrolls*; and Mansoor, *Thanksgiving Hymns*.

> Before him shall bend the knee
> 
> All who have gone down to the mud.
> 
> For the Victor himself restores to life.⁶

Two principal emendations lead to this reading. The difficult *dšny* is held to be composed of the "relative pronoun *dī* as in Ugaritic and Aramaic, and *šēnē* < *yᵉšēnē*, from *yāšēn*, 'to sleep.'" The "Victor," on the other hand, emerges from an audacious new interpretation of the lexeme *l'*, which now becomes a "stative participle . . . from *l'y*, a root frequently attested in Ugaritic and Phoenician."⁷

Many scholars have protested Dahood's basic assumption and practice, however, as an unjustified and uncontrolled use of cognate material,⁸ and it is unlikely that many of Dahood's proposals will in the final analysis prove satisfactory. Yet he has made a significant contribution by provoking debate concerning the value and applicability of the Ugaritic materials to the Hebrew Bible in particular and the value of comparative vocabulary and literature studies in general.

Although the Dead Sea Scrolls and Ugaritic tablets have at times clarified difficult Masoretic wording, textual criticism of the Hebrew lyrical literature has basically been proceeding at a slow pace and without spectacular changes. Undoubtedly, scholars will continue to use information derived from such extra-biblical documents, including the newly discovered Ebla texts. Primary emphasis for text-critical studies, however, will continue to be on the Masoretic tradition, with secondary emphasis on the LXX and other ancient versions. Representative examples of this continuing approach in text-critical studies are those of Leveen and Schmuttermayr in Psalms;⁹ Albrektson, Bergler, Dahood, Gottlieb, and Hillers in Lamentations;¹⁰ and Pope and Schneekloth in the Song of Songs.¹¹

---

6. Dahood, *Psalms I*, 138.
7. Dahood, *Psalms I*, 143–44.
8. See Loretz, *Psalmen*.
9. Leveen, "Textual Problems"; Schuttermayr, *Psalm 18*; See Gerstenberger, "Zur Interpretation," 23–26.
10. Albrektson, *Studies*; Bergler, "Threni V"; Dahood, "New Readings"; Gottlieb, *Study*; and Hillers, *Lamentations*.
11. Pope, *Song of Songs*; and Schneekloth, "Targum."

## Lyrical/Poetic Language

Language is the basic material with which modern interpreters of ancient texts must work. The question in our case, then, is this: Do we find a particular poetic or lyrical language and linguistic structure in the Hebrew Bible? This issue has increasingly entered scholarly consciousness and debate, and much study has been done on the way in which lexicographical and syntactical units are structured in Israel's poetic literature. This section will discuss these overall cultural patterns of lyrical language. The more individual stylistic elements will be considered in the following section.

As early as 1753, Bishop Lowth described in considerable detail the outstanding characteristic of Hebrew and other ancient Near Eastern poetry—the parallelism of words and ideas in a given poetic unit. Scholars have studied and reevaluated this phenomenon ever since, but the accuracy of Lowth's observation is still accepted.[12] As Norman Gottwald observes, "Parallelism of thought, and corresponding word-mass, is the substance and mode of Hebrew poetic expression."[13] The continuing study of parallelism has isolated three or four principal types: synonymous, antithetic, synthetic, and climactic.[14] For the most part, there has been little alteration or modification of this basic schema. Although further types of parallelism have been proposed (e.g., the "coordinating" and "summarizing" parallelism of Horst), they have not been generally accepted. Proposals of this type do not, of course, in any way alter the overall significance of parallel stichoi (or cola) as being the most characteristic elements of the Hebrew poetic line.

The intricate problems of Hebrew meter are, however, more difficult to resolve. The modern urge to investigate questions of meter and rhythm in Hebrew poetry seems to derive less from the Hebrew scriptures themselves than from our classical forebears. After all, if the Greeks and the Romans knew and used a quantifying and accentuating verse melody, why should the Hebrews not have employed it also? Assuming, then, that the Israelites did seek to achieve metrical equilibrium in their poetry, the issue is whether they attained this by counting syllables or by counting stresses.

Experts are divided on this question. Continuing the work done by Bickell in the last century, Mowinckel and others have defended an alternating system, a regular sequence of stressed and unstressed syllables. Most scholars, however, including Robinson, Kraus, and Feuillet,[15] and

---

12. See G. B. Gray, *Forms*; Robinson, "Hebrew Poetic Form"; and Boling "'Synonymous' Parallelism."
13. Gottwald, "Poetry," 835.
14. Alonso Schökel, *Estudios*; Ridderbos, *Psalmen*; and Kosmala, "Form."
15. Robinson, *Poetry*; Kraus, *Psalmen*; and Feuillet, *Cantique des Cantiques*.

going back to Ley and Sievers,[16] prefer to see a system of accentuation more in line with the present Masoretic punctuation. Thus, for them the number of stressed syllables, usually separated by some number of unstressed ones, determines the balance of the line. The difficulty with both these interpretations is that these scholars must presuppose more than a millennium of linguistic history with no major changes in speech habits and grammar. This would be most unlikely. Between the time of the judges and that of the Masoretes profound shifts in spoken and written Hebrew occurred, not to mention the transition that took place in the very beginning of Israel's history from Aramaic to the language of Canaan. Given this historical perspective, it is little wonder that there is growing dissatisfaction in the scholarly world with any ironclad or exclusive theory regarding the meter and rhythm of Hebrew poetry.[17]

Indeed, Segert has revised and elaborated an older hypothesis of his own allowing for change and development in Hebrew poetry. In the beginning, he argues, Hebrew meter depended on verbal units, without regard to quantity or quality of syllables. Only later did Israelite poets adopt an accentuating beat as a schema for their compositions.[18] While such hypotheses as these help in clarifying the issues regarding meter in Hebrew poetry, the material condition of our sources and the lack of any reliable information make it altogether inadvisable to hope for clear-cut solutions. As Freedman observes, no "magic key has ever been found, or is likely to be."[19]

Inspired both by metrical and structural considerations, Fohrer challenged the hegemony of parallelism in Hebrew poetry. He describes a poetic system based on autonomous semi-stichs (*Kurzverse*—short lines).[20] His evidence includes, besides some acrostic psalms (Pss 111; 112; etc.), parts of prophetic speeches such as Isa 63:10. Mowinckel, on the other hand, contests this interpretation, which in his opinion relies on exceptional and unusual passages.[21] So far, then, this theory has found little support from other scholars, although Piatti comes to similar conclusions and some other exegetes will admit, rather reluctantly, the existence of verses that do not obey the rule of parallelism.[22]

16. Ley, *Grundzüge*; Sievers, *Metrische Studien*.
17. See Alonso Schökel, *Estudios*; and Freedman, "Poetry."
18. Segert, "Problems."
19. Freedman, "Poetry," 10.
20. Fohrer, "Über den Kurzvers."
21. Mowinckel, *Real and Apparent Tricola*.
22. Piatti, "I carmi alfabetici"; W. Rudolph, *Buch Ruth*, 122, 124, 125; Ridderbos, *Psalmen*, 12–13.

The use of a strophic structure in Hebrew poetry also remains a more or less open question. Those who claim that such structuring devices were used can point to Isa 5:1–7, which falls neatly into four strophes,[23] or to the refrains of Psalm 42/43 and also to the Song of Songs generally. However, such examples of carefully structured strophic poetry appear to be the exception rather than the rule. Ridderbos, a dedicated scholar of all kinds of poetic phenomena, rightly observes that "only in relatively few cases can we detect a formal regularity."[24] Somewhat more optimism regarding the possible organization of Hebrew poetry in stanzas is shown by Mowinckel, Montgomery, Baumann, Skehan, Kunz, Cross, Freedman, and many others. Further, we may suspect that if the occidental predilection for seeing strophic order prevails, analysis could degenerate into the construction of artificial strophic arrangements.

A significant innovation occurred in postwar studies when researchers identified nearly self-sufficient poetic elements smaller than the colon or line. This discovery bears a certain resemblance to the isolation of those components which make up atomic nuclei. Like subatomic particles, these self-sufficient elements in Hebrew poetry have been seen as the basic structural elements, as the kernels of Hebrew poetry, the building blocks used in the constructions. Consequently, a good number of scholars, beginning with H. L. Ginsberg, have dedicated themselves to this research.[25] While some investigations, notably the recent monograph by Watters,[26] have been criticized because of questionable methodology,[27] on the whole scholars agree that fixed formulaic expressions of various kinds do constitute important poetic devices.

The use of such fixed formulas extends far beyond the cultures of the ancient Near East. As anthropologists and experts on compositional techniques have noted, standard phrases are part of the stock of creative elements used by all poets. Their use is especially prevalent, however, in the oral phase of poetic literature. Scholars of the Hebrew Bible have drawn on these general observations and have applied them to the questions of the setting and structure of Hebrew poetry. Thus, in the light of the general trend toward oral composition through the use of fixed formulas, Culley argued that the formulaic elements used in the psalms clearly

---

23. Willis, "Genre of Isaiah 5:1–7."
24. Ridderbos, *Psalmen*, 67.
25. Ginsberg, "Some Emendations."
26. Watters, *Formula Criticism*.
27. Good, Review of *Formula Criticism*.

demonstrate their oral origin.[28] Gevirtz followed Ginsberg in analyzing traditional word pairs in Israel's poetry,[29] and Dahood furthered this work significantly by considering Ugaritic parallels.[30] Whallon, after an extensive study of classical Greek, Old English, and Hebrew poetic compositions, explicitly linked word pairs with the wider phenomenon of parallelism: "The word pairs became formulaic because they assisted the poet in composing,"[31] and the act of composing in Hebrew poetry is tantamount to "creating parallelism."[32] We need to recognize, then, that societies create and provide, among other linguistic instruments for poetic work, fixed formulaic expressions which in some cultures, including Israel, included word pairs to be used in parallel lines. The conscious breakup or alteration of such fixed combinations is a matter of individual style, the significance and character of which will be discussed below.

In taking up other poetic devices we approach the realm of individual style, but since these linguistic features can be systematically identified they are at least partially collective in origin and function. While they may be distinctively altered and nuanced by individual poets, they are not the exclusive property of those poets or their times. From this perspective we may mention here further phenomena associated with Israelite poetry. Alonso Schökel's work will serve as a guide because his book on Hebrew poetry is the most comprehensive treatment written since 1945.[33]

According to Alonso Schökel, the first task of prosody should be a verification of the "sound material" (*material sonoro*) of a given language.[34] In the case of biblical Hebrew the difficulties of recovering sound values should not be overemphasized. After all, phonological investigations have revealed that the Hebrew script is phonetic in character and that "we can sufficiently trust in the extant text as far as consonants are concerned. In many cases this is true also for the vowels, and in general for the accents as well."[35] A second observation, based on specific texts, undergirds this optimistic conclusion. Certain sound-effects are universally known in all languages, and others we can extrapolate from semantic or symbolic values of the word or phrase concerned. Alonso Schökel observes that "Hebrew writers kept alive

---

28. Culley, *Oral Formulaic Language*.
29. Gevirtz, *Patterns*.
30. Dahood, *Psalms I, II, III*.
31. Whallon, *Formula*, 141.
32. Whallon, *Formula*, 154.
33. Alonso Schökel, *Estudios*; see also Alonso Schökel, *Manual*.
34. Alonso Schökel, *Estudios*, 71–117.
35. Alonso Schökel, *Estudios*, 80.

the predilection for sound-effects much more so than our modern writers do."³⁶ There must have been, then, an abundance of auditory devices at their disposal for use in both poetic and prose compositions.

In his analysis of selected texts in Isaiah, Alonso Schökel systematically examines the sound qualities of poetic language, drawing on previous work done by Boström, Saydon, Cross and Freedman,³⁷ and others on such devices as alliteration and assonance. But Alonso Schökel consistently places his research in the wider context of literary theory and stresses the importance of the general use of sound duplication—an "effective phonetic means of establishing the unity of two members, without however destroying their duality."³⁸ Repeated sounds function effectively in a variety of word combinations and stylistic settings. A second feature of Hebrew poetic language is the presence of "predominant sounds," that is, phonemes or clusters of phonemes which repeat themselves in a given poetic unit in order to underline the affirmation made. A good example of this phenomenon is Isa 17:12:

הוי המון עמים רבים כהמות ימים יהמיון

ושאון לאמים כשאון מים כבירים ישאון

Alonso Schökel further distinguishes particular uses of the application of sound dominance, notably onomatopoeic, metaphoric, and symbolic.³⁹

The use in poetry of the linguistic "raw material" dealt with above leads to various structural techniques and devices. Sound harmony can embellish all kinds of word arrangements within a poem: chiasm, antithesis, synonymy, etc. Sound dominance serves equally to enhance word play (paronomasia) and figurative meanings. To cite but one example, the repeated use of the consonants ל, and כ, in Isa 18:2 will, according to Alonso Schökel, effectively evoke the idea of הלך *hlk*, "to walk, to go."⁴⁰ While Alonso Schökel takes his examples for the most part from Isaiah, those researchers who have studied other poetic compositions in the Hebrew scriptures arrive at similar conclusions.⁴¹

The use of synonymy and antithesis is also a phenomenon that seems to belong to the realm of personal style. But inasmuch as they represent

---

36. Alonso Schökel, *Estudios*, 83.
37. Boström, *Paronomasi*; Saydon, "Assonance"; Cross and Freedman, *Studies*.
38. Alonso Schökel, *Estudios*, 110.
39. Alonso Schökel, *Estudios*, 113ff.
40. Alonso Schökel, *Estudios*, 114–15.
41. Boström, *Paronomasi*; Christian, *Untersuchungen*; Saydon, "Assonance"; and Díez Macho "La homonimia."

linguistic opportunities provided by existing speech patterns and vocabulary, they certainly belong to the general mass of poetic "raw material" which we are discussing here. Alonso Schökel sets these features apart from parallelism, justifying such treatment by asserting that "synonymy is a peculiar phenomenon which may exist with or without parallelism."[42] The same would hold true, of course, for antithesis. According to Staiger, to whom Alonso Schökel refers,[43] lyrical composition is based in a very special way on repetition, and repetition of emotional affirmations calls for synonymic expressions: "What keeps lyrical poetry from dissolution is, and exclusively so, repetition."[44] We should add that the evident overlapping of the phenomena of synonymy and antithesis with that of word pairs does not preclude their separate discussion. This is so because their construction and application constitute more than the simple use of conventionally predetermined formulas.

A weakness in Alonso Schökel's analysis must be noted, however. He tends to deal with stylistic antithesis principally under the rubric of antithetical thinking, a position now questioned by linguistic theorists. Consequently, his general conclusion—"In Hebrew literature synonymy or repetition is predominant; in Western literature it is antithesis or juxtaposition"[45]—should be received with caution.

Metaphors and symbols are widely used in all poetic language, and biblical poetry is no exception. Evidently, this preference for "nondirect" formulation has to do with the very nature of creative and inspired speech. The true poet of old was a powerful person, one who knew well how to synthesize reality in such a way as to give access to transcendental being.[46] Poetic language breaks through the confines of rationalistic world views, intuitively approaching the essence of things. Therefore, the use of comparative, inductive, indirect language is imperative for the poet. Every language possesses, from the very beginning, metaphors and symbols. Idioms are replete with them, and everyone who learns to speak a language at a given time learns to understand and handle their subtle meanings. Figurative speech, in this respect, is part of any given cultural heritage.

The importance of metaphors and symbols in Israel's poetry can hardly be overestimated. Unfortunately however, as Alonso Schökel observes, relatively little attention has been paid to these phenomena. Luckily, through

---

42. Alonso Schökel, *Estudios*, 231.
43. Alonso Schökel, *Estudios*, 235.
44. Staiger, *Grundbegriffe*, 31.
45. Alonso Schökel, *Estudios*, 267.
46. Weiss, "Wege"; Freedman, "Pottery"; Alonso Schökel, *Estudios*.

the work of Goodenough and of Keel,⁴⁷ a good part of Hebrew symbolism has become visible, enabling us to avoid the excessive rationalism and materialism that have often characterized our approach.

The sheer number of poetic linguistic devices quite naturally leads to the question of whether there existed anything like a genuine lyrical language in Israel. Those specialists whose work we have been discussing are by and large aware of this problem, although most commentaries on the biblical poetic books ignore it. A few basic differences between poetry and prose, in fact, have long been noted. Thus, the accusative particle rarely appears in poetic texts; a relative clause often remains formally unrelated to the main clause; the copulative we is sometimes missing.⁴⁸ Poetic language in the Hebrew scriptures, furthermore, tends at times to archaisms (Robertson),⁴⁹ exquisite vocabulary, and inverted word order. But all these are minor divergences that do not constitute sufficient reason to speak of a separate lyrical dialect, in contrast to the situation found in Sumerian literature.

One specific point in question, however, could be the verbal system employed in Hebrew poetry. As can be expected, the narrating forms of the verb occur only in historical psalms and similar texts (see Pss 78; 105). Typical for most lyrical materials are simple perfects and imperfects, which occasionally pose problems if viewed with reference to the traditional schema of time sequence. The thorough study of Diethelm Michel,⁵⁰ departing from earlier work done by E. Kuhr, H. S. Nyberg, Joachim Begrich, and Ludwig Köhler, demonstrates a distinctive use of verbal tempora and word order (position of subject and predicate) in poetic language. Finite verbs, according to Michel,⁵¹ do not indicate a fixed spot in a simple schema of past, present, or future time. Rather, they relate to the beginning, duration, and modalities of the action involved. Michel further insists that the usual classification of sentence structure into nominal and verbal sentences does not apply to poetic language. Instead, the basic sentence forms need to be redefined, and their functions in composite sentence clusters must be investigated.

An example of the importance of the clarification of these grammatical issues is the thorny problem of divine enthronement psalms. How should we translate *yhwh mlk* (Ps 93:1) and related expressions? Michel applies his general rules concerning word sequence and type of phrase: verbal clauses

---

47. Goodenough, *Jewish Symbols*; and Keel, *Symbolism*.
48. Freedman, "Pottery."
49. Robertson, *Linguistic Evidence*.
50. Michel, *Tempora und Satzstellung*.
51. Michel, *Tempora und Satzstellung*, 177ff.

"do not predicate a subject, but indicate an action"; a nominal clause "makes a statement about a subject... Normally its sentence is subject-predicate."[52] Therefore, Michel concludes, the affirmation *yhwh mālāk* "does not indicate how Yahweh became king, but rather how he acted as king."[53]

It is not surprising that it was Dahood who hinted at more far-reaching conclusions regarding a grammar of poetic language. At the end of his commentary on Psalms he summarizes (in more than eighty pages, divided into nine chapters) his linguistic observations on the poems. After dealing with orthography and phonetics,[54] he presents poetic peculiarities according to the different word classes—pronouns, nouns, verbs, prepositions, particles—and uncovers in each a variety of hitherto unknown expressions and meanings.[55] The longest chapter is "Syntax and Poetic Devices."[56] Among the newly discovered phenomena discussed in this chapter are the precative perfect[57] and a good number of double-duty lexemes.[58]

However, as has been stated before, Dahood's suggestions are still in the experimental phase and are being hotly contested by other scholars. The grammatical appendix to his Psalms commentary, therefore, is not the final word on poetic language in the Hebrew scriptures. Consisting primarily of lists of passages, without discussion of the evidence or answers to opposing views such as the one just cited, this "Grammar of the Psalter" still lacks the plausibility it wishes to attain.

The idiosyncrasies of Hebrew poetic language also lead to the question of possible foreign influences on the language. Albright and his followers have long pointed out the affinities between Hebrew poetry and the Ugaritic literature. Kramer goes much further,[59] insinuating that early Sumerian poetic practices established the patterns for poetic expression later to be employed throughout the ancient Near East. Other scholars have noted the above-average stock of Aramaic loanwords in Hebrew poetry. These and other observations leave us with the question of whether there was anything like an international poetic tradition in the ancient world.[60]

---

52. Michel, *Tempora und Satzstellung*, 178; see also Michel, "Studien."
53. Michel, "Studien," 395.
54. Dahood, *Psalms III*, 370–74.
55. Dahood, *Psalms III*, 374–410.
56. Dahood, *Psalms III*, 410–44.
57. Dahood, *Psalms III*, 414–17.
58. Dahood, *Psalms III*, 429–39.
59. Kramer, "Sumerian Literature."
60. See below, Settings and Genres.

A summary description of all the research done on and the features discovered in Hebrew poetry could yield not only a "handbook" of poetic grammar but also a kind of semantic synthesis, a dictionary of lyrical terms and usage. In fact, such a work, *A Lexicon of Accadian Prayers* by C. J. Mullo Weir, was published in 1934. Initial steps in this direction have also been taken in regard to the Hebrew poetic literature. The various lexical studies of the special terminology of the psalms demonstrate the necessity for further research in this field.[61] In addition, given the basic importance the poetic materials in the Hebrew scriptures have for theology and for the message of the church and synagogue today, we might even speak of an urgent need for an independent dictionary of poetry. N. D. Williams's *A Lexicon for the Poetic Books* is a sign that this need is being recognized.

## Stylistic Features

The Western concept of literary style is ambiguous. On the one hand, it usually assumes that there are figures and patterns of speech that are characteristic of a given cultural context. On the other hand, it reckons with the numerous varieties of individual articulations that result in an unmistakable profile of literary expression. This oscillation between social and individual traits is by no means arbitrary. On the contrary, it has its roots in the problem of language itself. Language has always been a prefabricated instrument handed over to be used (and abused) by individuals. In other words, the poets of all times have created their poetic realities in the midst of—not outside of—that conditioning network of social relations and linguistic structures which is their physical and spiritual home. In turning to the aspect of individual creativity in the Hebrew scriptures, it should be clear then that all the linguistic features discussed above may and do serve as vehicles of personal expression. If there were room enough to do so, we would treat them again in this section. Under the circumstances, however, we shall limit ourselves to a discussion of personal authorship in Israelite lyrical literature and of typical elements of lyrical style frequently considered in research on the Hebrew scriptures.

The question of authorship is a central issue in the discussion of lyrical poetry. Nineteenth-century criticism emphasized individual authorship to the extent of virtually equating the poet and the product; thus it tended to ignore the significance and influence of social and communal factors. However, with the rise of new areas of research (history of religions, cultic history,

---

61. See Mowinckel, *The Psalms*, 2:207-17; Delekat, "Probleme"; Delekat, "Zum hebräischen Wörterbuch."

mythological research, folklore studies, form criticism, tradition history, etc.) attention became focused on the popular, anonymous, and collective origin of many ancient literary genres. It seems that in our times the pendulum is starting to swing back toward assuming individual authorship of Israel's poetry. One should expect, however, a better solution to the enigmatic problem of the individual/collective interplay in forming poems and lyrical literature. A wide variety of opinion still remains on this issue.

The Song of Songs, though occasionally still considered an authentic work of King Solomon,[62] is for the most part interpreted in terms of folkloristic or royal religious ideology. Pope's surprising, but by no means absurd, localization of this cycle of love songs in funeral celebrations suggests a popular and religious background for them.[63] On the whole, modern exegetes tend to stress the ritual character (in its broadest sense) of the book rather than to insist on its origin as a piece of individual artistry (Audet; Bentzen; Dubarle; Feuillet; Kramer, 1969; Schmökel; Widengren, 1948).[64] The same interpretation also applies to the book of Lamentations. Modern research rarely attributes this book to Jeremiah, as did the LXX. Instead, the origin of these "communal dirges" is traced back to public laments after the fall of Jerusalem in 587 BCE.[65] Suggestions concerning the real poets behind these texts remain extremely tenuous.

With Psalms the situation is more complicated. Biblical tradition seeks to identify historical figures as the authors of various poems: David, Asaph, Korah, and others are mentioned in the superscriptions. Modern theological interest often unconsciously follows the same path and so tries to secure the testimony of faith in a psalm by assigning it to one particular witness. Small wonder, then, that conservative scholars still cling to Davidic authorship, while other critics, although abandoning the literal interpretation of the titles, opt for anonymous but still well defined individual artists. Given this orientation, there seem to be two alternatives regarding the quest for the authors of the psalms: either our extant psalms are to be seen as private compositions, even though they are indebted to older liturgical poetry,[66] or they are the more professional compositions of

---

62. Thieberger, *King Solomon*.

63. Pope, *Song of Songs*.

64. Audet, "Le sens"; Bentzen, *Messias* (ET *King and Messiah*); Dubarle, "L'amour humain"; Feuillet, *Cantique des Cantiques*; Kramer, *Sacred Marriage Rite*; Schmökel, *Heilige Hochzeit*; Widengren, "Hieros gamos."

65. Albrektson, *Studies*; Kraus, *Klagelieder*; and Hillers, *Lamentations*.

66. Beyerlin, *Rettung*; Kraus, *Psalmen* (ET *Psalms*); Sabourin, *Psalms*; Delekat, *Asylie und Schutzorakel*; Weiss, "Wege"; and others.

temple singers and were destined for cultic use.[67] Behind this controversy, however, there still lies the unresolved problem of how to evaluate justly the relative proportions of individual creativity and social convention in the process of poetic composition.

Lyrical poetry in the Hebrew scriptures outside of the poetic books is obviously subject to the same kind of uncertainty. A good illustration of this is the discussion that centers on the so-called Confessions of Jeremiah (Jer 11:19—12:6; 15:10-21; 17:12-18; 18:19-23; 20:7-18), lyrical compositions akin to the individual laments in the Psalter. The vast majority of experts insist on the personal authorship of these laments by the prophet. However, if the history of compilation and transmission of prophetic books is taken into consideration, their autobiographical character and intention must be doubted. Thus Reventlow and this writer have contested the private character of Jeremiah's laments, postulating instead a cultic and liturgical background.[68] This latter interpretation has so far found little sympathy in scholarly circles but rather has provoked vehement protests from, among others, Bright, Berridge, and Holladay.[69]

Similarly, other lyrical compositions in the Hebrew scriptures are, with varying degrees of probability, seen as the work of individual authors. They are attributed variously to particular historical figures (Judges 5 to Deborah; Exod 15:21 to Miriam; Deuteronomy 32 to Moses; 2 Sam 1:19-24 to David), are left to the anonymity of preliterary history (Gen 4:23-24; Gen 49; Num 23:7-10), or are treated as interpolations by later editors or redactors (2 Sam 2:1-10; Isa 5:1-7; 38:9-20; cf. also the citation of biblical psalms in 2 Sam 22 and 1 Chr 16). With regard to this issue, the Servant Songs in Deutero-Isaiah pose very specific problems.[70]

Unfortunately, there has been little discussion of the problem of how to recognize the personal involvement of poets in the emotions expressed in ancient texts. Are observations of style and content really sufficient to address this issue? The hidden presupposition behind studies of this kind seems to be that the emotional participation of the author is directly reflected in the surface or depth structure of the poem. But the results of intensive studies on this subject are, at best, ambiguous. As with the Confessions of Jeremiah, all the emotions expressed in ancient poetry can be understood in terms of individual emotional involvement, but these emotions are perhaps better

---

67. Mowinckel, *The Psalms*; Ridderbos, *Psalmen*; Ringgren, *Faith*; Keel, *Symbolism*; A. R. Johnson, *Cultic Prophet*; and others.
68. Reventlow, *Liturgie*; and Gerstenberger, "Jeremiah's Complaints."
69. Bright, "Jeremiah's Complaints"; Berridge, *Prophet*; and Holladay, *Jeremiah*.
70. Seybold, "Thesen."

understood as stylized liturgical language. Scholars almost unanimously emphasize the virtual absence of historical and biographical references in Psalms, the Song of Songs, and Lamentations. They readily admit a certain vagueness and generality of expression in the lyrical literature of the Hebrew scriptures.[71] How can we verify, then, any "real" emotional involvement by the authors with the feelings communicated by their poetry?

The same question arises in regard to all stylistic devices employed by ancient poets. In order to be able to distinguish personal style from general usage we need a far more thorough knowledge of Hebrew literature than we can ever hope to attain. The Hebrew scriptures, after all, preserve only a tiny percentage of the lyrical poetry actually used in Israel; note, for example, the lost collections mentioned in Num 21:14 or 2 Sam 1:18. In this connection modern observers like to point to the hold individualistic use of metaphors and symbols, comparisons and parables in the prophetic books. There is some justification for such statements, as a parallel study of Amos and Hosea or Isaiah and Jeremiah demonstrates. Nevertheless, can we be so certain of their individual styles? Not knowing much of the language of their immediate environment, it is extremely difficult for us to risk a final conclusion. Lyrical language, on the other hand, is not less hold in its imagery and structure. Yet it is, according to all experts, much more dependent on conventional patterns of speech and expression. What is the significance of this divergent evaluation regarding the role of "literary creativity" in prophetic as opposed to lyrical compositions? Is it justified, or has the appeal of the prophets as hold and innovative messengers of the word of God unduly influenced our perceptions and opinions?

We must be aware of all these difficulties posed by ancient poetic texts. Proceeding with caution, however, we can detect certain "individualizing" features in Israel's lyrical materials, if it is understood that by "individualizing" we do not here mean individual in the modern solipsistic sense. Rather, throughout Israel's history, stylistic traits were in all likelihood the property of temple schools, groups of prophets or sages, and guilds of singers, as well as of particular regions, social classes, and historical periods. With this in mind, we may point out a few modes of lyrical expression on which research has focused its attention and which complement the observations made above.

The simple repetition of words or phrases within one poem is a stylistic device known in all literatures. This form of expression in Hebrew lyrical literature has been studied by Muilenburg, Alonso Schökel, Ridderbos, and others. Martin Buber and Franz Rosenzweig have also

---

71. See Ridderbos, "Psalmen und Kult," 265ff.

frequently called attention to biblical repetitious styles. Albright, looking at the historical development of Israelite poetry, has stressed the fact that the Canaanite style of literal repetition of expressions and lines in a poem soon gave way in Israel to more sophisticated and varying types of restatements. Functionally, all the phenomena related to parallelism, alliteration, assonance, paronomasia, etc. can be seen as nothing more than specialized versions of the simple reiteration of words. Further, by these means of simple repetition, the ancient poet readily found innumerable possibilities for driving home a particular point of view, concern, or aspiration. Thus, Ps 13:2–3 repeats reproachful questions; Ps 29:1–2 sounds like a jubilant call to praise; Ps 29:3–5 uniformly describes the "voice of the Lord"; and Ps 136:1–26 shows, in the second colon of each verse, a type of antiphonal repetition apparently sung by the congregation.

Probably very early in the history of ancient Near Eastern poetry the widely used repetitious style began to employ an antithetic or chiastic structure. That is, poets learned to juxtapose, within a given poetic unit, words, ideas, and phrases in order to heighten expectation and suspense in the listener or reader. There is an infinite variety of chiastic arrangement in the lyrical materials of the Hebrew scriptures.[72] Psalm 1 is structured in terms of polar ideas (blessed-wicked; tree-chaff; prosper-perish; etc.), and the whole poem is construed accordingly. In Isa 6:10 there are, altogether, seven cola. The first three speak about "heart," "ear," "eye"—a sequence exactly inverted in the following three units. And similarly, but on the level of entire lines, Ps 9:12–15 "shows chiastic structure. Verse 12 corresponds to v. 15, v. 13 to v. 14; this correspondence applies to contents as well as to vocabulary . . ."[73]

Another artistic feature sometimes imitated in our own hymns is the acrostic structuring of a poem. In this arrangement, each line or group of lines begins with another letter of the alphabet, or even with one special word which forms part of a phrase. Psalms 25, 34, 37, 111, 112, 119, and 145; as well as Lamentations 3, are examples of alphabetic acrostics in the Old Testament. It is doubtful that there are word acrostics in the Bible, although they are definitely to be found in the cuneiform materials. Acrostic arrangement is often considered artificial by modern exegetes. To us it looks contrived, it is true; we must remember, however, that our use of end rhyme in poetry would undoubtedly appear just as forced to the ancient Israelites.[74]

---

72. See G. B. Gray, *Forms*; Kosmala, "Form"; Ridderbos, *Psalmen*; Weiss, "Wege," 425ff.

73. Ridderbos, *Psalmen*, 143.

74. See Gottwald, "Poetry"; Freedman, "Pottery"; Bergler, "Threni V."

*Inclusio* is the term used to identify an arrangement of complete units of poetry in which the beginning and end correspond to each other (see Pss 8; 12; 20; etc.). In its most sophisticated form, thoughts and words ascend and descend to and from a climax that is reached in the middle of the poem. For more details regarding this literary device, see Liebreich and Ridderbos.[75]

The so-called break-up of composite phrases or word units has been studied only recently.[76] The theory underlying such inquiry is that, if we can find parts of standard formulations separated by alien words or grammatical elements, we can assume that the author of the poem must have consciously broken up the traditional unit in order to achieve a special effect. For Dahood, typical examples of this device are such expressions as עצה רוח, ("spirit of counsel") in Isa 11:2, which is dismembered in Isa 19:3, and קדשו כסא ("his holy throne") in Ps 47:9, which is taken apart in Ps 11:4. Taken by itself, the search for such dismembered standard expressions would seem to be an optimal means of identifying individual creativity in poetry. After all, does it not require unusual courage to counteract common linguistic usage? The whole theory, however, rests on shaky foundations, for the combination of two words does not necessarily make them a standard phrase, nor does the use of any word within a fixed expression preclude its further employment either individually or in combination with other words.

The list of stylistic features given above remains incomplete. There are more phenomena presently under discussion, as a study of the literature cited demonstrates. Moreover, continuing research will discover even more characteristics of the Hebrew lyrical materials. We must stop here, however, and draw an interim conclusion. On the one hand, we can be extremely grateful for the wealth of insights won so far in postwar research. Israel's lyrical literature is today far better known than it was before 1945. That knowledge has enhanced sympathetic understanding of these ancient texts, with the result that the poetic and lyric portions of the Hebrew scriptures have entered a new cycle of use and acceptance as valid expressions of faith and life experience.[77]

On the other hand, there certainly remain problems and uncertainties with regard to these ancient materials. Many formal, cultural, and religious traits of Hebrew prayers, hymns, laments, love-songs, incantations, and so forth are not easily accessible to modern investigations. Therefore, all our interpretive efforts are subject to the very natural temptation to ignore that

---

75. Liebreich, "Psalm 34"; and Ridderbos, *Psalmen*.
76. Melamed, "Break-up"; Dahood, "Breakup."
77. See below.

which is alien or offensive in the texts and to impose on them exegetical schemes that produce the answers subconsciously desired by the interpreter. This danger is the motive for undertaking (below) a brief self-critical reflection on the different standpoints or perspectives of modern research.

## Opinions and Schools of Interpretation

The old positivistic, historically oriented school of thought is all but extinct in our time. Previously, Duhm had sought that historical and religious objectivity which the past century was hopeful and proud to conquer.[78] Gunkel, however, in his commentary on Psalms rejected this orientation and sought to uncover the innermost religious sentiments of Israel's psalmists.[79] In our day, objectivity is still a cherished working premise in technical and scientific studies, whereas in the humanities its role has gradually been deemphasized. Spiritually speaking, we are living in an age of growing concern for the state of humanity. Our thinking is inner-directed and overshadowed by great uncertainties regarding our true calling. So far as research in the Hebrew scriptures is concerned, historical objectivity lingers on only in our unintentional efforts to create a purely academic world of scientific facts and prestige. In other words, the continuing temptation, always present in scholarly undertakings, to rely excessively on external data—philological, historical, archaeological, or stylistic—is a leftover of that earlier positivistic age.

Gunkel and Mowinckel, working within an intellectual tradition that valued the emotional and mythical dimensions of being, were, as noted above, able to overcome the historical and literary positivism of their age. Their pioneering work in the field of Hebrew poetry is still very much alive, and their method continues to produce new fruits in terms of modified approaches to the texts of the Hebrew scriptures. It seems that, after a period which focused on analyses of poetic surface structures, a greater concern for the life situations that gave birth to the texts is now again coming to the fore. Gunkel's triad of methodological avenues—observation of literary form, situation in life, and religious sentiments—still offers ample room for further investigation. Form-critical work, in this sense, is just beginning.[80]

Notable shifts of emphases have also occurred in the so-called archaeological school of interpretation so closely aligned with the name of W. F. Albright. Its roots lie both in Christian concepts of salvation history

---

78. Duhm, *Psalmen*.
79. Gunkel, *Psalmen*.
80. Gerstenberger, "Psalms."

and in liberal theology's concern for human progress. The Bible is seen as God's revelation, and the poetic strata within the Old Testament constitute, because of their age and authenticity, the very fundamentals of Israel's faith. The task of modern research according to this school is clear: to reconstruct, as fully as possible, the literary history of Israel's poetry by assigning each individual poem to its appropriate historical situation. It is impressive to me the amount of work put to this task—and the optimism expressed concerning its final results. But, within this school, there has been an increasing openness to other approaches to biblical poetry.[81]

Another methodology that has arisen in the last decades and has rapidly won adherents among researchers of the poetic literature of Israel is often called "New Literary Criticism." It is based on recent developments in literary science represented, for example, by the work of Kayser as well as Wellek and Warren.[82] Each poem, for these scholars, is an independent work of art that speaks for itself. Not even the life of the poet may serve as a guideline for interpretation, much less all the accidental facts of history or general social background. Therefore, researchers following this line of thinking, notably Weiss and Alonso Schökel, challenge traditional exegesis of Israel's poetry as being distractive. The modern exegete, they insist, has to pay attention to that poetic reality that the author created in the poem—and to nothing else. Among the questions that should be raised concerning this interpretation, two are especially significant. First, can we assume that these poems were the conscious work of gifted individuals as we visualize it today? Second, with regard to those charismatic creations of modern poets, might we not be missing something of their value and intent unless we set them in the context of the cultural patterns and social relations of their respective times?

Although the following methods of biblical interpretation have so far shown little concern for Hebrew poetry in particular, they should be watched. The first is that exegetical method which grows out of philosophical structuralism. In this approach, each text is taken as a linguistic expression of depth-structures of the mind, i.e., of being itself. Interest, therefore, does not rest with the poetic forms at all but rather with the underlying patterns of life, which we can readily compare with our own experiences and thus elucidate further our existence. The second method, the psychological, works basically with the same frame of reference as structuralism, so far as surface- and depth-structures of the text are concerned. But it goes further by applying the theories of Freud, Jung, Fromm, and others

---

81. See Cross and Freedman, *Studies*.
82. Kayser, *Das sprachliche Kunstwerk*; Wellek and Warren, *Theory of Literature*.

to the analysis of those depth-structures. And finally, there is a growing awareness among Old Testament scholars that biblical texts in general and lyrical poetry in particular (because of its ritualistic character) have to a large extent been conditioned by the social and environmental factors of Israelite life. This last method is, of course, diametrically opposed to the new literary criticism summarized above.[83]

## Music, Instruments, and Ritual

In addition to all the problems discussed above, scholars are facing considerable difficulties in attempting to verify the musical and ritual accompaniment of Israel's poetic materials. That there was a great number of activities accompanying poetic "recitations" is clear from allusions within the poems themselves. There are also passing references to this effect in narrative and prophetic books. However, there is not a single complete ritual preserved in the Hebrew scriptures that would indicate exactly the place and kind of accompaniment of prayer or song. The sacrificial texts of Leviticus and the well-known ordeal ceremony in Num 5:11-31, both of which are common genres in the ancient Near East, are closest to this type of description. "Prophetic liturgies" preserve mainly the spoken parts (see Isa 63:7—64:11; Jer 14:1-22; Joel 1-2). However, painstaking scrutiny of the available evidence, deriving to a large extent from wider studies of the ancient Near East, has yielded valuable information regarding probable musical and ritual accompaniment in Israel.

Lyrical poems have from time immemorial been accompanied by musical instruments. The name of the Psalter (from the Greek *psalterion*, "harp," "lyre," from *psallo*, "to tug") is a witness to this fact. It attests that stringed instruments often were a favorite means of accompaniment; many such have, in fact, been recovered from tombs and other archaeological sites.[84] In addition, numerous other types of instruments were also used in musical and ritual settings. Hand drums accompanied the songs of victory (Exod 15:20); horns and trumpets apparently had their place in larger temple rituals (see Num 10:1ff.; Isa 27:13; Zech 9:14). Psalm 150:3-5 gives the impression of a fully orchestrated hymn. Of course, the music produced by these instruments has been lost. Quite recently, however, the

---

83. See Gottwald, "Poetry"; Albertz, *Persönliche Frömmigkeit*; and Gerstenberger, *Der bittende Mensch*.

84. Kolari, *Musikinstrumente*; Werner, "Music," and "Musical Instruments"; and Stauder, *Die Harfen und Leiern*.

first piece of music written on a clay tablet has come to light,[85] an Ugaritic hymn with musical notes. Working with these various clues we can now reconstruct, at least approximately, the sound of a recital. Musical instruments served to reinforce and embellish the voices of singers and choirs. Percussion and wind instruments were used probably because the music also had an apotropaic (exorcistic) and charming function in ritual. We can assume also that wedding songs had their own special instrumentation (see Jer 7:34; 16:8–9; Ezek 33:32).

If instrumentation played an important part in ritual, vocal articulation of lyrical poems was indispensable to any correct performance. A recent attempt has been made by Haïk Vantoura to reconstruct the ritual songs and melodies used in Israel on the basis of the Masoretic accentuation.[86] In the book of Chronicles especially, temple functionaries such as singers and choirs are mentioned as playing an important role in the vocal portions of the worship services. Modem research has revealed that very probably there never was anything like communal song during worship. Rather, the people would respond by refrains and shouts, leaving the presentation of the texts and the leading of chants to the experts (see Exod 32:18; 2 Sam 18:7, 10).[87] The same pattern was very likely followed in profane ceremonies.

In speaking about musical accompaniment and vocal expression we must not overlook all the rites that were, in one way or another, integral parts of ritual performances, sacred and profane. For Israel's various festivities our sources refer to dance, processions, gestures, and mime (2 Sam 6:14; Pss 26:6; 48:13; 68:26; etc.). There have been many efforts in postwar research to describe in more detail various great annual feasts in order to achieve a plausible background for one or the other group of lyrical poems. Thus, Mowinckel elaborated the ritual of the New Year festival with its royal ascension ceremonies.[88] Weiser concentrated on a great renewal of the covenant between Yahweh and Israel, which could have provided the setting for the majority of the psalms.[89] Beyerlin investigated the judgment before a temple court of those unjustly accused.[90] Seybold explained the psalms of the sick as a part of the praxis of rehabilitation.[91] Gerstenberger has tried to

---

85. Draffkorn-Kilmer, "Cult Song."

86. Haïk Vantoura, *La musique*.

87. See also Werner, "Music," and "Musical Instruments"; and Draffkorn-Kilmer, "Cult Song."

88. Mowinckel, *The Psalms*, 106–92.

89. Weiser, *Psalmen* (ET *The Psalms*).

90. Beyerlin, *Die Rettung*.

91. Seybold, *Das Gebet*.

place individual laments in the context of a prayer service of the primary group.[92] Kramer and Schmökel interpreted the Song of Songs against the background of Mesopotamian sacred marriage rites.[93]

In view of the diversity of such proposals, how can we understand and identify the settings and genres of the poetic materials in the Hebrew scriptures?

## Settings and Genres

The quest for genre definitions has been very intense in postwar research. It is motivated not only by form-critical methodology but also by new literary considerations. We may correctly say that genre classification of Israelite poetry has for the most part become commonplace, replacing the older identification of material on the basis of content or sentiment. Obviously, this does not mean that scholars are unanimous in applying categories or in evaluating the classification of individual texts. Nevertheless, even widely diverging opinions have a common denominator: everyone wishes to recognize the genre affiliation of a given lyrical text. Assuming this concern, we may now discuss briefly profane and then sacred poetry, knowing well that in Israel this distinction was not an absolute one.

The first group of poems are work songs, chanteys, harvest songs, and the like. Examples of this type of poetry are the song celebrating the construction of a well (Num 21:13-14) and a watchman's call, possibly preserved in Isa 21:11-12. Although such compositions are poorly represented in the Hebrew scriptures, all researchers and commentators pay at least passing attention to them. There has not, however, been any extensive study done on this topic.

Without doubt there were songs for all kinds of social gatherings in Israel. Even if such gatherings were possibly connected with a religious ceremony (the sacrifice in 1 Sam 9:12, 19-20), emphasis could be placed on the noncultic aspects and activities. From rare allusions in the texts (Judg 21:11; Isa 5:11-12; 24:8-9; etc.) we may surmise that there was a variety of chants connected with festivities of the family, clan, or neighborhood. Considering the Israelites' predilection for their own history, it would be legitimate to think also of more epical poems which might have been recited at such occasions (see Ps 78; Deut 32; Hab 3). The larger introductions to

---

92. Gerstenberger, *Der bittende Mensch*.
93. Kramer, *Sacred Marriage Rite*; Schmökel, *Heilige Hochzeit*.

the Old Testament, such as those of Eissfeldt and Sellin/Fohrer, give more information on this matter.[94]

A well-known genre in secular lyrics is the wedding song. Extant examples are Psalm 45 and the Song of Songs; these poems should be put into life settings such as those indicated by Genesis 24 or Judges 14 and 16. Moreover, the comparative Egyptian and Mesopotamian material has to be taken into account. The work done so far shows similar poetic practice all over the ancient Near East concerning the profane (and sacred!) setting of love poetry, the possible involvement of the king, and the social significance of such poetry.[95] Exegesis of the Song of Songs has by now abandoned its doctrinal, messianic, and allegorical outlook.[96] Yet there are still some differences of opinion regarding its interpretation—most notably between those who advance secular and those who propose cultic interpretations. Thus the picture is far from uniform. There are also laudable and creative efforts being made to compare these ancient love songs with corresponding situations in our own time.[97]

The dirge is the other lyrical type we can study directly in the Old Testament. Examples preserved include 2 Sam 1:19–27; 3:33–34, and some prophetic imitations (see Amos 5:1–3; Isa 14:4–21). Ever since Budde and Jahnow did the pioneering work that identified this genre,[98] there has been near agreement among scholars about its form and setting. Therefore, fundamentally new developments are not to be expected. Future research will tend to refine observations already made:[99] to discuss the function and transfer of the genre,[100] and most of all to compare more ancient and modern material.[101]

As can be expected from the nature of biblical writings, the sacred lyrical poetry is far better represented than the secular and has received much more attention in research. This writer has previously discussed the situation of scholarship in this particular field.[102] Therefore, we will limit ourselves here to the most essential observations.

---

94. Eissfeldt, *Old Testament*; Fohrer, *Introduction*.

95. W. Rudolph, *Hohelied*; Kramer, *Sacred Marriage Rite*; Schmökel, *Heilige Hochzeit*; Pope, *Song of Songs*; Murphy, "Towards a Commentary"; White, *Study*.

96. Würthwein, "Zum Verständnis."

97. Lys, "Une histoire d'amour"; Müller, "Die lyrische Reproduktion"; Segal, "Song of Songs"; Dubarle, "L'amour humain"; Dryburgh, *Lessons for Lovers*.

98. Budde, "Das hebräische Klagelied"; Jahnow, *Das hebräische Leichenlied*.

99. Gevirtz, *Patterns*.

100. Long, "Divine Funeral Lament."

101. Littmann, *Abessinische Klagelieder*.

102. Gerstenberger, "Psalms"; Gerstenberger, "Zur Interpretation."

Laments and thanksgivings, both of the individual and communal types, form a block of genres interrelated by analogous and corresponding life situations. They have been under careful scrutiny in the past decades, and there are numerous relevant publications. The purely literary and non-cultic interpretations have found some support.[103] The vast majority of scholars, however, still accepts the cultic or semi-cultic interpretation of Gunkel and Mowinckel.

The analysis of linguistic forms and structures within the four genres has been greatly refined.[104] Occasionally, someone wants to rename lamentation "supplication,"[105] or to eliminate the communal thanksgiving for formal and theological reasons.[106] However, on the whole the genre picture is quite stable, even if attribution of some psalms to a determined category is controversial.

It is regarding the imagined and reconstructed life situations that most debate occurs. What was, after all, the ritual setting of the complaint prayer of the individual? Where should we locate public lament? To the first question there are at least four types of answers. The sufferer took the prayer to the great temple service,[107] as apparently Elkanah did in 1 Samuel 1. Others insist that it must have been a special tribunal at the temple that tried and rehabilitated the falsely accused.[108] Still others deny the existence of an appeal to divine justice, suggesting that the laments are really thanksgivings; they complain of past misery in order to celebrate recovery.[109] Finally, those who defend the royal interpretation declare all individual and communal prayers the work of the monarch acting in the name of the people.[110] In opposition to all these hypotheses, Gerstenberger advances his own, reconstructing on the basis of Mesopotamian rituals a healing ceremony in the family circle, independent of the temple and official cult. Whatever other settings are identified, however, communal laments would obviously have their place within rituals of public fasting and mourning.[111]

103. Tur-Sinai, "Zum literarischen Charakter"; Becker, *Wege der Psalmenexegese*, 75: "laments are pious literature; they do not have a life-setting but are rooted in literature."
104. Westermann, *Das Loben*; Crüsemann, *Studien*; Ridderbos, *Psalmen*.
105. Beyerlin, *Die Rettung*; Gese, "Psalm 22."
106. Crüsemann, *Studien*; contra Mand, "Die Eigenständigkeit."
107. Mowinckel, *The Psalms*; Weiser, *Psalmen* (ET *Psalms*); etc.
108. Delekat, *Asylie und Schutzorakel*; Beyerlin, *Die Rettung*.
109. Weiser, *Psalmen* (ET *Psalms*); Gese, "Psalm 22"; Seybold, *Das Gebet*.
110. Bentzen, *Messias* (ET *King and Messiah*); Engnell, *Studies*; Soggin, "Il canto"; Widengren, *Sakrales Königtum*; and Mowinckel in his later works.
111. Kraus, *Klagelieder*; Gottwald, *Studies*; Hillers, *Lamentations*; Wolff, "Der Aufruf."

The setting of the thanksgiving song seems to be less disputed. Thanksgiving songs, at least those for the individual, are clearly attested in special worship services after a decisive salvation event had been experienced.

The hymns of praise form a second large and diversified group of sacral poems. Again, the groundwork of structural analysis and identification of genre and setting was laid by Gunkel and Mowinckel. Since 1945 their theories have been amplified but seldom challenged. Modifications of hymnic attributes such as those proposed by Westermann ("narrating" vs. "affirming" praise)[112] or Crüsemann ("imperative" vs. "participle" hymn)[113] did not have much impact on the scholarly world.

It also remains a common opinion that Israel's hymns grew out of larger community festivities. For the most part these were cultic celebrations. As noted above, the Chronicler is essentially correct in making families of temple singers responsible for hymn singing. In this regard scholarly attention is especially captured by the figures of Asaph and Korah, Levitical (?) singers known both from Psalms and from Chronicles.[114]

Modern scholarship singles out several main types of hymns associated with the different feasts and festivals in Israel. The first of these is the victory song. These songs were part of the celebrations after military victories and are marked by the significant participation of women (Judges 5; Exod 15:21; Psalm 68).[115] The second type, royal hymns, adorned those festivities in which the king played a significant role. Some experts, especially from northern European countries, attribute to these festivals a formative influence on virtually all psalmic genres (Mowinckel; Engnell; Widengren; Bentzen; Birkeland). The idea of a royal ideology was repudiated, however, by Bernhardt. The third type is the Zion songs, hymns about the holy city of Jerusalem (Pss 46; 48; 76; 87; 132). There must have existed, during Israel's long history, various festive occasions to commemorate Yahweh's presence on Mount Zion (see Psalms 24 and 122). The Yahweh-kingship hymns, celebrating the supreme power of Israel's deity certainly belong in this context also (Pss 47; 93; 96–99).[116] Most of the hymns, notably those which glorify Yahweh's creative and salvific power, probably belong to the seasonal cycle

---

112. Westermann, *Das Loben*.

113. Crüsemann, *Studien*.

114. See Mowinckel, *The Psalms*; Buss, "Psalms of Asaph"; Gese, "Zur Geschichte"; Wanke, *Zionstheologie*.

115. See Globe, "Literary Structure"; J. Gray, "Contata"; Soggin, "Il canto."

116. Kraus, *Psalmen* (ET *Psalms*); Asensio, "El Yahweh Malak"; Coppens, "La royaute de Yahve"; Lipinski, *La royaute de Yahwe*; de Moor, *New Year*; and Widengren, *Sakrales Königtum*.

of feasts.[117] Unfortunately, we can no longer say where exactly they would have been used in the liturgy of these events.[118]

The last comprehensive group of lyrical poems contained in the Psalter apparently is not cultic in origin, but it nevertheless shows a marked theological orientation. Sapiential psalms (see Psalms 1; 19B; 37; 49; 73; 119) derive from circles of sages, which may in some instances be identified with priestly or levitical groups. Wisdom psalms focus on ethical problems. They try to define the position of humanity in this world and wrestle with Yahweh's apparent injustice. One of the main critical questions to be clarified is the identity and function of the sages in relation to the cult and religious education.[119] For now, we cannot go much beyond the affirmations of Mowinckel,[120] who considered some of these psalms to be authentic prayers, although free from cultic functions.[121]

## Parallels from Outside Israel

We have repeatedly referred to literary, cultural, and religious analogies taken from Israel's neighbors. These references were neither accidental nor arbitrary. They reveal the historical truth that Israel's lyrical poetry, although a cultural and theological phenomenon in its own right, still remained part of the larger ancient Near Eastern civilization. There are too many cross-connections and correspondences between the poetry of the OT and that of Israel's neighbors to allow them to be ignored by modern scholarship. In fact, research since 1945 has widely accepted this, utilizing with caution and prudence that vast material available in the relevant disciplines.

Where can we expect to find contributions to research on Israel's lyrical poetry? Relevant ancient Near Eastern texts normally come from archaeological excavations. It is impossible to enumerate all the important sites or, for that matter, to mention only the most important text publications. Suffice it to say that all of the four large regions that make up the arena of ancient Near Eastern history — Egypt, Syria-Palestine, Asia Minor, and Mesopotamia — have already yielded valuable comparative material and will continue to do so. In fact, every year the avalanche of relevant texts

117. Halbe, "Passa-Massot."
118. See Weiser, *Psalmen* (ET *Psalms*); Kraus, *Psalmen* (ET *Psalms*); Leslie, *Psalms*; van der Ploeg, *Psalmen*; Podechard, *Psautier*.
119. Perdue, *Wisdom and Cult*.
120. Mowinckel, "Psalms and Wisdom."
121. See Murphy, "Consideration"; Skehan, *Studies*; Trible, "Wisdom"; Crenshaw, *Hymnic Affirmation*; Gemser, "Gesinnungsethik."

is increasing, and the next substantial amount of material will likely come from the clay tablets found at Ebla in Syria.

What types of texts (genres) are available for comparative study? The answer is simple. All the poetic genres found in the Hebrew Bible are also known from the neighboring cultures, from love song to individual prayer, from blessing to hymn, from thanksgiving to pun, from lament and dirge to incantation. To mention but a few examples from literally hundreds of important publications of comparative material, we can point to the new collection of Babylonian and Assyrian hymns and prayers edited by Seux[122] and the more recent monograph on Babylonian prayer formulations by Mayer.[123] A widely used collection of translated hymns and prayers is that of Falkenstein and von Soden.[124]

How can we legitimately compare Israelite poetry with extant texts from elsewhere in the ancient Near East? We should admit that grave errors have been committed in the past. The attempt at schematic comparison in order to demonstrate the superiority of one culture over the other (Israelite vs. Babylonian vs. Egyptian, etc.) is certainly not adequate. Each culture, in spite of all affinities, has its own character and value. Nevertheless, we are able to juxtapose carefully the texts of one culture with the corresponding texts of another, to compare life situations, genre profiles, intentions, social conditions and so forth, and to come to valid internal conclusions, using the insights gained on one side as leads to discover inherent traits in the other. It should be added that this writer has the firm conviction that this same cautious method of comparison is also applicable to texts from cultures other than those of the ancient Near East, be they ancient or modern.

## Dating Lyrical Texts

Our historically minded age has been bent on dating the texts of antiquity, and there is some good reason for this. Fixation in a particular epoch can be a useful instrument in determining the message of a document. Lyrical texts, however, by definition lack historical and biographical references and therefore are very hard to date. Further, if one views the "point of origin" in terms of a transmission process, dating is again problematic. For these reasons Gunkel and his followers substituted references to genre and setting for specific historical dates. Yet as Gunkel's commentary on Psalms

---

122. Seux, *Hymnes*.
123. Mayer, *Untersuchungen*.
124. Falkenstein and von Soden, *Sumerische und akkadische Hymnen*.

clearly shows, even if this is done there still remains a certain tendency to look for historical points of fixation.

The late dating of the psalms and other lyrical poetry so characteristic of the Wellhausen school[125] has been practically abandoned in research since World War II. In general, the date of poems has been pushed backward, and pre-exilic dates for Israel's poems today are the rule, not the exception. The most interesting recent attempt in research is that of sequence-dating, inaugurated by Albright and used extensively by Cross, Freedman, and others. The assumption underlying this approach is that linguistic and stylistic features give clues to the formative epoch for a given poem. After establishing a sequence from archaic to more "modern" poems, one can then try to tie the whole network to historical events, thus gaining a reliable chronological order for the development of Hebrew poetry.

In addition to studying the dates of individual poems, scholars have also invested much energy in seeking to illuminate the complex processes that resulted in the present shape and collection of lyrical materials in the Hebrew Bible. This has involved the study of their transmission, the efforts that led to the compilation of biblical books, and the developments that brought about their final canonization.[126]

## Anthropology, Theology, and Influence

There is growing awareness that Israel's poetry bears direct witness to human suffering and joy, faith and hope. This anthropological dimension is becoming ever more important in OT exegesis. Furthermore, small-group relations and to a certain extent also secondary social organization are reflected in our texts.[127] Of course, the poems in question do not contain treatises on social subjects. Yet their informal and unintentional information is therefore all the more valid, especially with regard to the life and cult of the small group.[128]

The lyrical poems do not speak only about human beings; rather, they speak primarily to and about God. They do so on many levels— implicitly in much of the "profane" poetry, explicitly and with audacity in cultic and liturgical compositions. Depending on the life situation,

---

125. See Duhm, *Psalmen*.
126. Gese, "Entstehung."
127. See Turner, *Ritual Process*.
128. See Westermann, *Das Loben*; Albertz, *Persönliche Frömmigkeit*; Gerstenberger, *Der bittende Mensch*; Muntingh, "A Few Social Concepts"; Anderson, *Out of the Depths*; Gottwald, "Poetry"; Trible, *God and the Rhetoric*.

affirmations about God can be extremely scathing and desperate or highly exuberant and almost ecstatic with happiness. There are in many of these poems marvelous manifestations of confidence and admiration; indeed, quite often they make statements about God so sublime that we are immediately impressed by their truth and depth (e.g., Ps 139:1–12). A good theology of lyrical poetry would have to distinguish, therefore, among the different human situations and recreate for each one of them that freedom of communication with God that we encounter throughout the Hebrew scriptures. Von Rad, in his *Old Testament Theology*, gave a sensible exposition of the psalmists' faith; research should pursue this direction further.[129] Most recently Kraus, in the newest edition of his commentary, devotes extensive treatment to the theology of the psalms.[130]

Any text that is preserved and used has an "after-life." In a very deep sense, this process of being utilized and interpreted is an integral part of the text. Therefore, research in the Hebrew Bible must not overlook the interpretive history of the texts. In the case of the lyrical literature we see three main areas in which research is occurring and where it should be strengthened even further. In the first place, each poem has to be followed through its interpretive history within a community of faith, be it Jewish, Christian, or other.[131] Second, we are witnessing today, especially in the Third World, the birth of a new singing by the often oppressed communities of faith, and this "new song" is greatly indebted to the old poems of Israel.[132] Finally, throughout the course of cultural history the lyrics of the Hebrew scriptures have spread their influence far beyond the confines of organized religion. The art and literature of many nations reveal the impact of these poems.[133] Quite often the recognition of such unexpected aftereffects will deepen and enhance our understanding of the ancient texts.

---

129. See also Ringgren, *Faith*; Albertz, *Persönliche Frömmigkeit*; Vorländer, *Mein Gott*; Westermann, *Das Loben*.

130. Kraus, *Theologie* (ET *Theology*).

131. See Knuth, *Zur Auslegungsgeschichte*; Arens, *Psalmen*; Cohen, "Song of Songs"; Fischer, "Christliches Psalmenverständnis"; Schneekloth, "Targum."

132. Cardenal, *Zerschneide*; Sciadini, *Salmos*.

133. See Kurz, *Psalmen*.

# 2

# The Psalms in Form-Critical Perspective

## History of Research and Development of Method

### Hermann Gunkel and Sigmund Mowinckel: Parents of Form-Critical Work

D. R. Ap-Thomas, "An Appreciation of Sigmund Mowinckel" (1966)

H. Gunkel, *Die Psalmen* (1926)

H. Gunkel and J. Begrich, *Einleitung in die Psalmen* (1933)
  ET *Introduction to Psalms* (1998/2020)

F. Heiler, *Das Gebet* (1923)
  ET *Prayer* (1932)

A. R. Johnson, "The Psalms" (1951)

A. S. Kapelrud, "Die skandinavische Einleitungswissenschaft zu den Psalmen." (1966)

W. Klatt, *Hermann Gunkel* (1969)

S. Mowinckel, *Psalmenstudien*, 6 vols. (1921–1924)
  ET *Psalm Studies*, 2 vols. (2014)

S. Mowickel, *Offersang og sangoffer* (1951)
  ET *The Psalms in Israel's Worship*, 2 vols. (1962/2004)

MODERN PSALM EXEGESIS UNTIL the 1920s traveled in the wake of scholars like Heinrich Ewald, W. M. L. de Wette, and Julius Wellhausen in Germany, Abraham Kuenen in the Netherlands, S. R. Driver in Great Britain, Adolphe Lods in France, Frants Buhl in Denmark, and G. F. Moore in the United States, all of whom were outstanding literary critics. This meant that in prevailing academic fashion most OT exegetes would look upon even the Psalter as a product of literary art. Each psalm was considered first and foremost the written proclamation of a poet. Focal points of interest, consequently, were, in the first place, the author's historical situation, the events and the environment to which he reacted in his poem, and secondly, his inner feelings, the psychological and religious condition he presumably lived in. Thus OT scholars between 1800 and 1920 mainly dedicated themselves to uncovering in each psalm traces of the history of Israel; and they were eager to learn how the psalmists put their personal experiences of national affairs into words and poetic structures. Of course this "literary," "historical," and "psychological" preoccupation (as all our exegetical endeavors always are) was prompted by presuppositions virulent in that period. History and psyche were of burning interest to nineteenth-century thinkers, philosophers and theologians alike, since F. W. Hegel had so masterfully described the rolling movements of human progress and the spirit propelling them. Small wonder, then, that essays and commentaries on the Psalter would, as a rule, concentrate on the personal and historical features in each poem and on literary techniques used. Notable examples are the expositions of T. K. Cheyne, C. A. Briggs, Rudolf Kittel, and Bernhard Duhm. Their commentaries on the psalms still can be used with profit, if their limitations are kept in mind. No doubt, nineteenth-century exegetes tended to take their own way of producing written work as the overall matrix for literary activity. (Later generations will discover, probably, the same affinity between culture and exegesis in our present time.)

Close to the turn of the century some basic attitudes started to change. Cause and effect, people felt, were not the only categories in comprehending history; emphasis on literary and poetic forms alone would not suffice to reveal the meaning of ancient documents. A new romantic movement rediscovered "mystery" and "unpredictability" as constitutive factors of reality. So it happened that in Germany a number of angry young men gathered in opposition against the prevailing Wellhausen school with its literary approach to the documents. Albert Eichhorn, William Wrede, Wilhelm Bousset, and Ernst Troeltsch became their leaders, and by the turn of the century they were known as the "religionsgeschichtliche Schule." Hugo Gressmann, a close friend of Gunkel's and an important member of that movement, bluntly described the feelings of the group: "We are fed up with being treated with literary criticism only."[1] The point was: the new school demanded—on top of literary criticism, or better, preceding it—a comprehensive analysis of history, culture, and religion. The rebels could not content themselves with reconstructions of conceptual systems or historical surface structures. They were searching for the very soul of the ancient writers, and, what is even more important, they took into account both general

---

1. Klatt, *Hermann Gunkel*, 74.

cultural and religious backgrounds and all those social factors which influence the growth of oral traditions.

Hermann Gunkel (1862-1932) became a member and a leading figure of this "religious-historical" circle, and since the new school of thought was suspect by the church and state authorities he had to fight for recognition and promotion almost to the end of his life. Gunkel indeed took a different avenue also to psalm exegesis. "Religion" and "History" were his watchwords; he aimed at retelling the story of Israel's faith in the context of the ancient Near East. Old Testament poetry and prose no longer were considered a product of literary activity, the work of authors, redactors, and publishers, but the fruit of long processes of transmission. Group life and institutionalized customs were considered instrumental in bringing about the variety of "literary" forms preserved in the Old Testament. Writing down the old traditions was only a final step, usually signalizing the end of a period in which a text was used naturally. The composition of written literature, according to Gunkel, was in most cases indicative of the fact that some learned author had cut the umbilical cord of a particular genre severing its connection to its source of life. To reduce a living text to writing in ancient times was artificial, even decadent. Gunkel wanted to portray the history of Israel's literature from the dawn of its existence in popular sayings, songs, and narrations through its period of living use to its final disintegration and codification.

How did this "religious and historical" breakthrough affect psalm interpretation in particular? Gunkel, referring back to old and new romanticists (e.g., Robert Lowth, J. G. Herder, G. Wünsch), located ancient poetry in popular activities, in various feasts and gatherings. More specifically, the majority of psalms for him clearly reflect cultic happenings: the exuberant joy or the deadly dejection of the community or individual who felt in close alliance with their God, Yahweh. There were plenty of references in the psalms, Gunkel felt, to cultic music, to processions and ritual acts, to temple and divine throne to support this genealogy. The language of the songs, furthermore, showed marks of communal and cultic use. It was repetitious and full of religious imagery. Some psalms even betrayed the activities of choirs and temple personnel as part of a worship service (cf. Pss 24; 48; 136; 1 Chr 16). Gunkel, especially after an exchange of arguments with Sigmund Mowinckel, was fully convinced that the temple cult was the ultimate source for most of Israel's psalms.[2]

By what technique did Gunkel establish his far-reaching conclusion? Several qualities had to come together in one man to insure any results in

---

2. Gunkel and Begrich, *Einleitung*, 175-80 (ET *Introduction*, 123-27).

form-critical psalm exegesis: a keen observation of linguistic patterns; a new evaluation of the formulaic character of the poems; a vivid sympathy with their "authors"; and a deep sensitivity to ancient life situations. Gunkel was able to apply his talents to the work. Because of our remoteness from the ancient scene, grammatical and syntactical analysis had to take precedence. But the listing and description of recurring phrases immediately went hand in hand with a depiction of form elements and genres and their function in real-life settings. All these different steps of investigation belong close together. The written documents were the material with which he began, but the vision of specific cult situations was always in focus whenever Gunkel worked on the psalms. There were, in short, five major psalm genres and settings for Gunkel: festive hymns, communal complaints, individual complaints, royal psalms, and thanksgiving songs—each connected with their respective worship services. Discovery of the existence and usage of the types prior to the beginning of their so-called "literary history," their generic description, and their cultic foundation were most important impulses for subsequent research.

Gunkel's way of looking at the psalms soon gained some reputation among younger scholars. His most eminent and most independent pupil in this field became Sigmund Mowinckel (1884–1965). The young Norwegian had studied with two prominent Danish teachers, Vilhelm Grønbech and Johannes Pedersen, before he met Gunkel and became intrigued by the new method. Grønbech and Pedersen both had emphasized the mysterious faculties of the soul, individual and communal, as creative powers of religion. Thus Mowinckel's background prepared him to add a new dimension to Gunkel's work and to move even more resolutely into the new direction of psalm research.

As early as 1921 Mowinckel's first volume of *Psalmenstudien* appeared, to be followed by five more weighty essays on topics in the same area. Together with his later comprehensive survey *Offersang og sangoffer* and numerous articles, these books constitute the most challenging ventures in the newer psalm research. Mowinckel's basic ideas may be summarized as follows:

1. Form-critical analysis and generic classification of the psalms as inaugurated by Gunkel are sound methods.

2. Many hymns, royal psalms, and even complaint songs can be understood only within the framework of a comprehensive Israelite festival celebrated in the fall, at the beginning of the New Year.

3. Psalms with a more individualistic outlook (e.g., psalms of sickness) are to be connected with more private services in the temple.

4. The remaining psalms are stamped by reflection, by instructional rather than cultic use and may be attributed to learned psalmographers and wise men who possibly were involved in composing and collecting liturgical texts.

It was his emphasis on specific cultic situations and his distinct conception of the ancient mentality which made Mowinckel's work such a valuable contribution to psalm research. Sometimes his approach is labeled "cult-historical" in contradistinction to Gunkel's method. But there is no real need to separate the two aspects of modern psalm exegesis that distinctly. They belong together in that Gunkel worked from literary documents towards the institutions, while Mowinckel concentrated his attention on cultic and sociological problems. Both men, as it were, called the tunes of today's psalm interpretation. The main problem still seems to be how well scholarship—even after fifty years of form-critical investigation of the psalms—can cope with the double challenge brought forth by the parents of modern psalm interpretation.

### Formal Analysis: From Begrich to Westermann and Beyond

E. Balla, *Das Ich der Psalmen* (1912)

C. Barth, *Einführung in die Psalmen* (1961)
 ET *Introduction to the Psalms* (1966)

W. Baumgartner, *Die Klagegedichte des Jeremia* (1917)

D. J. A. Clines, "Psalm Research since 1955" (1967, 1969)

P. Drijvers, *Over de Psalmen* (1956)
 ET *The Psalms* (1965)

H. Jahnow, *Das hebräische Leichenlied* (1923)

A. S. Kapelrud, "Scandinavian Research in the Psalms after Mowinckel" (1965)

H.-J. Kraus, *Psalmen*, 2 vols. (1978);
 ET *Psalms*, 2 vols. (1988, 1989)

E. A. Leslie, *The Psalms* (1949)

L. Sabourin, *The Psalms*, 2 vols. (1969)

H. Schmidt, *Die Psalmen* (1934)

W. Staerk, *Lyrik* (1920)

J. J. Stamm, "Ein Vierteljahrhundert Psalmenforschung" (1955)

C. Westermann, *Das Loben Gottes in der Psalmen*, 2nd ed. (1961)
ET *The Praise of God in the Psalms* (1981)

C. Westermann, *Der Psalter*, 2nd ed. (1967)
ET *The Psalms* (1980)

We shall now look at the first step of form-critical exegesis of the psalms and try to sketch the development from Gunkel to our present time. In Germany, no doubt, this aspect of analyzing and defining formal elements retained a certain predominance, which does not mean, of course, that German scholars altogether neglected the social backgrounds and cultic settings of the psalms.[3]

Gunkel, who in his own way was a sociable man with many friends,[4] influenced some of his colleagues with his methods. Rudolf Kittel, for instance, at least took note of the program, and Willi Staerk as early as 1911 tried to arrange his whole psalm exegesis according to Gunkel's principles. More important, however, were Gunkel's pupils. Among those who received firsthand instruction in form-critical analysis were scholars like Hans Schmidt, Emil Balla, Walter Baumgartner, Joachim Begrich, Hedwig Jahnow, all of whom later contributed pioneering studies in the area of Hebrew poetry.

But first-generation form criticism in the Psalter came to an abrupt end as a result of the Second World War. Begrich, for example, was killed in action; Schmidt in 1945 lost his chair at Halle University on account of his former political leanings, while Baumgartner had withdrawn to Basel before the Nazis took power. Thus there was a long break in German psalm research, and when the studies were renewed after the war theological presuppositions had drastically changed. Karl Barth's theology of the "Word of God" had captured the minds of those who tried to resist the devastating political dictatorship. The "Word" was set apart from any other religious phenomenon, it (or HE, as many theologians preferred to say) had become a genre all by itself, incomparable and incompatible with anything else. Most of all, it was Gerhard von Rad who influenced Psalm investigation in this direction. In addition to his lectures at Göttingen and Heidelberg Universities, several of his publications made significant contributions to form-critical research on the Psalms.[5] Other scholars with somewhat differing outlook who flourished in the fifties were Claus Westermann, Artur Weiser,[6] and Friedrich Horst. Hans-Joachim Kraus, theologically speaking, although not in terms of age, firmly belongs to this older group. In the next decade,

---

3. See below, pp. 44-48.
4. Baumgartner, "Zum 100. Geburtstag."
5. For bibliographical data, see below, pp. 44-45.
6. See below, pp. 44-48.

another shift in psalms research becomes discernible. The Barthian school of thought loses ground, and younger form critics take over, scholars like Klaus Koch, Ernst Kutsch, Hartmut Gese, Diethelm Michel, Lienhard Delekat, Walter Beyerlin, Gunther Wanke, and Frank Crüsemann. Thus form-critical work on the psalms after Gunkel can be roughly divided into three periods which are characterized by their own theological principles. A real problem is to understand how form-critical method survived the basic shifts that occurred between 1920 and 1970.[7]

The first decade of psalm research after Gunkel (roughly 1930–1940) was filled with enthusiastic work along the trail the master had blazed. Begrich and Schmidt were prototypes of faithful pupils. They worked independently and sometimes insisted on details not to Gunkel's liking,[8] but they completely shared all the fundamental persuasions of their master. Begrich, for instance, finished the important *Einleitung* in such a way that there is hardly any break between his own contribution and Gunkel's. Schmidt, among other things, edited a two-volume "Festschrift" for Gunkel's sixtieth birthday and completed a full commentary on the psalms along his master's lines. Form-critical method, therefore, as applied by these early "practitioners" in the main was identical with that of Gunkel. It was he who had laid down the three necessary requirements:[9] first, to classify the psalms by their respective life situations; second, to recognize that psalms of the same genre are governed by "a common treasure of thoughts and moods"; and third, to analyze the linguistic and poetic structures of each psalm, because this "form" of the literary text is a reflection of life conditions, thoughts, and moods.

Now, it is important to note that when Gunkel and his first pupils are talking about the "outward form" of a poem, they do not aim at a philologic explanation but an aesthetic description of phraseology, structure, and genre. Take the hymnic language for an example. Early form critics would carefully note the use of imperatives, the vocabulary, verbal tenses, number of nouns and the like, and then delineate the function and impact of such language in the context of a presupposed life situation. They noted the change of speaker or addressee in many psalms and the shift from dejection to exuberance in some complaints as well as a good number of more formal observations. These were all understood to reveal underlying sentiments and religious feelings. Linguistic surface structures emphatically are not exploited for the sake of their theological contents or concepts, but because

---

7. Klatt, *Hermann Gunkel*, 13.
8. Gunkel and Begrich, *Einleitung*, 195 (ET *Introduction*, 139).
9. Gunkel and Begrich, *Einleitung*, 22–23 (ET *Introduction*, 15–16).

they are outpourings of religious beings. And these sentiments are basically common to all peoples; in the particular case of the OT they are tied to ancient-more specifically, to ancient Near Eastern-group life, and to those religious feelings which were dominant in the respective cultural groups. Thus Gunkel and his first generation offspring could freely draw on ancient Near Eastern analogies in form and content. Israel, in their opinion, had reached a higher level of religion, but she still used the outward structures common to all in order to communicate her deeper insights and experiences. Linguistic forms, especially in the psalms, have to be placed back into full-blooded religious life according to Gunkel and his pupils, and form-critical analysis in their opinion was doing just that.

After the Second World War the scene had changed. Linguistic surface structures no longer were searched for their human sentiments by Protestant theologians but rather for revelations of the divine will. Of course there are certain difficulties in regarding prayers such as the psalms as the direct word of God. But they certainly may be taken as responses to God's will and action. Consequently, von Rad, in his famous theology of the Old Testament, puts the psalms in juxtaposition to salvation history. And form-critical method used along this line now is applied to quite different ends, namely to clarify the message of Yahweh to his people, and, secondly, to determine the role of the believer vis-à-vis this absolutely unique God. Westermann's book *The Praise of God in the Psalms* is quite a typical example. Surface structures are to be investigated because of their underlying word events. "It is therefore not the fact of the oracle as such that created this special type of Psalms of petition, but the word which in these oracles came from God."[10]

Sometimes one cannot help feeling that outright trinitarian structures are visualized behind the texts.[11] In consequence, real life situations seem to be sacrificed in favor of those mysterious "basic modes of that which occurs when man turns to God with words."[12] Words and structures, form elements, and genres become indicators of divine "occurrences." Formal analysis remains a tool of exegesis, but the theological perspective is a new one. There are some brilliant studies in ancient Near Eastern comparative materials, notably Christoph Barth's *Die Errettung vom Tode in den individuellen Klage- und Dankliedern des Alten Testaments* (1947). But as a rule, comparisons are kept to a minimum in this period, and they sometimes

---

10. Westermann, *Praise of God*, 65–70.

11. Westermann, "Struktur und Geschichte der Klage," 47: "the three-fold subject of complaint."

12. Westermann, *Praise of God*, 153.

look rather strained. Small wonder, because God's activity in this world supposedly was confined to Israel's history, and from this perspective all formal and structural affinities to Israel's neighbors must pose a problem. Hans-Joachim Kraus' commentary on the psalms and Christoph Barth's introduction to the psalms are good examples of form-critical work governed by a theology of the "Word of God."

In the sixties a new consciousness gradually came to the fore in Protestant Germany while form criticism as a method in psalm research was catching on also among Roman Catholic exegetes.[13] The influence of Karl Barth's theology has since been receding. The old problems of general religious history and development again are debated, and psalm research has been slowly drawn into this discussion. Among younger scholars there is an increasing feeling that the results of the preceding decade have to be rechecked. There is pressure to go back to Gunkel, to study again the individual genres of the psalms and their life settings,[14] and to avoid hasty and general conclusions in regard to theological purpose and meaning. Gunkel's genre classifications are subject to minor changes and relabeling. In general, they still stand, or at least they can serve as a point of departure. The same holds true for form-critical method. Strangely enough the same techniques of observation and classification, the same theories of language, of oral transmission, of genre growth and decay are still in vogue, although some skepticism seems to be seeping in and the goals of research again are shifting. Today's exegetes care less about the pious soul or the "Word of God" behind the psalm texts. Apparently they are rediscovering the importance of sociological settings, even though the older schemes and methods are still lingering on. If it is religiosity upon which attention is focused, it will be group religiosity rather than Gunkel's aesthetic and individualistic piety. And if the group itself is looked for, it will be some cultic gathering in Israel which may be illuminated by analogies from other cultures.

## Near Eastern Ritual and the Biblical Psalms

J. Aistleitner, *Die mythologischen und kultischen Texte aus Ras Schamra*, 2nd ed. (1964)

A. Bentzen, *Messias–Moses redivivus–Menschensohn* (1948; 1975)
ET *King and Messiah* (1955)

---

13. Nötscher, *Die Psalmen*; Deissler, *Die Psalmen*.
14. See below, pp. 49–71 and Chapter 3.

K.-H. Bernhardt, *Das Problem der altorientalischen Königsideologie im Alten Testament* (1961)

G. R. Driver, "The Psalms in the Light of Babylonian Research" (1926)

G. R. Driver, *Canaanite Myths and Legends* (1956)

C. M. Edsman, "Zum sakralen Königtum in der Forschung der letzten hundert Jahre" (1959)

M. Eliade, *Le Mythe de l'éternel retour* (1949)
ET *The Myth of the Eternal Return* (1954)
ET *Cosmos and History* (1959)

I. Engnell, *Studies in Divine Kingship in the Ancient Near East* (1943; 2nd ed. 1967)

H. Frankfort, *Kingship and the Gods* (1948)

T. H. Gaster, *Thespis: Ritual, Myth, and Drama in the Ancient Near East*, 2nd ed. (1961)

S. H. Hooke, ed., *Myth and Ritual* (1933)

S. H. Hooke, ed., *The Labyrinth* (1935)

S. H. Hooke, ed., *Myth, Ritual, and Kingship* (1958)

A. R. Johnson, "Divine Kingship and the Old Testament" (1950/51)

A. R. Johnson, *Sacral Kingship in Ancient Israel*, 2nd ed. (1967)

S. Mowinckel, *Psalmenstudien*, vol. 2 (1922)
ET *Psalm Studies*, vol. 1:175–490 (2014)

S. Mowinckel, *Han som kommer* (1951)
ET *He That Cometh* (1956/2005)

M. Noth, "Gott, König, Volk im Alten Testament" (1950/1957)
ET "God, King, People in the Old Testament" (1966)

H. Schmidt, *Die Thronfahrt Jahves am Fest der Jahreswende im alten Israel* (1927)

P. Volz, *Das Neujahrsfest Jahwes* (1912)

G. Widengren, *Sakrales Königtum im Alten Testament und im Judentum* (1955)

J. T. Willis, "I. Engnell's Contribution to Old Testament Scholarship" (1970)

The nineteenth century had witnessed a tremendous rise in ethnological and anthropological studies.[15] Since early romanticism and the pioneering work of the Grimm brothers, as well as that of J. G. Herder, there had been a steady increase in scholarly dedication to the study of folk tales, folk customs, and folk beliefs. Primitive man became the subject of investigation. Illumination of the lowest stages of human development promised

---

15. Evans-Pritchard, *Social Anthropology*, esp. 21–42.

to shed light also on the destinies of present-day generations.[16] In the course of such studies, quite naturally, theories emerged about the origin and nature of religious thinking. In contradistinction to earlier views the explanation of "religion" now included not only the psychic conditions of the individual but the life of the group or nation in which religious ideas were actually practiced. The sociological basis of all religious thinking came to be emphasized; rituals and customs, patterns of behavior, and structures of society were more and more taken into account. To mention but three outstanding scholars who paved the way to fuller investigations of religious rites and ceremonies: Sir E. B. Tylor (1832–1917),[17] Sir James G. Frazer (1854–1941),[18] Émile Durkheim (1858–1917).[19]

It is first against this background and second in the context of contemporaneous archaeological discoveries in the ancient Near East that the ritualistic approach to psalm research has to be seen. As the mounds of Mesopotamia were opened and innumerable tablets, temple ruins, and religious artifacts found, it became clear that the Sumerians and Akkadians had been great liturgists.[20] What could be more logical than looking for connections to and affinities with the mythological and cultic world of the Hebrews? Soon, indeed, and partly in opposition to narrowminded orthodox Christian militants, pan-Babylonian ideas sprang up. Some scholars, especially Alfred Jeremias and Hugo Winckler, with verve promoted the thesis that Mesopotamian cult and culture had permeated those of all the other peoples of the ancient Near East and had perhaps extended their influence beyond this area. Israel, they held, also had copied the ritual patterns of the Babylonians; the OT was but a dim reflection of the light emanating from the vast literatures of the Mesopotamian civilizations.

Thus we find the ritualistic interpretation of the psalms does emerge from a different direction. But we also have to realize some converging lines in ethnological and form-critical research. Form critics starting out from a purely literary point of view had discovered the importance of social relationships and ceremonial practices. Were ethnologists—at least those working in the OT field—ready to concede the merits of form-critical analysis?

16. Note two titles that were the fruit of nineteenth-century research: Boas, *The Mind of Primitive Man*; Levy-Bruhl, *Les fonctions mentales dans les sociétés inférieurs*, (ET *How Natives Think*).

17. Tylor, *Primitive Culture*.

18. Frazer, *The Golden Bough*.

19. Durkheim, *Les formes élémentaires de la vie religieuse* (ET *The Elementary Forms of the Religious Life*).

20. Zimmern, *Beiträge zur Kenntnis der babylonischen Religion*; and *ANET*, 325–401, 573–86.

Paul Volz and Sigmund Mowinckel were the first to draw special attention to the central affair in the Babylonian festive calendar, namely the New Year Festival. The evil powers of the past year had to be defeated and the good fortunes, fertility, and happiness of the coming year had to be procured annually in twelve days of celebrations and ceremonies. The king and the priesthood of the capital were the main actors in the dramatic performances; the populace took part in mourning and feasting and accompanied the processions of the god Marduk. For, in fact, the New Year Festival at Babylon was the feast of Marduk. The suffering, death, and resurrection of this deity were reenacted during those crucial days at the beginning of each new year. The elaborate ritual has come down to us,[21] as well as the mythological background of the event, contained in *Enuma Eliš*, the poem of the chaos battle and world creation.[22] Main elements of the feast, then, were the death and resurrection of the deity according to seasonal archetypes, the fixing of destinies for the new year, the performance of the sacred marriage, the enthronement of the victorious god on his olympic seat, and the acclamation of the subordinate deities.

Paul Volz and Sigmund Mowinckel took up the results of Near Eastern studies in cultic matters and looked for traces of similar rituals and festivals in ancient Israel. Even if the OT should yield only fragmentary glimpses of a ceremony comparable to the Babylonian New Year, the two scholars (independently of each other) felt encouraged by much later evidence such as Mishnaic texts (cf. e.g., the rites described in tractate Sukkah). Late Jewish rituals could help to fill in details of that ancient Israelite festival, the outlines of which could be found in the OT itself. And there were quite formidable hints in the Bible, especially in the book of Psalms, which would suggest some big cultic event also at the beginning of the Hebrew New Year. The autumn celebration (the Feast of Tabernacles, cf. Exod 34:22; Lev 23:34–44) in early times may have had that particular purpose. A good number of psalms could be interpreted—in the light of Babylonian motifs—as reflecting the ceremonials of a New Year celebration. Thus Mowinckel forcefully pointed out that those songs acclaiming Yahweh's enthronement (cf. "Yahweh has become king!" in Pss 47; 93; 96; 97; 99) fell in line with the Babylonian idea of reinstating the victorious Marduk. And there were other traits in the book of Psalms: the procession of the ark (cf. Ps 132), the taming of chaos powers (cf. Ps 77), the creation of heaven and earth (cf. Ps 104), the revitalization of

---

21. Thureau-Dangin, *Rituels accadiens*.

22. Lambert and Parker, *Enuma Eliš*. [ED: see also Lambert, *Babylonian Creation Myths*.]

the parched fields by rain (cf. Ps 65), and the charge of the Davidic king with divine and liturgical responsibilities (cf. Pss 2; 45; 110).

At first sight the methodology implied in all this is purely ethnological: a comparison of motifs, ideas, and individual ritualistic practices. But Mowinckel at least had recognized the value of form-critical analysis. His studies in the psalms demonstrate that he was able and willing to employ the "literary" tools furnished by Gunkel. Analysis of the structure of a given text and subsequent working back towards its intention and life setting were imperative for Mowinckel.

In the decades to come this integration of methods was not always mastered by the scholars of the "cult-functional" schools. By and large those who stressed the common ritualistic pattern in the ancient Near East tended to come to rash and generalized conclusions, while their more formalistic opponents (notably Martin Noth and Karl-Heinz Bernhardt) sometimes were in danger of overemphasizing literary structures and what they thought could be deduced from them.

The ritualistic approach to the psalms was boosted by the discoveries at the site of ancient Ugarit. Excavations started in 1928 and soon brought forth, together with invaluable other documents, the well-known mythological texts which gave rise to a whole new branch of studies and decisively influenced OT research. Scholars like Cyrus H. Gordon, G. R. Driver, and Joseph Aistleitner gained well-deserved merit in editing and interpreting this material. Its cultic origin and use soon had become apparent. Here was Baal, the deity of fertility, waging battle against Mot, the power of death. We read about Baal's death and resurrection, of concomitant weeping and rejoicing on earth. Baal is made king over the whole universe; banquets and exuberant joy among his fellow deities mark his victory. These and many more details fit the scheme of a New Year festival according to the Babylonian pattern. One has to imagine that the myths were enacted by king, priestesses, and priests and adorned by various ritual activities, like processions, sacrifices, meals, prayers, recitations and the like. British and Scandinavian OT scholars were quick to point out the affinities of the Ugaritic myths to the Babylonian ritual on the one hand and the OT practices on the other hand. The works of S. H. Hooke, Aubrey R. Johnson, Aage Bentzen, Ivan Engnell, Geo Widengren, and others bear witness to the virtuosity with which the Babylonian and Canaanite patterns were applied to the OT. The direct consequence for the studies of the OT psalms are that virtually all the genres and even most of the individual texts are assigned to the New Year Festival. And since the king was the central figure in the life-creating drama he was supposed to have been the reciter of most of the psalms.

This is precisely the point where the form critics like to launch their most severe attacks against "patternism." Aside from the many problems surrounding the "comparability of cultures" or their "uniformity," the specific question in our case may be: Is it possible to visualize a king in Israel or Judah who as a divine representative restaged the tale of a dying and revitalized Yahweh? Certainly, the ancient (and nomadic!) Israelite traditions did not embrace such seasonal myths. Certainly, the Hebrews were hesitant to copy the institution of kingship once they had settled among the Canaanites. But eventually they did, and we may be sure that some elements in the ancient Near Eastern kingship ideology and royal ritual as well as the belief in the renewal of the year came in at the very same time. The psalms and other OT texts do show that Israel was touched by these foreign influences, although it is very hard to estimate how deeply they penetrated or whether they came to dominate the cultic life of the people of Yahweh.

## Covenant Theology and the Psalms

A. Arens, *Die Psalmen im Gottesdienst des alten Bundes* (1961)

A. Deissler, *Die Psalmen*, 3 vols. (1963–1965)

F. C. Fensham, "Psalm 21—A Covenant Song?" (1965)

K. Koch, "Tempeleinlassliturgien und Dekaloge" (1961)

G. E. Mendenhall, "Ancient Oriental and Biblical Law" (1954/70)

E. Nielsen, *Shechem: A Traditio-Historical Investigation* (1955)

Q. Quell, *Das kultische Problem der Psalmen* (1926)

G. von Rad, *Das formgeschichtliche Problem des Hexateuch* (1938/1958)
    ET "The Form-critical Problem of the Hexateuch" (1966)

G. von Rad, "Das jüdische Königsritual" (1947/1958)
    ET "The Judean Royal Ritual" (1966)

G. von Rad, "'Gerechtigkeit' und 'Leben' in der Kultsprache der Psalmen" (1950/1958)
    ET "'Righteousness' and 'Life' in the Cultic Speech of the Psalms" (1966)

G. von Rad, "Israel vor Jahwe (Die Antwort Israels)" (1957)
    ET "Israel before Yahweh (The Answer of Israel)" (1962)

A. Weiser, "Die Darstellung der Theophanie in den Psalmen und im Festkult" (1950)

A. Weiser, *Die Psalmen*, 2 vols. (1950)
    ET *The Psalms* (1962)

The decisive role theological thinking played even in form-critical psalm research has already been referred to above. It is fascinating to study this problem in more detail and in doing so provide a sequel to the discussion of feasts in OT scholarship. The discovery of ancient Near Eastern ceremonialism in fact did influence even those form critics who worked on the basis of a "pure theology of the Word of God." The result was a peculiar understanding of those ancient Israelite customs which were considered the life setting of the OT psalms.

Between 1933 and 1939 Walther Eichrodt published his three-volume *Theologie des Alten Testaments*. The author then was Professor of OT Scriptures at Basel University and a colleague of Karl Barth. In what we may call a remarkable synchronization of events, Eichrodt pointed out that the covenant between Yahweh and Israel—a unique institution in the ancient world—was the focal point for all theological thinking in the OT.[23] Consequently he proceeded to explain systematically all OT life and literature from this perspective. When Gerhard von Rad established the existence of the *Fest der Bundeserneuerung* ("the feast of covenant renewal") of the Hebrew tribal amphictyony as the background of the hexateuchal traditions, Eichrodt's ideas seemed to be reinforced. Later George E. Mendenhall, Klaus Baltzer, and others gave form-critical assistance to this prevailing taste in OT interpretation cherished at least in Germany and the United States. They tried to demonstrate that an overall ancient Near Eastern treaty scheme had been adopted by the Israelites in order to express their belief in a covenantal relationship to Yahweh. As a result, "covenant" really became the master key for some circles of OT exegetes; covenantal interpretations sprang up like a torrent; and there was hardly any text in the OT which could escape being incorporated into the fashionable scheme. The specter lasted until Dennis J. McCarthy analyzed more soberly the pros and cons of the treaty form,[24] and Lothar Perlitt finally proved that covenant theology in the OT is basically the result of the critical developments of the sixth and seventh centuries.[25]

The surge of "covenantalism" had to affect form-critical psalm research as well. One typical example is presented by A. Weiser and his interpretation of the OT Psalter. There are several observations and presuppositions which led him to assume that the fall festival in Israel was centered around the renewal of the covenant. First of all he finds evidence within the psalms themselves: Yahweh's self-revelation looms large in some of the liturgical texts.[26] Secondly, other features fall in line with

---

23. K. Barth, *Church Dogmatics* I/1, e.g., §§41, 57.
24. See McCarthy, *Treaty and Covenant*.
25. See Perlitt, *Bundestheologie im Alten Testament*.
26. See the description of a theophany in Pss 18; 50; 81; etc., as well as the critical assessment of this pivotal point by J. Jeremias, *Theophanie*.

and are subordinate to this central act of revelation: the proclamation of apodictic, divine commandments (cf. Ps 81);[27] the enumeration of saving acts in history (cf. Ps 78); the celebration of Yahweh's creative power and royal rule (cf. Pss 47; 104); the universal judgment over peoples and nations (cf. Pss 68; 82; 99); the enthronement of the Judaean king (cf. Pss 2; 45), and many more. For Weiser, all these motifs perfectly fit the covenant ideology. He argues that the cultic tradition of Yahweh's covenant festival had a distinctive character of its own which dominated all the essential thoughts in the book of Psalms.[28] Thirdly, Weiser freely draws upon every bit of information in the historical and legal books of the OT which might pertain to the autumnal covenant festival. Thus he hopes to convince the reader that the comprehensive celebration at the end of the year really was designed by the ancient Israelites to reestablish their formal alliance with Yahweh rather than renewing the potencies of nature.

Small wonder, then, that according to Weiser virtually all the genres of OT psalmody should be attributed to the covenant festival; at least they should be seen in close proximity to the ideology of the covenant. That means that those form elements and genres which cannot originally be tied to covenantal customs and ceremonies have been adapted to it at a later stage. They, too, need to be interpreted in the light of Israel's covenant faith.

Festive hymns of all sorts raise small difficulties for Weiser. If they praise Yahweh's deeds in history, Yahweh's victories over the enemy, or Yahweh's chastisement of Israel, they are automatically earmarked for the covenant liturgy. In cases where they are prayers for rain and fertility (cf. Ps 65) or adoration of sky and sun (cf. Ps 19A) or reminiscent of the chaos battle and other nature mythology (cf. Pss 29; 77), these hymns have been drawn in from a pagan environment and incorporated into the covenantal (and genuinely Israelite) framework. Likewise, all the hymns concerning "kingship," be it heavenly or earthly, are basically of foreign provenance but fully adapted to covenant ideology. Complaint psalms and thanksgiving songs too can easily be claimed for the covenant festival as long as they are communal in character. Israel—suffering under the punishment of a "jealous" covenant partner whenever breaking away from him—would turn to her God at the fall festival or on special days of mourning and confess her sins or complain about injustice done to her in order to be restored to a good standing within the covenant relationship (cf. Pss 44; 106). Communal thanksgivings, according to Weiser, come close to hymns in style and character (cf. Pss 67; 124; 129).

---

27. Gerstenberger, "Covenant and Commandment."
28. Weiser, *Psalms*, 23–35.

The individual complaint poses much more serious problems, however. Weiser recognizes that in these prayers a real individual is pouring out his sorrows before Yahweh (cf. Ps 102:1), and there is no doubt in his mind that the earlier collective interpretation held by the elder R. Smend and others is not tenable. How then can individual prayers be connected to anything as comprehensive as the covenant ceremony of all Israelite tribes? Weiser in the main has a twofold answer. The individual Israelite is part and parcel of the covenant community; he cannot possibly exist on his own and thus *per definitionem* can approach his God only by way of the communal cult. Weiser uses 1 Sam 1, Hannah's distress and prayer, as one strong argument in this context. The covenant community on the other hand is highly interested to see its covenant God also help the individual member. This mutual interdependence of individual and community Weiser takes as a warrant for the idea that communal and individual worship are tied together in the very same way. Within some individual prayers he indeed discovers communal traits, and quite a number of motifs and terms in such songs prove to be identical with their communal variety.[29]

Finally there are the so-called wisdom poems, notorious especially among German form critics for their "natural theology," their black and white cliches of the pious and the wicked man, their legalism, their speculative theodicy, and their total lack of interest in matters of cult or salvation history. For Weiser all these features do not pose insurmountable obstacles. He simply believes that the covenant cult in Israel also made use of wisdom forms and topics in order to illuminate genuine covenant structures by wisdom elements.[30]

There should be some concluding and critical comments at this point on what has been said so far about the development of form-critical psalm research.

a. From the very outset, form-critical work on the OT psalms got entangled with other methods of research, that is with other interests, aspects, and presuppositions, with value judgments and theological assumptions. And, in fact, nobody should expect it to be otherwise; there is no way of avoiding a merger of methods. The reason is quite apparent. Form-critical analysis *has* to search for life situations which in themselves are satisfactory explanations for the origin and growth of a given genre. Settings like these, however, cannot be grasped by mere analyses of linguistic structures; they call for appropriate application of sociological, anthropological, historical, and even theological methods. This is why Gunkel and Mowinckel would

---

29. Weiser, *Psalms*, 66–72.
30. Weiser, *Psalms*, 88–89.

not limit form-critical work to stupefying vivisection of literary remains but included all possible avenues which might lead back towards a fuller understanding of the pertinent life situations. Naturally, the path backwards into the shadows of history is long and arduous and there are many places where direct and precise information is lacking so that mere speculation can intervene. Basically, however, form-critical method in its wider sense as visualized by Gunkel and Mowinckel is a sound one to serve psalm research now and in the future. All the evidence gathered until now furthermore points to the fact that cultic performances of some kind have been background and fertile soil for most of the OT psalms.

b. Scandinavian and British ceremonialists and continental covenantalists as pictured above are both correct in pursuing form-critical work on the psalms towards possible fountainheads for the different genres. Again, they are both perfectly correct in singling out cultic activities as the life settings for the psalms. But they are overzealous in postulating, each group according to its own upbringing and mentality only one point of origin for a great variety of psalm types. Perhaps they both miss their point because they employ too many general truths and hypotheses, combining them freely, instead of looking for empirical and full-blooded details. A seasonal feast probably cannot be reconstructed by means of motifs and ideas supposedly inherent in the rituals but by assembling data about the real performances. Since such data are lacking in the OT the ceremonialists and covenantalists fill in the gaps with their preconceived ideas of what could have happened at the grand autumnal festival in Israel. And their feast, be it called New Year/Enthronement Festival or Covenant Renewal Festival, at times looks like a specter or a bag of bubbles.

c. Maybe there is a way to be more realistic in portraying ancient life situations in general and those cultic ceremonies in particular which gave birth to our OT psalms. We can possibly find much needed information outside the OT. Of course many sources, especially in the ancient Near East, have been tapped already. What is meant here is this: More data about rites and feasts, songs and liturgies, taken from Israel's neighbors as well as from other times and cultures could give us a better idea of what was feasible in the field of cultic activities. In other words, the vast information about cult and ritual which is at our disposal as the product of scores of anthropological and historical investigations should be used by OT scholars to narrow down the number of choices we have for depicting or reconstructing the cultic affairs of ancient Israel. To give but one example, by way of careful comparison with other cultures one could perhaps establish that worship services catering to the needs of individuals (even though they are considered members of a religious group) need not be tied to a communal cult pertaining to the affairs of tribe, nation, or community at large the way our "ceremonialists" or "covenantalists" would like to make us believe.

## Classification of Psalms: The Genres

### Complaints and Thanksgivings

G. W. Anderson, "Enemies and Evildoers in the Book of Psalms" (1965)

G. W. Ahlström, *Psalm 89: Eine Liturgie aus dem Ritual des leidenden Königs* (1959)

C. Barth, *Die Errettung vom Tode in den individuellen Klage- und Dank-liedern des Alten Testaments* (1947)

W. Beyerlin, *Die Rettung der Bedrängten in den Feindpsalmen der Einzelnen auf institutionelle Zusammenhänge untersucht* (1970)

H. Birkeland, *The Evildoers in the Book of Psalms* (1955)

R. L. Caplice, "Namburbi Texts in the British Museum" (1965, 1967, 1970, 1971)

R. L. Caplice, "Participants in the Namburbi-Rituals" (1967)

G. R. Castillino, *Le lamentazioni individuali e gli inni in Babilonia e in Israele* (1939)

E. R. Dalglish, *Psalm Fifty-One* (1962)

L. Delekat, *Asylie und Schutzorakel an Zionheiligtum* (1967)

E. S. Gerstenberger, *Der bittende Mensch* (1980/2010)

W. W. Hallo, "Individual Prayer in Sumerian" (1968)

J. Krecher, *Sumerische Kultlyrik* (1966)

S. Mowinckel, *Psalmenstudien* I: *Awän und die individuellen Klagesalmen* (1921)
ET *Psalm Studies*, vol. 1, 1–173 (2014)

E. K. Ritter, "Magical-Expert and Physician in Babylonian Medicine" (1965)

H. Schmidt, *Das Gebet der Angeklagten im Alten Testament* (1929)

C. Westermann, *Das Loben Gottes in den Psalmen*, 2nd ed. (1961)
ET *The Praise of God in the Psalms* (1965); also included in *Praise and Lament in the Psalms* (1981)

C. Westermann, "Struktur und Geschichte der Klage im Alten Testament" (1954)
ET included in *Praise and Lament in the Psalms*, 165–213 (1981)

J. W. Wevers, "A Study in the Form-Criticism of Individual Complaint Psalms" (1956)

G. Widengren, *The Accadian and Hebrew Psalms of Lamentation as Religious Documents* (1936)

H. W. Wolff, "Der Aufruf zur Volksklage" (1964)

Gunkel's fourfold design of complaint psalms and thanksgiving songs still is fundamental to all discussions of the matter today. He distinguished between individual and communal complaints, provoked by personal or collective danger and distress and performed in appropriate worship services at the temple. Correspondence of genres seems to be very reasonable and in agreement with what we know about ancient (and modern for that matter) cultic practices. Unfortunately our OT source material is not so unambiguous that we can take things for granted.

A strange phenomenon, to begin with, is the fact that in the extant body of material we realize a great preponderance of individual prayers. There are in the OT Psalter about fifty complaint psalms of the private type and nearly twenty thanksgiving songs to go with them according to Gunkel's count. Communal complaints, although clearly attested in terms of structure and life setting by quite a number of OT passages, comprise less than ten specimens in the book of Psalms, and communal thanksgivings pretty much merge with the hymnic genre.[31] Looking, then, at the four genres at hand, it is certainly impressive to see the large number of psalms destined to serve the needs of individuals. Most form critics so far have been overly fascinated by the communal or national aspects of Israel's faith. Following Gunkel, they dealt with hymns and congregational songs in the first place and attribute to this order of things quite a bit of theological significance. A better starting point is individual prayers and their settings.

Of course this view can be maintained only after an express refutation of that contrary opinion which seeks to eliminate all "private" psalms from the OT scene. Mainly, the Scandinavian and British scholars referred to above as "ceremonialists" hold that all complaints and thanksgivings which on the surface use the personal "I" were originally national psalms sung by the king. He, representing the corporate personality, the soul of his people, would stand up before Yahweh in national services, probably at the New Year celebrations. Only later on, after the kingdom had vanished in Israel, so this opinion goes, did such psalms become "democratized" and handed over to "everyman" for "private" use. Birkeland went to the extreme in defending this view, and Mowinckel in his later years followed his pupil rather closely.[32]

Granted, there is a whole cluster of presuppositions and observations that make up the fabric of this collective scheme. Nevertheless it may be sufficient to point to a few cardinal errors in order to establish the legitimacy

---

31. Gunkel and Begrich, *Einleitung*, 314-23 (ET *Introduction*, 240-47); Crüsemann, *Studien*, 202-6; see below, pp. 58-68.

32. Mowinckel, *The Psalms*, 1:225-46.

of dealing with individual prayers in the OT psalter. For example, the "enemy" in OT complaint songs by no means can be construed as a national foe in the majority of cases. The "king" cannot simply be taken out of royal psalms like Pss 20; 45; or 110 and transplanted into all the other texts. Most important, worship services for individuals in the OT are unquestionable. Also there is positive evidence from many other cultures that the official and national cult quite often goes side by side with the more "private" rites (*rites de passage*, etc.) without too much interference or interdependence.

## *Individual Complaints and Thanksgivings*

Form critics of differing schools of thought show significant agreement regarding the structure and formal elements of the psalms to be discussed here. According to Gunkel, individual complaints may roughly display the following outline and setup (we have to keep in mind, however, that there is no fixed order to these texts and that each element may be more or less elaborate within one poem or, at times, missing altogether):

1. Invocation (usually including an appellation to Yahweh and initial plea); cf. Pss 6:2; 26:1; 38:2.

2. Complaints (description of suffering, reproachful questions, etc.); cf. Pss 22:1–9, 13–19; 38:1–9, 11–15, 18, 20–21; 69:2b–5, 8–13, 20–22.

3. Plea or petition for help (usually imperatives: "help, save me, wake up, have mercy," etc.); cf. Pss 3:8; 26:11; 57:2; 86:2.

4. Condemnation of enemies or imprecation against wrong-doers; cf. Pss 35:1–8; 69:23–29; 109:6–20.

5. Affirmation of confidence (Gunkel considered this part as the outstanding example of a more general category of elements, namely the "motives for Yahweh's intervention."[33] But the general label is hardly of any use, for, in fact, all the form elements thus brought together can be aligned with either plea or complaint); cf. Pss 13:6; 22:10–11; 31:2–6; 142:6.

6. Confession of sins or assertion of innocence; cf. Pss 26:4–6; 51:5–7.

7. Acknowledgment of divine response; vow or pledge; cf. Pss 6:10; 7:18; 56:13; 109:30.

8. Hymnic elements, blessings; cf. Pss 5:5–7; 31:20–25; 69:33–37.

---

33. Gunkel and Begrich, *Einleitung*, 231–32 (ET *Introduction*, 168–70).

Reading through Gunkel's and Begrich's treatment of the matter,[34] one cannot help but be amazed at the immense variety of forms, the proliferation of formulaic expressions,[35] and syntactical structures. It is equally astonishing to see Gunkel's mind at work bringing about a plausible and comprehensible order without pressing the material into rigid patterns. Gunkel was never a formalist; he always paid due tribute to life conditions. In fact he was bent on recovering the *Sitz im Leben* in as vivid and colorful details as possible. So up to this day there is little reason to take issue with his formal analysis of the individual complaints. Only minor questions may be raised. Is it really necessary to distinguish between "wish" and "plea" the way he does on the strength of different Hebrew grammatical forms (imperative versus jussive)?[36] "These wishes contain all the motifs we already found in the request forms."[37] Both forms furthermore can serve the same end within the complaint structure. So, why keep them segregated that strictly? Or another question already raised above: Should we retain the general category of "motives for Yahweh's intervention" which seems so vague and elusive? While such minor corrections without doubt are necessary, Gunkel's analysis of the individual complaint must still stand basically uncontested. Scholars as different as Widengren, Kraus, Mowinckel, Westermann, Sabourin, Deissler, Wevers,[38] and many others are almost unanimous in following Gunkel's lead in so far as structural observations are concerned.

The same holds true in a small degree for the individual thanksgiving songs. Gunkel's analysis here has come under more critical scrutiny and has been sharpened and modified to a certain extent.[39] Nevertheless, his basic insights still hold true.

Gunkel quite correctly pointed out: "It is this genre in particular which we are able to locate with complete certainty in its original setting, the worship service."[40] There are clear records in the OT showing Israelites who bring their offerings after being heard and helped by God. Before or during presentation of the offering, they recited their thanksgiving prayer (cf. 1 Sam

34. Gunkel and Begrich, *Einleitung*, 212–50 (ET *Introduction*, 152–86).

35. Culley, *Oral Formulaic Language in the Biblical Psalms*.

36. See Gunkel and Begrich, *Einleitung*, 218–29 (ET *Introduction*, 157–68).

37. Gunkel and Begrich, *Einleitung*, 224 (ET *Introduction*, 164).

38. Widengren, *Akkadian and Babylonian Psalms of Lamentation*; Kraus, *Psalmen* 1:XLV–XLVI; Mowinckel, *The Psalms*, 2:9–11; Westermann, *Struktur und Geschichte*, 48; Sabourin, *Psalms*, 2:1–4; Deissler, *Psalmen*, 1:16–18; Wevers, "A Study."

39. Westermann, *Praise*; Mand, "Die Eigenständigkeit der Danklieder"; Beyerlin, "Die *toda*"; and especially Crüsemann, *Studien*, 210–84.

40. Gunkel and Begrich, *Einleitung*, 265 (ET *Introduction*, 199).

1:24—2:10). There is such an intricate connection between thanksgiving and preceding complaint ceremonies that occasionally it seems thanks are offered immediately after the complaint has been "filed" and Yahweh's favorable answer received. The connecting link in this situation between the complaint and the thanksgiving is the *Heilsorakel*, the salvation oracle,[41] and Ps 22:23–32 is a telling example that should also warn us not to draw the dividing line between thanksgiving song and hymn too sharply.[42]

The following are the structural elements of the personal thanksgiving song as Gunkel visualized them:

1. Call to sing, give thanks, etc. (directed either to the supplicant's own seif or to the participants in the ritual; akin to the hymnic introduction); cf. Pss 30:2; 107:1; 118:1–4.

2. Account of trouble and salvation (narration to the worshipping community, usually talks of the great danger to which the supplicant was about to succumb and of Yahweh's merciful help); cf. Pss 18:5–20; 30:3–4, 9–12; 40:3–4.

3. Praise of Yahweh the savior; cf. Pss 18:2–4, 47–49; 40:6; 118:28.

4. Announcement of sacrifice; cf. Pss 66:13–15; Jonah 2:10.

5. Blessings upon participants; cf. Pss 40:5; 118:8–9, 26.

6. Hymnic elements (general praises of Yahweh); cf. Pss 30:5–6; 138:2, 4–6.

For this basic structure, reference must be made first of all to Gunkel and Begrich, *Einleitung*.[43] For modifications of this scheme one has to turn to Westermann. Presupposing that "the 'categories' of the Psalms are not first of all literary or cultic in nature" but "basic modes of that which occurs when man turns to God with words," or "basic occurrences,"[44] he resolutely merges personal hymns and personal thanksgivings (as well as the corresponding communal genres) into one new type,[45] and with equal resolution divides it again into two new categories, namely, the declarative and the descriptive psalms of praise.[46] Crüsemann, on the other hand, refutes Westermann's efforts and postulates two original types of thanksgivings

---

41. Begrich, "Das priesterliche Heilsorakel."
42. See also Ps 92 and Crüsemann's *Studien*, which attempts to clarify the matter.
43. Gunkel and Begrich, *Einleitung*, 267–74 (ET *Introduction*, 201–7).
44. Westermann, *Praise*, 153.
45. Westermann, *Praise*, 18.
46. Westermann, *Praise*, 102–42.

distinguished by their usage of "thou" and "he" styles respectively when addressing Yahweh.[47] Those differences supposedly reflect two stages in the thanksgiving ceremony, the address of the worshipping community before the sacrifice (the "he" style) and the address to Yahweh when the sacrifice is offered (the "thou" style) . In spite of these and other contributions, Gunkel's structural arrangement of the thanksgiving song of the individual may still serve as the starting point for our discussion.

While the structural problems of individual complaints and thanksgivings are not too severe, a heated debate has been going on since the days of Gunkel as to the proper occasions and life settings to be attributed to these prayers. What precisely were the cultic ceremonies in which these texts were performed? Who were the performers and participants? Several theories have been advanced, of which the two main types will be sketched here. They both of course refer initially to the complaint psalm.

We have to leave Gunkel behind at this point, for in his opinion the extant texts already are far removed from their original cultic situation. The complaint psalms in the OT, he assumed, had been composed by a later, more "spiritual" and less "cultic" generation. ("Spiritualization" ever since has been a catchword among Continental form critics, possibly because of their subconscious distrust of all cultic affairs.)[48] But there are scholars who have overcome their aversion to the cult. Insofar as they believe in personal OT prayers and rites they agree that the individual complaints were answering deadly perils against personal life and well-being such as sickness, slander, persecution, and misfortune. Most experts favor one or the other of these as the cause for the individual prayer.

Mowinckel was the first to publish a detailed situational analysis of the personal complaint. For the most part he considered these prayers as psalms of sickness.[49] Although he later restated his case,[50] hazards to physical or mental health remain for him predominant motivations for personal prayer. Among those hazards, less known to modern man, are evil deeds performed by word of mouth, by secret or open curse and slanderous talk. All of these in ancient times were held to be contributory causes of sickness and misfortune. Mowinckel in particular singled out the phrase *poale' 'awen*, evildoers (cf. Pss 6:9; 59:3, 8; 64:3-7) and their machinations. Sickness could be inflicted by sorcerers, and the only way to counteract their evil deeds was by

---

47. Crüsemann, *Studien*, 225-67.

48. Von Rad, *Theologie des Alten Testaments*, 1:400-405 (ET *Old Testament Theology*, 1:402-8); Hermisson, *Sprache und Ritus*.

49. Mowinkel, *Psalmenstudien* I (ET *Psalm Studies*, vol. 1:1-173.)

50. Mowinckel, *The Psalms*, 1:225-46; 2:1-25.

supplication to Yahweh.[51] Complaint psalms of the individual, then, are integral liturgical parts of a ritual performed at the request of people suffering from severe ills, especially in cases where an evil spell had been diagnosed as the root of the trouble. Thanksgiving songs which were enjoined when a sick person had been healed belong to the ritual of the thanksgiving sacrificial service. Mowinckel's view has much to commend it and in fact has been taken into account by most exegetes with more or less enthusiasm as far as the sorcery part is concerned.

Hans Schmidt discovered another location for individual complaints, which he tended to overstress at times. There are psalms which can rightly be called "protestations of innocence" (cf. Pss 7; 17; 26). Supported by chance references in the OT, like 1 Kgs 8:30-32, Schmidt concluded that persons indicted, imprisoned, or sentenced subjected themselves to some kind of ordeal (cf. Num 5:11-31) and were given a chance to appeal to Yahweh in prayer. Mesmerized by his idea, be found numerous vestiges of judicial procedures. According to him, even the psalms of sickness might have carried this additional feature; the sick person being shunned and even accused for his alleged contact with evil deeds or powers.

Lienhard Delekat and Walter Beyerlin each in bis own way carry the judicial aspects of the individual complaints some steps further. Delekat considers most texts of this genre to be mural inscriptions scribbled on the temple wall by people who sought refuge in the sanctuary (cf. Deut 19:1-13). Complaints and thanksgivings added later even tell him exactly how the refugee subsequently fared. He held his "sleep of incubation" in the temple, received oracles, experienced dreams, had to undergo ordeals, and was finally hired and put under contract as a temple worker. Beyerlin is more elusive and general in his descriptions. He talks about an institution attached to the temple which promulgated and enforced divine jurisdiction in special cases. The complaints of the individual partly are to be understood as appeals to this *kultische Gottesgerichtsinstitution*, a divine court of justice at the temple.

The "judicial" approach to the complaints of the individual also has something to recommend it. After being rid of some hypothetical exaggerations, especially those of Delekat, one cannot help but admit that "protestations of innocence" may have been used in worship services or ordeal ceremonies which were considered as appeals to Yahweh the supreme judge. What kind of "institution" really acted as recipient of the plea or took action to implement a divine sentence is hard to tell. Possibly there was no one but a priest leading a given complaint ceremony, and all

---

51. For excellent comparative material from a far-away culture, see Fortune, *Sorcerers of Dobu*.

the judicial terms were nothing but profane imagery adapted to a religious rite. And yet, the judicial aspect should not be neglected; it deserves notice along with the "medical" type which Mowinckel inaugurated. Most scholars actually regard both explanations as legitimate, and there are numerous variations and nuances to each of them as well as various combinations and exegetical operations on every single text.[52]

## Royal Complaints and Thanksgivings

A few remarks concerning royal complaints and thanksgivings may be in order at this point because we do not want to classify the royal psalms as an altogether new and separate genre. Gunkel and Begrich did,[53] and most commentators and exegetes accept their view.[54] Gunkel himself, however, knew quite well that the royal psalms are no homogeneous group but songs of different origin and function which happen to be used with royal festivities.[55] Therefore royal complaints and thanksgivings should be placed in between individual and communal prayers of that type. The court had adapted such psalms for its own needs to be used in royal worship services. We may say that all the extant psalms which are clearly designed to be spoken by or for the king and which can best be explained against the background of a ritual petition or thanksgiving to Yahweh may be claimed as royal complaints, petitions, or thanksgivings. This interpretation, of course, is in direct contrast to that which rates all royal ceremonies as first and much older than "private" rites. For Israel we may safely assume, however, that popular use of complaint and thanksgiving prayers has a longer tradition and that the masters of ceremony at the northern and southern court drew from this tradition.

In the area of complaint, petition, and thanksgiving we find a few good examples: Pss 18; 20; 21; 72; 89; 101; 132; and 144. Careful analysis of each text would reveal that a great number of structural elements, formulaic expressions and motifs from "popular" counterparts have gone into the royal psalms of petition and thanksgiving.[56] On the other hand the influence of imperial court tradition of the ancient Near East can be

---

52. Cf. Kraus, *Psalmen*; Deissler, *Psalmen*; Weiser, *Psalms*; Leslie, *Psalms*; Sabourin, *Psalms*; C. Barth, *Einführung* (ET *Introduction*); Wevers, "A Study"; et al.

53. Gunkel and Begrich, *Einleitung*, 140–71 (ET *Introduction*, 99–120).

54. Cf. bibliographical references above, pp. 39–40; and Crim, *The Royal Psalms*.

55. Gunkel and Begrich, *Einleitung*, 146–47 (ET *Introduction*, 103).

56. Cf. most of all the commentaries by Gunkel, Schmidt, Leslie, Weiser, Kraus, Sabourin, et al.

detected. Yahweh's theophany (cf. Ps 18) certainly was not to be expected to honor some plain Israelite; supplication for the king and thanksgiving for him (cf. Pss 20; 21), with due reverence for the anointed, are reminiscent of ancient Near Eastern court etiquette; references to the king's enthronement (cf. Ps 89; 101) reflect ritual features of this important event, as well as the divine promise to the new king (Ps 89:20-38) and the royal oath (Ps 101). The presence of hymnic elements also may point to the exuberance and national dimension of court festivities. Still, the royal psalms should be seen in conjunction with their "popular" counterparts.

## Communal Complaints and Thanksgivings

Communal complaints in their structure and setting are comparable to individual prayers of the same sort, the basic difference being that now "all kinds of community distress: war, captivity, plague, drought, famine ..."[57] are prompting religious activities. A day of fasting is called (cf. Judg 20:26-28; 21:2-3; Jer 14:2; Neh 9:1), sacrifices are prepared, and communal complaints are sung by choirs, priests, or all the congregation, perhaps in a repetitious ceremony which may have included many rites of which we no longer have knowledge. The contents of the communal prayer we know from the individual complaint: An invocation, a complaint, plea, or petition, an affirmation of confidence, a confession of guilt or protestation of innocence, and hymnic elements. The main formal distinction between the two genres is the fact that collective complaints usually speak in the first person plural, and quite often the national calamity is clearly referred to (cf. Pss 44; 74). This is not to deny that there may be communal complaints in the "I" form.[58] Because the situation of danger, threat, and fear is so much alike whether one person or a whole community is affected, there is a good chance that elements and motifs of the individual and communal liturgies may have been interchanged or mutually influenced. Indeed we witness the same sort of wandering of texts in our hymnbooks and church services. Individual expressions of faith are used by a whole congregation, and communal poems may be read or sung by one person who includes himself in the "we" form of the text. In spite of all affinities between OT complaints, be it individual or collective, it should be taken for granted that the "I" psalms are basically personal in character and reflect services for an individual. Because communal complaints "are recognizable partly by the use of 'we,' partly by the

---

57. Gunkel and Begrich, *Einleitung*, 118 (ET *Introduction*, 82).
58. Mowinckel, *The Psalms*, 1:225-46.

occasion which produced them,"[59] scholars in large measure agree as to the concrete texts which are to be so named: Pss 44; 58; 60; 74; 79; 80; 83. Even so, a more substantial group of psalms remains under debate.[60]

About congregational thanksgivings there is no need to say very much more. Since it is perfectly clear that there were in Israel public fasting days with complaint services, there is no reason whatsoever to doubt that public thanksgiving days were also observed. It is especially awkward to argue from a dogmatic viewpoint as follows: Israel continuously praised her Lord; the eternal praise was interrupted by complaint days only in time of grave danger; there was no need to celebrate special thanksgivings, as it was entirely sufficient to resume the normal praise after the crisis had been overcome.[61] We may safely assume that special thanksgiving days were held in Israel in the ordinary course of events. It is an entirely different problem whether or not these special days "gave birth" to a separate genre of psalms. Judging from the evidence preserved in the OT Psalter we indeed may be pessimistic. Only Pss 66:8-12; 67; 124; 129 have a chance to qualify as national thanksgiving songs. But the OT, we must remember, preserves only a tiny selection of all the songs actually used in the long history of Israel. And, furthermore, hymns proper could very well take the place and function of a thanksgiving song in a day of feasting and joy over Yahweh's help.

### Hymns of Praise

W. F. Albright, "A Catalogue of Early Hebrew Lyric Poems (Ps 68)" (1950/51)

J. Blenkinsopp, "Ballad Style and Psalm Style in the Song of Deborah" (1961)

F. Crüsemann, *Studien zur Formgeschichte von Hymnus und Danklied in Israel* (1969)

A. Deissler, "Zur Datierung und Situierung der 'kosmischen' Hymnen Pss 8, 19, 29" (1961)

T. E. Fretheim, "Psalm 132: A Form-Critical Study" (1967)

T. H. Gaster, "Psalm 45" (1955)

H. L. Ginsberg, "A Phoenician Hymn in the Psalter" (1938)

J. Gray, "The Kingship of God in the Prophets and Psalms" (1961)

K. Koch, "Denn seine Güte währet ewiglich" (1961)

H.-J. Kraus, *Die Königsherrschaft Gottes im Alten Testament* (1951)

---

59. Mowinckel, *The Psalms*, 1:194

60. Sabourin, *Psalms*, 2:141-43.

61. Thus, in all seriousness, Crüsemann, *Studien*, 204-6, following von Rad and Westermann.

L. Krinetzki, "Zur Poetik und Exegese von Psalm 48" (1960)

E. Lipinski, *La royaute de Yahwe dans la poesie et le culte de l'ancien Israel* (1965)

E. Lipinski, *Le Poeme royal du Psaume LXXXIX, 1-5, 20-38* (1967)

J. Morgenstern, "The Cultic Setting of the Enthronement Psalms" (1964)

S. Mowinckel, *Der achtundsechzigste Psalm* (1953)

J. Patterson, *Praises of Israel* (1950)

H. G. Reventlow, "Der Psalm 8" (1967)

H. H. Rowley, "The Text and Structure of Psalm 2" (1941)

N. H. Snaith, *Hymns of the Temple* (1951)

W. S. Towner, "'Blessed be YHWH' and 'Blessed art thou, YHWH': The Modulation of a Biblical Formula" (1968)

A hymn, in our understanding, is a "song of praise to God" (Merriam-Webster), and not only the name but also the contents of this definition have come down to us in the stream of Greco-Christian tradition. We think of melodious presentations, of solemn and joyful crowds, of colorful clergy, festive congregations, lofty domes. Not many of the traits customary to us may hold true when we discuss Israelite hymnody. What is even more troublesome in form-critical research is the fact that the term "hymn" from the very beginning proved too general and too vague and, on top of this, too heavily freighted with emotional values. "The basic moods of these poems are enthusiasm, adoration, reverence, praise and laudation..."[62] "The core of the hymn of praise is the consciousness of the poet and congregation that they are standing face to face with the Lord himself... and worshipping him with praise and adoration."[63]

A common stock of phrases and moods alone is not sufficient to delineate a genre.[64] Westermann's futile search for some "basic occurrence" beyond cultic affairs[65] only proves that thus far the first condition of form-critical investigation, namely to locate a recurring event that can be considered the fountainhead of a literary genre, has not been fulfilled. For the "hymn" does not imply any specific event of praise; it rather encompasses a very wide range of possible occasions: weddings and dedications, victories in battle, harvest times and seasonal feasts, as well as spontaneous gatherings after a plague or drought had come to an end. Therefore, form

62. Gunkel and Begrich, *Einleitung*, 68 (ET *Introduction*, 47).

63. Mowinckel, *The Psalms*, 1:81.

64. This is Gunkel's own insight; cf. Gunkel and Begrich, *Einleitung*, 22-23 (ET *Introduction*, 15-16).

65. Cf. above, p. 38.

critics all along have been wrestling with the "hymn" and the appropriate life situations.

Unfortunately, precise knowledge about the different festive occasions in Israel is hard to attain. Furthermore, we may be sure that during the centuries feasts and their liturgies underwent substantial changes and that those texts which survived the process of transmission to be incorporated into the OT had possibly migrated through a number of life settings.[66]

In spite of all the difficulties at hand we should try to subdivide the general category of "hymn of praise" according to the specific situations to which each owes its existence instead of dealing with one broad group only. We keep in mind that indeed there is a certain common mood to all the hymns and that we may consider the following three-part structure as a kind of basic pattern which seems to fit most of the hymns preserved:

1. Call to praise (usually understood as an exhortation by a choir leader or the like to a group or the whole of the congregation);

2. Account of Yahweh's deeds or qualities (the body of the hymn may feature various styles and formulaic expressions); and

3. Conclusion (renewed call to praise; blessings; petitions; or other forms).

Again, this general structural analysis already suggested by Gunkel, has been widely adopted as valid.[67] If we take it as a working scheme and, in addition, ask for possible settings, we may get a clearer picture of Israel's hymns.

## Victory Songs

Cultic activities of any human group tend to be determined by seasonal needs. The OT festival calendars (cf. Exod 23:14-17; 34:22-23; Lev 23; Deut 16:1-7) make it perfectly clear that Israel was no exception to the general rule. Yahweh's people in Canaan adopted quite naturally the local seasonal cultic patterns and probably merged them with their own tradition. The fixed cycle of yearly events, however, does not extinguish spontaneous religious activities.

---

66. This is the grain of truth in Beyerlin's attempt to redefine the concept of literary genre; cf. *Rettung*, 154-58.

67. Cf. Gunkel and Begrich, *Einleitung*, 38-58 (ET *Introduction*, 26-41); Mowinckel, *The Psalms*, 1:81-89; Kraus, *Psalmen*, XLI-XLII; Sabourin, *Psalms*, 1:181; etc.

In the OT we find some beautiful examples of such spontaneous praise in the victory songs performed after a battle had been won. Exodus 15:21 (cf. the short phrases in Judg 16:23-24); Judg 5:2-31; and Ps 68 are specimens of this type of hymn. What Crüsemann considers the most basic form of all genuinely Israelite hymn singing is located in this situation.[68]

> Sing to the Lord!
> Yea, he rose high!
> Horse and rider he threw into the sea! (Exod 15:21)

Two out of our three hymnic elements are present—the call to sing and the account of Yahweh's deeds (Hebrew *ki*, according to Crüsemann, does not introduce a mere appendix to the exhortation but as a deictic particle starts off the communal refrain). This is all there is to a hymn: In endless repetition, accompanied by drums and dancing (cf. Exod 15:20; Judg 11:34) and with terrific noise, the Israelites may have celebrated their small and big victories.

Of course, virtually all of this spontaneous poetry has been lost. There was nobody to take notes in ancient times. If some examples were preserved, the reason must be that they by some chance got into the stream of recurring events. Judges 5 for instance probably became part of the historical tradition put to memory; Ps 68, with its "spontaneous" verses 12-15, was drawn into the liturgy of some regular festival (cf. Ps 68:25-26) but may at some time have commemorated an historical event. The same may be true for Exod 15:21 in relation to Exod 15:1-19; and even Pss 118:15-16; 78:65-66; 18:33-49 may go back to some spontaneous lines composed and sung after victorious battles.[69] The other way around also may hold some truth: There is absolutely no reason to exclude the possibility that Israelite warriors (and their women-folk) in the course of victory celebrations did sing older hymns, even taken out of different contexts. (Soccer fans on the continent sometimes behave that way.)

We can think of more occasions in which spontaneous hymnic poetry was used to praise Yahweh: When the harvest was reaped in the fields or vineyards; when a caravan successfully returned home, etc. But we do not have sufficient information about such customs. The only other situation we can speak of with some certainty is the public thanksgiving ceremony in general.[70] If there were festivities to celebrate deliverance from some evil, spontaneous hymns certainly may have been used. But again, poems

---

68. Crüsemann, *Studien*, 34.
69. Thus Westermann, *BHHW*, III, 1790-91.
70. Cf. above, section "Communal Complaints and Thanksgivings."

historically unique and specific to the event are easily lost from tradition; fixed formulations expressing gratitude and adoration will usually suffice in such "emergencies."

### Pilgrim Songs and Processional Hymns

Some hymns, it is quite obvious, were not sung by a congregation standing in a sanctuary but rather by people on. the move. Whether performed during the pilgrimage to Jerusalem to attend one of the major festivals or for some more private occasion, or during a procession around the holy city or the temple grounds, these hymns should be considered separately according to their specific life situation. We have to keep in mind, however, that again the borderline between different kinds of hymns may be uncertain and that the songs could be used across genre classification.

One of the earlier collections within the Psalter (Pss 120–134) preserves, in the psalm superscriptions, the memory of those "ascents" to Jerusalem.[71] At least one of these psalms (Ps 122) is a true pilgrimage song, as is Ps 84.[72] Judging from just two examples little can be said about the specific structure of these psalms. However, within them the "moods" of the pilgrims are quite clear: They long for the holy city and the presence of Yahweh; they dwell on their strenuous journey and the joy of arriving at their destination. A direct formal outcome of these sentiments may be seen in their predilection for blessings and benedictions (cf. Pss 84:5–6; 122:6–9), the praise of city and temple (cf. Pss 84:2, 11; 122:3), and the description of personal longings (cf. Pss 84:3; 122:1). There are numerous other psalms that allude to such pilgrimages or betray the same sentiments (e.g., Pss 87; 121; 126; Isa 2:3), so that the life setting "pilgrimage" should be recognized as the formative factor for a category of hymns.

Closely connected with either pilgrimage or local procession were the entrance liturgies in Pss 15 and 24. Arriving groups would ritually inquire about the conditions of being admitted into the sanctuary.[73] Finally, processions also played a great role in the ancient Israelite cult (cf. 2 Sam 6), and a good number of psalms belonging to different genres refer to them (e.g., Pss

---

71. Keet, *A Study of the Psalms of Ascent*, a learned philological and historical treatise with little reference to form criticism; the superscriptions are discussed on pp. 1–17)

72. Gunkel and Begrich, *Einleitung*, 309–11(ET *Introduction*, 235–37); Kraus, *Psalmen*, 2:581–87; 838–42.

73. Cf. Mowinckel, *Le Decalogue*; Koch, "Tempeleinlassliturgien und Dekaloge"; Delekat, *Asylie*, chap. III/2.

42:5; 55:15; 118:19-20). Psalms 48; 68; and 132 may be named as possible examples of processional hymns.[74]

Pilgrimages and processions, religious communities on the move, of course are tied to those cultic affairs proper which are happening at the sanctuary. They deserve, however, to be recognized as special settings for a distinct category of hymns. We can easily imagine that psalms first composed for one particular pageant became adapted to other occasions and even incorporated into the liturgy of the festival itself.[75]

## Hymns of the Festival Cycle

We possess some knowledge of Israel's main yearly festivals, namely those three seasonal assemblies that very probably had been taken over from the Canaanites.[76] Precise historical developments and liturgical details of these celebrations are unknown. All we can be reasonably sure of is that the seasonal pattern of feasts set the stage for most of the hymns preserved in the OT Psalter. And a second point is even more important: The oldest cultic calendars found in the OT[77] already betray the complex traditions which were combined in Israel's cult. We discover traits of agricultural as well as of nomadic ways of life; the intertwining of motifs is particularly apparent in the Passover-Mazzot tradition.[78]

We cannot possibly discuss the difficult problem of whether or not it is legitimate to distinguish in OT scholarship between a religious mentality which was mythical in character and bent on preserving or revitalizing all "natural" powers and Israel's faith which kept in touch with the historic acts of Yahweh. Let it be sufficient here to note that both aspects reflect fundamental human needs and that both are integral parts of OT hymnic tradition. We use this distinction only because it is impossible any more to attribute the individual texts of the hymns to this or that one of the three Israelite festivals.

After settling in Canaan one of the main concerns of the Israelite farming communities had to be rain and fertility of the fields. Psalms 65 and 67 are thanksgiving hymns after bountiful harvests; they may have

---

74. Cf. Oesterley, *The Sacred Dance*; Alt, "Die Wallfahrt von Sichern nach Bethel"; Mowinckel, *The Psalms*, 1:169-82.

75. Cf. the Zion Songs, below pp. 67-68.

76. Cf. de Vaux, *Les institutions de l'Ancien Testament*, 2:383-413 (ET *Ancient Israel: Its Life and Institutions*, 484-506).

77. Cf. Exod 23:14-17; Kraus, *Gottesdienst*, 40-88 (ET *Worship*, 26-76).

78. Cf. Kutsch, "Erwägungen."

belonged to either of the old ingathering festivals.[79] Which hymns were intoned when the sowing season started we do not know. Maybe Ps 126:5 is a quotation from this kind of opening hymn. The god Yahweh who proved his creative powers by providing a good year for the farmers was of course the same god who once "had made heaven and earth" (cf. Pss 8; 19A; 33; 104; 136:1–9). Creation "once upon a time" is reexperienced in nature's growth and crops. Mowinckel's idea therefore that creation was dramatically reenacted at some point in the festive cycle (he prefers the New Year celebrations) is quite plausible. Yahweh had become for Israel a God who also gave "grain, wine and oil" (Hos 2:10). He was responsible for the fertility of the fields and herds. The agricultural festivals celebrated his powers; the hymns sung praised him as a fertility deity. Small wonder that numerous features and formulations used in neighboring cults were adopted by Israel to glorify Yahweh. Egyptian, Babylonian, and Canaanite influences have been increasingly discovered in Israelite hymns of this type. Most ancient Near Eastern cults knew one deity which procured growth and fertility, which commanded the winds and weathers, which defeated the primeval chaotic powers, etc. Israel's indebtedness to the older traditions of her neighbors has always been admitted by all form critics, and it has been corroborated by outstanding Ugaritic scholars.[80]

The fact of "foreign" influence on Israel's hymnody does not entitle us to draw a line between forms or genres which have been contaminated and those which remain totally Israelite. Crüsemann, for example, in his painstaking analyses wants to separate hymns of imperative provenience, participle style, and direct address forms,[81] restricting the concerns for fertility to one kind only. Distinctions of this sort are dogmatic in character; they are not tenable because they are not provable. Concerning the forms used in the "nature" hymns we have to stay with the observation of Gunkel and Mowinckel, namely that the songs in their praising parts use a variety of expressions side by side in the very same function, and that each "composition itself is very far from following any set pattern or schedule."[82]

Yahweh was Israel's God; his faculties and qualities were praised at the major festivals. The praise centered on Yahweh's providing fertility and produce, but also to him who revealed himself in terrifying phenomena, in lightning, storm, fire, and clouds and who commanded the forces of war

79. Kutsch, "Erwägungen."

80. G. R. Driver, Gordon, Aistleitner, Pope, Dahood, et al.; see, e.g., the discussion of Ps 29 by Ginsberg, "A Phoenician Hymn in the Psalter"; and in the commentaries.

81. Crüsemann, *Studien*, 135–52, esp. 153: "Hymnic participles ... in general describe such divine acts as are materializing in creation and natural events."

82. Mowinckel, *The Psalms*, 1:88.

and pestilence. Yahweh's deeds only happened in relation to his people; that is why the hymns tell of his saving acts in history (cf. Pss 66:1–12; 77; 78; 105; 114; 115; 126; 135; 136). From other parts of the Old Testament it is known that the seasonal cycle, if it did not feature such motifs from the beginning, later attracted historical reminiscences. We can recognize in the "historical" psalms the counterparts to the "nature" hymns. They both have their original setting in the great Israelite festivals which determined the yearly cultic activities of the people. All efforts to introduce basic differences between these types of hymns are of little avail. This is true for Mowinckel's distinction between hymns celebrating general and others praising special deeds of Yahweh[83] as well as for Westermann's artificial operation to gain "declarative" and "descriptive" psalms of praise.[84]

## *Yahweh Kingship Hymns and Royal Psalms*

Few psalms have received more attention among biblical scholars and prompted greater changes in psalm research than the small group of "enthronement" hymns—Pss 47; 93; 96–99.[85] They form a distinct and separate group in the Psalter in that their structure, imagery, and motifs are very much alike. They all center around Yahweh's enthronement as the universal king over all the nations.[86] Because of their characteristic features we are simply compelled to concede that these psalms had a special life setting; a festival that Mowinckel and the "patternists" claim was intimately linked with the New Year's celebrations. We are uncertain as to the date of this festival of Yahweh's assuming regal authority over the whole world, but a festive occasion of this sort must have existed in Israel. Babylonian parallels indeed point to the New Year's celebration; Ugaritic mythology seems to strengthen the argument. We leave the dating open and just state that the Yahweh kingship psalms are sufficient evidence for an Israelite festival that praised Yahweh's taking power over the nations and which probably was tied to the seasonal cycle of cultic activities. If the day of "enthronement"

---

83. Cf. Mowinckel, *The Psalms*, 1:85.

84. Cf. Westermann, *The Praise*, 31: descriptive praise "praises God for a specific deed."

85. See above, pp. 39–44.

86. Note the one central phrase: *yahweh malak*, "Yahweh has become king," Pss 93:1; 97:1, and the very description of his ascension in Ps 47:6. In spite of Michel, "Studien zu den sogenannten Thronbesteigungspsalmen," these passages speak of a real enthronement; they are not merely describing an eternal state of affairs.

was part of some other agricultural cultic event, it certainly has brought forth this particular genre of hymns we mentioned above.[87]

The main form elements of the psalms of Yahweh's kingship are (and this pattern fits perfectly the general hymnic structure having been adapted to the singular event in minor details):

1. Exhortation to praise, directed to the nations and nature; c. Pss. 47:2, 7; 96:1–3, 7–9; 98:4–8.
2. Praise of Yahweh as the new world ruler (including: praise of his strength, Pss 47:3; 99:4; glory, Ps 96:6; justice, Ps 97:6; victory, Ps 47:4; epiphany, Ps 97:2–5; former deeds for Israel, Ps 99:6–7; accepted acts of salvation, Ps 97:7, etc.).

The hymns belonging to this type truly show cosmic dimensions, and this must reflect the outlook and content of the festivities behind the text. It is perfectly clear that Israel learned to praise Yahweh in this way from her neighbors, but, as Mowinckel has adroitly pointed out, the changes which the ancient Near Eastern kingship ideology underwent in Israel are equally remarkable. No trace is left, for instance, of the mythical story of a dying and resurrected deity within our psalms.[88]

The so-called "royal psalms" pertaining to a human ruler, for the most part the Davidic king in Jerusalem, are only loosely connected with the hymns celebrating Yahweh's kingship. For, as was pointed out above, we may safely assume (even under the protest of quite a number of eminent scholars) that the needs of the royal court in terms of liturgical items and texts were met partly by using popular prototypes and partly by drawing from neighboring ancient Near Eastern court etiquette. The former way may hold true for complaint psalms and thanksgiving in particular, while the latter may have been followed for ceremonial enthronement and the like. This is the point where we might find some connection with the Yahweh kingship hymns: Taking office certainly was no mean affair for an heir to David's throne (cf. Pss 2; 110; 89; 101). He was the "son of God" (2 Sam 7:14; Ps 2:7); he may have taken the place of Yahweh in ritual drama, as the "patternists" strongly suggest, or he may have celebrated his own coronation in conjunction with the New Year festival of Yahweh either yearly or at the beginning of his reign. In any case, some of the glory

---

87. The best summaries of all the problems involved are found in Mowinckel, *The Psalms*, 1:106–92; and A. R. Johnson, *Sacral Kingship*. For some corrective points of view one should consult Bernhardt, *Königsideologie*; and W. Schmidt, *Königtum Gottes in Ugarit und Israel*.

88. Mowinckel, *The Psalms*, 1:136–40.

of Yahweh's own enthronement seems to reflect on that of his anointed, and the coronation hymns bear witness to this. That the wedding song Ps 45 should be indicative of a sacred marriage, according to Babylonian ritual, is hard to believe; we would prefer rather to interpret it as a piece out of a real wedding ceremony.[89]

## Zion Songs

When discussing the pilgrim songs[90] we touched upon hymns that hailed the holy city as Yahweh's sacred dwelling place. A small group of texts, viz. Pss 46; 48; 76, have been set apart by virtually all form critics from all the other psalms referring to Zion.[91] Although various scholars would add to the three poems mentioned one or more related songs (e.g., Pss 84; 87; 122; 132; etc.) we will restrict ourselves to the examples which are most characteristic and recognized by all experts in the field.

The formal structure of Pss 46; 48; and 76 betrays just one conspicuous deviation from the hymn structure in general: a proper introit ("exhortation to praise") is missing (Gunkel). This may be accidental, because the texts do have an occasional address to the congregation (cf. Pss 46:9; 76:12). The body of the hymn celebrates Yahweh, Israel's powerful God, who has taken his abode on Mount Zion which is likened to a mythical sacred mountain (cf. Ps 48:3). Zion and Jerusalem thus become the invincible fortress of Yahweh and his people. The praise of Yahweh is expressed in various ways: as an affirmation of confidence (Ps 46:2-8), in direct-address form (Ps 76:8: "But, thou, terrible art thou! . . ."), as well as in third person formulations (Ps 48:2: "Great is the Lord and greatly to be praised") . What makes these psalms so extraordinary, therefore, is not their formal structure but their content. They all speak of a kind of primeval attack upon the holy city, of Yahweh fighting back against the evil powers and securing victory.[92] This fact, together with some signs of special rites to be performed in connection with the hymn singing (e.g., Ps 48:13-14), has sparked the idea that there must have been some peculiar festive occasion celebrated in the Zion songs.

89. For a different interpretation of the royal psalms as reflections of a festival of the "election of Zion and of David" and a subsequent understanding of the Yahweh kingship developing from a celebration of Yahweh's eternal kingship with only the ark moving into city and temple, see Kraus, *Königsherrschaft Gottes*.

90. See above, pp. 62-63.

91. Gunkel and Begrich, *Einleitung*, 80-82 (ET *Introduction*, 55-57); Mowinckel, *The Psalms*, 1:90; Sabourin, *Psalms*, 1:230-43.

92. Cf. von Rad, *Theologie des Alten Testaments*, 2:166-79 (ET *Old Testament Theology*, 2:155-69).

It is the life setting which again is most important in determining a genre of psalms. Unfortunately we do not know about any regular Zion festival outside of these psalms. Speculations which find some support in archaic texts such as Gen 14:18 (Melchizedek of Salem; see Ps 110:4) assume that the sacred traditions of Jerusalem were taken over by the Israelites when David took possession of this Canaanite city. One essential part of the pre-Israelite cult then would have been a Zion festival centering around an ancient belief in a sacred mountain and the god's eternal presence. In the light of these theories, Wanke's suggestion that the Zion songs are exilic or post-exilic in origin would seem rather improbable.[93] For an extensive discussion of the Jerusalem cultic traditions, see H. Schmid.[94]

Even if we take into consideration a possible Zion festival that, however, cannot now be located in the seasonal cycle of cultic festivities, the problem of how to interpret the Zion hymns has still not been solved. It is reasonably clear that Israelite beliefs have merged with Canaanite traditions. But the very intention of the psalms remains an enigma. Historical interpretations of attacking nations (Krinetzki), the cult dramatic understanding (Mowinckel), and an eschatological view (Gunkel) are in tension. Mowinckel still seems to have opened up the most likely avenue to grasp the meaning of these hymns.

Hymn singing, we may conclude, in Israel as well as among most other people, belongs to communal cultic festivals. This does not preclude the possibility that congregational hymns could also be used in rites which served the needs of individual persons. But, on the whole, we are dealing with collective praises of Yahweh, when trying to understand OT hymns. While the formal structure of all the hymns is plain enough, and while the moods of joy, exuberance, and adoration are to be met in all types of hymns, the real distinctions can be made only when we get some notion of the original setting of a given psalm or, better, group of psalms. We need to know more about Israel's feasts in order to be more confident of the life situations of the hymns.

## Didactic or Wisdom Psalms

A. Deissler, *Psalm 119 (118) und seine Theologie* (1955)

W. G. Lambert, *Babylonian Wisdom Literature* (1960)

S. Mowinckel, "Psalms and Wisdom" (1955)

---

93. Cf. Wanke, *Die Zionstheologie der Korachiten.*
94. H. Schmid, "Jahwe und die Kulttraditionen von Jerusalem."

R. E. Murphy, "A Consideration of the Classification 'Wisdom Psalms'" (1963)

R. E. Murphy, "The Interpretation of Old Testament Wisdom Literature" (1969)

G. von Rad, *Weisheit in Israel* (1970)
ET *Wisdom in Israel* (1972)

H. Reinelt, "Die altorientalische und biblische Weisheit und ihr Einfluss auf den Psalter" (1966)

H. Ringgren, "Einige Bemerkungen zum LXXIII. Psalm" (1953)

P. W. Skehan, "Borrowings from the Psalms in the Book of Wisdom" (1948)

E. Würthwein, "Erwägungen zu Psalm 73" (1950/1970)

Since it has come to be a fundamental belief among form critics and cult historians that the vast majority of the psalms reflect ceremonial activities, "a problem arises when we find in the Psalter some poems which do not seem to have been composed for cultic use."[95] The influence of the "sages" on some. of the extant psalms cannot possibly be overlooked, however, and since "wisdom" in OT scholarly terminology is tantamount to acultic or even anti-cultic attitudes, form critics really are in some trouble. How could these bastard compositions sneak into a collection of liturgical and strictly cultic songs? Even worse, how could they exert influence on otherwise clean-cut cultic poems?

In the first place, we have to ask ourselves in what way wisdom influence on the psalms can be established, and second, we should raise the question of setting in regard to wisdom poems preserved in the Psalter.

There are, in fact, enough criteria to tell with some degree of certainty which psalms have grown out of that wide (and still fairly unknown) realm of the "wise man."[96] Firstly, formulaic expressions and form elements quite common in wisdom writings reappear in some psalms.[97] The mode of addressing people sometimes is directly gleaned from instruction (cf. Pss 34:12; 49:2-5; 78:1-2); there are typical makarisms ("Lucky the man who . . . ," cf. Pss 1:1; 112:1); sentences structured as numerical sayings (Ps 62:12); proverbial sayings which seem almost to be quoted from Proverbs (Ps 37:16; Prov 15:16; Ps 37:21); and exhortations so common in wisdom literature (cf. Pss 34:14-15; 37:1-8). Larger literary devices out of the treasury of the sages are the acrostic arrangement of a poem (in the psalms the alphabet is used as the artistic guideline, cf. Pss 9/10; 25; 34; 37; 112; 119; and 145) and the

---

95. Mowinckel, "Psalms and Wisdom," 205.

96. Cf. Hermisson, *Studien zur israelitischen Spruchweisheit*; and Gerstenberger, "Zur alttestamentlichen Weisheit."

97. Cf. Gunkel and Begrich, *Einleitung*, 389-90 (ET *Introduction*, 299-300).

so-called anthological style whereby sayings are strung together by certain catchwords (cf. Pss 33; 119).

Second we find outspoken didactic interests and intentions, sometimes in the introduction of a poem (cf. Pss 49; 78) or in its whole tone and structure (cf. Pss 1; 19; 34; 119). Instruction in fact can be surmised to be the driving force behind most of the wisdom poems. Whether or not this instruction is flowing out of (royal) schools or coming from more or less professional sages is an open question. It seems most probable that guidance concerning the right or wrong life was primarily communicated within families and clans. However that may be, didactic overtones and undertones in most of the wisdom psalms are obvious.

There is a third point to be made. The topics and motifs of the psalms concerned are those also present in other wisdom literature. The problem of good and evil men and their respective fates is inherent in Pss 1; 9/10; 14; 119 for example; the vexing question of why a righteous person has to suffer comes to the fore in Pss 37; 49; and 73. Reverence for a God-given and already written *torah* (cf. Pss 1; 19B; 119) may point towards theological circles as to authorship and into late post-exilic times when the scrolls of Moses already were considered holy scriptures. The wisdom psalms, in short, are substantially molded by a characteristic language, the reflective mood and didactic intention, and the imagery, topics, and motifs of Israel's sages, whoever they were. Language, structure, and themes of complaints, thanksgivings, and hymns on the other hand are conspicuously absent. Full recognition of these facts is certainly a merit of form-critical research.

Again, the problem which remains is one concerning the life setting of these psalms. Since the wisdom genre in the Psalter was form-critically assessed,[98] the wise man in Israel was visualized as the counterpart of an ancient Greek philosopher or a self-sufficient nineteenth-century German idealist—an Immanuel Kant walking around Königsberg. That is to say, the concept of a sage was quite academic and abstract; there was little sociological flesh and blood to it. The sage and his wisdom, in Gunkel's mind, were private and personalistic, uncultic, and ahistoric; humanistic and cosmopolitan in nature. And this view is *communis opinio* up to our own time encompassing even von Rad and Hermisson.

Wisdom is depicted as aloof from religious practice and attributable to rather "spiritual" schools, court circles, and wise individuals.

There may be something wrong with this picture that we project into Israel's life. Gunkel was the first to feel this way. When contemplating Ps 91

---

98. See especially Gunkel and Begrich, *Einleitung*, 381–97 (ET *Introduction*, 293–305); Mowinckel, *The Psalms*, 2:104–25; and Mowinckel, "Psalms and Wisdom."

as a possible wisdom poem, he remarks: "It is remarkable that in vv. 14–16 a divine oracle was added to the wisdom poem ... This would indicate that the poem was performed in a worship service."[99] Mowinckel barely airs the thought that "learned psalmographers" would have anything to do with the cult. Murphy has asked the decisive question: "Is there any good reason to rule out cultic use and cultic life setting" for the wisdom psalms?[100] Indeed, this question must be raised even if a positive answer cannot be easily found. If Mowinckel's assertion is correct: "The psalmists have learnt from the learned men and the learned men have learnt from the psalmists ... ,"[101] and if Murphy's suggestion that wisdom influence penetrated deeply into other psalm genres should prove right ("the psalmists found wisdom themes useful and ... exploited the wisdom style as an apt mode of expression")[102] then we could postulate a much closer connection between the genres and their authors than has hitherto been assumed.

A striking Babylonian parallel to the biblical material may point in the right direction. The poem known under the title "The Babylonian Theodicy" is an acrostic one,[103] and the author gives his name and profession: "I, Saggilkinam-ubbib, the incantation priest, an adorant of the god and the king."[104] The professional performer of ritual prayers for individual and community[105] certainly did not compose such a poem for his private edification. The number of copies found in Babylonia and Assyria alone would witness to a widespread use, probably in cultic rites. Thus we may seriously ask whether the authors of Israelite wisdom psalms could not be found among those priests who were responsible for complaint and thanksgiving ceremonies. Of course this is a mere hypothesis which might draw some of the wisdom psalms over into the group of cultic poems.

## Whither Psalm Research

After more than half a century of form-critical studies on the psalms, an evaluation of achieved ends and further goals should go into greater detail than is possible here. The brief sketch of some main trends in scholarly thinking given above demonstrates one thing: Form-critical work on the psalms

---

99. Gunkel and Begrich, *Einleitung*, 394 (ET *Introduction*, 303).
100. Murphy, "A Consideration," 161.
101. Mowinckel, "Psalms and Wisdom," 208.
102. Murphy, "A Consideration," 167.
103. Lambert, *Babylonian Wisdom Literature*, 63–91; *ANET*, 601–4.
104. Lambert, *Babylonian Wisdom Literature*, 63.
105. See Caplice, "Participants in the Namburbi-Rituals."

has not yet come to an end but rather stands at a new beginning. There is no real "beyond" to form-critical psalm exegesis. The method itself certainly has changed through the decades because those unavoidable ideological presuppositions and outlooks have also changed. Gunkel's basic idea that the psalms for the most part have grown out of cultic activities and that their linguistic and sentimental structure is indicative of their liturgical background is still as valid as ever. And while formal analysis in many instances has reached a final stage, the exploration of settings is still very much a task of the future. Of course, in the past decades some important books have been published concerning the institutional life of ancient Israel, studies which would have been impossible without form-critical work also in the area of OT psalms.[106] A wealth of information concerning cultic practices has been collected, but still there are too many questions open. They can be answered only by further resolute research along form-critical lines; all the other modes of investigation naturally tie in with this approach.

Form-critical work on the psalms means that an all-inclusive method has to be applied on the basis of those principles established by Gunkel and Mowinckel. The fact that queries from other than literary and formal standpoints have to join "form" critical investigation has been touched upon occasionally but not sufficiently stressed. It will gain more importance in future research. For example: Modes of investigation which do not start out from "form" analysis in the strict sense can still promote in a high degree recognition of both formal structures and settings. Philological and lexical studies will help to illuminate dark passages that so far cannot be classified according to genre characteristics; statistical (even computerized) counts of vocabulary will help to circumscribe more exactly specific layers of language and usages typical for fixed life situations (so far these efforts often are based on literary units of the OT which in reality are very "unoriginal" conglomerates of various genres); stylistic and literary investigations, particularly in the field of comparative literature, will enhance our understanding of analogies and peculiarities in the OT psalms; ancient Near Eastern scholarship in general and form-critical exploitation of cuneiform materials, as well as archaeological discoveries in particular, will increasingly shed light on all matters relevant to OT psalm exegesis (the special role of Ugaritic studies has been mentioned earlier).

Most important of all, however, and already pointed out above, is the fact that the social sciences of our day have given and will further supply invaluable insights into the nature of rites, feasts, and cultic activities which will help us to understand better Israel's ceremonial ways. Anthropological field studies, for instance, can tell us how rites function in a given, living society, what roles officials and participants play in ritual

---

106. E.g., de Vaux, *Ancient Israel*; Kraus, *Worship*; Rowley, *Worship*.

activities, etc. Won by direct observation of life performances, this knowledge will enable us by careful comparison and inference to arrive at a better estimation of Israel's analogous activities.

Thus, form-critical research on the psalms, much more so than Gunkel or Mowinckel could know, today has to be augmented by probes into life settings. If the latter become sufficiently clear for each main genre, analyses of formal structures again can move out of some formalistic impasses and become oriented towards living reality once more. This is to reemphasize the fact that formal analysis alone cannot possibly be sufficient in form-critical research. The term "form critical" has been misleading in this regard in that it signalized only one (for Gunkel, the most natural) starting point of investigation. Although the term "form critical" does not say anything about Gunkel's real intention in its original meaning, it always included the "cult functional" aspects as propagated by Mowinckel. Formal analysis, then, gives us clues as to which direction to look for the appropriate life situation. Formal analysis can be a corrective if a life setting has been postulated for a given text and the OT scholar needs to check the validity of his hypothesis. Only if life settings can be reconstructed with sufficient clarity and plausibility is formal analysis worth the effort.

Another string of thoughts seems to follow from this intimate connection between formal structures and life settings. We must not look upon life situations in a rigid, schematic fashion. A setting for a literary genre is no slot machine that produces standardized items without end. Life always, even in recurring situations governed by custom and ritual, allows for a certain latitude of verbal expression. Certainly, there are guidelines that cannot be overruled without risking serious misunderstandings. But even very formalized situations and genres show a certain flexibility, a variety of accepted formulas and expressions which can be used to fulfill a particular communicative function. This flexibility implies a slow and gradual change going on always in all "settings" and their ritualistic paraphernalia, a shift that even in ancient times makes itself felt over long periods.

Another observation is also true: Verbal expressions and texts born in one particular life situation by accident or on purpose may be used in quite different situations and there sink their roots. In other words, all texts and words transmitted in human groups are themselves alive in the sense that they are prone to migrate from one original setting into other settings, and it may be difficult or impossible in each individual case to pinpoint the different stations of a given psalm.

The result is simply this: Form-critical psalm research is still extremely young and promises to be a very exciting pursuit in the decades to come.

# 3

# The Psalms—
# Genres, Life Situations, and Theologies

*Towards a Hermeneutics of Social Stratification*

How may we get to some plausible order while facing a seemingly disorganized assemblage of quite different songs, meditations, and prayers brought together in the Old Testament Psalter? In my opinion, distinctions according to moods, forms, thought patterns, literary and stylistic features, literary structures, and so on—although interesting and useful—are insufficient. One decisive aspect would be missing, that of *Sitz im Leben*, as Hermann Gunkel and Sigmund Mowinckel did not cease to emphasize.[1] All those theories of literature, which take into account the social conditioning of texts, in a way corroborate this stance. But why should this be true? Because—thus my basic axiom, debatable as it is—all human discourse is communicative action. There is always a speaker (sender) of messages and a recipient. The words pass from one to the other, they are anchored in determined life situations, they make sense in relationships between real people who speak and listen to each other, deities included. The invention of writing systems, of course, seemingly changed that situation. Words, so to speak, emancipated themselves from flesh and blood, and became self-sufficient and universal. They overcame the limits of time and space, were accessible in distant regions and among subsequent generations. But this concept of free-floating discourses, without any ties to social life and real people, is a mere illusion. Sure enough, "life-situations" wherein words can

---

1. Cf. my earlier efforts to elaborate a hermeneutical and theological approach to Scripture heeding the social roots of biblical testimony: Gerstenberger, "Canon Criticism and the Meaning of Sitz im Leben"; Gerstenberger, "Social Sciences and Form-Criticism"; and Gerstenberger, *Theologies in the Old Testament*.

acquire meaning, suffer an extension of sorts. The reader of written texts just the same is a receiver of distinct messages, and he will be able to understand adequately any given discourse only if he grasps the one-time *Sitz im Leben* and/or if he places it resolutely into his own societal environment. Given the great historical distance of ancient texts it surely becomes difficult to evaluate life settings for specific utterances. Still, exegetes cannot neglect attempting serious soundings into the real communicative situations of old. If they ignore those earthly ties, the text becomes an object of arbitrary interpretations solely in the light of present day configurations. One may say: Any text in and of itself is completely without life and meaning, as long as it is hidden away in archives or mounds. It is the reader, listener, peruser who revivifies old messages by drawing them into his or her own environment. The text becomes text only in belonging to a living discourse. And it is able to exercise a critical function only as far as it is experienced within its older, bygone mental and social configurations.

## Four Settings

To get down to the specifics of genre and life situation in the Psalter, I should like to present four broader settings responsible for a variety of psalm types. Naturally, one would be able to subdivide each of the four societal layers according to more specific rituals. But for the sake of perspicuity I want, at this point, to limit myself to the larger, communicative backgrounds of Psalm poetry.

## The Family

Family has been, over the millennia, the most basic social conglomerate, at least since the "Neolithic" Revolution, when humankind settled for sedentary life, beginning already to create norms and rules of cohabitation in trans-familiar social entities. But the bonds of family relationships go back much further, into Stone Age periods; they became so strong that they were the backbone for most social developments, even quite complex, anonymous social configurations. Family structures have been predominant even in the West until the industrial, individualistic age severely challenged their "reason to be" by the end of the eighteenth century CE. The reasons for the extremely long preponderance of familial patterns and values certainly rests with the fact that human life always needed a network of small group relations in order to develop. Family groups have been (and to a certain extent still are) the berth and shelter of decent living. In agrarian societies, they organize work and sustenance for its members to the point that isolated individuals hardly have a chance of survival. Families in this environment furthermore constitute basic juridical, cultural, and religious entities. In this way, the lives of individuals may be encompassed perfectly in familial grids of meaning, orientation, and protection. The Shunamite woman declines an attractive offer of assistance by saying: "I live among my own people" (2 Kgs 4:13). Thus the well-being of any person through biblical times rested with the destiny of his or her family.

The religious dimension of family life is of particular interest for investigations into the psalms. It is fairly well known that throughout the ancient Near East there have been domestic cults dedicated to family deities. There may have been also prayers and hymns used within the circle of household worship. The psalms of the "individual" (better: "familial" psalms of complaint and thanksgiving), however, contained in the biblical Psalter, actually seem to be products of ritual experts outside the family realm. Babylonian incantations do prove this analysis: shamanistic figures would address special situations of distress (and salvation, healing, etc.?) within the family compound. As a rule, they would come to the sick person's house, perform the proper rituals of reconciliation with the deity, and exorcise demonic powers, that is, undertake purification. Traces of such visitations remain visible in the Hebrew Scripture (cf. Job 33:23–28; Isaiah attending Hezekiah in Isa 38:1, 21; Elisha in 2 Kgs 4). A different model of petitionary prayer for families is shown in 1 Sam 1–2. A person stricken by some bad luck or dire distress could turn to a local or regional sanctuary, offer supplication, and wait for a favorable response by the clergy at hand. In either case the needs of family members are taken care of by professional healers. They determine which rituals are necessary and they lead the ceremonies. Because of close affinities between incantation prayers of ancient Mesopotamia and biblical psalms of complaint we may be sure that the latter specimens, preserved in the Psalter, originally were part and parcel of old Hebrew rites of healing or rehabilitation. They were oriented towards family needs, thus they may be claimed for this elementary association of human beings.

Clearly, the sheer number of psalms of individual supplication in the Psalter (some thirty to forty examples) speaks in favor of their importance. Human experience and anthropological research corroborate this fact. One of the most frequent and serious motives for seeking contact with the gods are situations of grave illness, danger, and distress. The family was the natural group to take care of its troubled members. In cases of sickness or bad luck, domestic means and cures very probably were tried first to achieve health, tranquility, and well-being. If they failed, the only possible solution would lie with healing experts. They would bring to the case their wider knowledge and religious know-how. Of course, they were geared to family situations, just as any shaman today takes into account the basic social structures in his rituals. (My imagination has been inspired also by Navajo singers, who convene the family in its hogan to chant over a sick person. Today's ambulant treatments by medical, psychological, and psychosomatic experts still bear some basic features of ancient incantation ceremonies.) Now, if we consider Old Testament psalms in this real-life context, we have a better chance to understand what prayers of individual complaint and thanksgiving are about. Analogous set-ups in medical and psychological diagnosis and treatment today are obvious.

## The Village or Town

Life changes considerably whenever several families constitute a settlement, be it a village or small town. Family ties continue to be of utmost importance, because the basic unit remains that intimate living-and-working-together group. Property belongs to families or, nominally, to the male head of the small group. But living with other families as neighbors poses certain problems of determining rights and responsibilities across the family fence. There is a lesser degree of solidarity owed to neighbors than to family members. Only the latter applies the strict principle "one for all, and all for one." Yet, there also exist mutual obligations, and infractions of rules and norms have to be taken care of; common undertakings must be organized.

One of the most salient features of common life in settlements during the Old Testament period has been the religious duty to serve the local deities at an open air sanctuary. First Samuel 9:11–13 or 20:6 give us a hint of this custom. Annual sacrifices in a town or village perhaps coincided with seasonal harvest festivals. Since fertility of soil and herds was a great concern in such settlements, we may surmise that the center of religious activities at local shrines were seasonal celebrations (cf. also Judg 21:19–21). If this is reasonable, we can take such festivals as being the background for psalms of nature, harvest, and procreation. Psalm 65 may serve as an example.

> You visit the earth and water it,
>    you greatly enrich it;
> The river of God is full of water;
>    you provide the people with grain,
>    for so you have prepared it.

> You water its furrows abundantly,
>> settling its ridges,
> softening it with showers,
>> and blessing its growth.
> You crown the year with your bounty;
>> your wagon tracks overflow with richness.
> The pastures of the wilderness overflow,
>> the hills gird themselves with joy,
> the meadows clothe themselves with flocks,
>> the valleys deck themselves with grain,
> they shout and sing together for joy. (Ps 65:10–14, NRSV 9–13)

The address goes, to be true, to the "God of Zion" in his "holy temple" (Ps 65:2–5, NRSV 1–4), but this state of affairs is probably reflecting later tradition, namely incorporation of the text into the temple community of post-exilic times. The original outlook was that of local agrarian settlers giving thanks for bountiful harvests (cf. Ps 67:7, NRSV 6). One might speculate whether or not other hymns of the Psalter originally belong with village life and its cultic rites, such as Ps 8, a eulogy of human capacities (puberty ritual?); Ps 29, an adaptation of a Canaanite praise of the weather god; Ps 104, poetry in the vein of Egyptian sun hymns. The question, of course, arises as to what extent local groups did employ cultic experts to organize and administer sacred rites for the community. The example of Samuel in 1 Sam 9 suggests occasional participation of special personnel; sanctuaries like Shiloh, Nob, Gibeon, Arad, or others of regional importance were presumably run by professionals. Judges 17:5, 10 pictures a family sanctuary first operated by a family member, and thereafter by a paid priest. Other stories suggest ordinary leadership at local shrines (cf. Judg 6:25–32). Thus we may assume a wide range of lay and expert cultic performers on the level of local ceremonialism.

## The Monarchy

Coming to larger secondary social organizations, tribal structures first should be mentioned, because traces of ritual practice and pertaining psalmic texts are still extant in the Old Testament (cf. Ps 68; Judg 5). My proposal, however, is to leave out this level of socialization and only consider the monarchic state as an example of larger, anonymous, and bureaucratic institutions. The special problem we have to face with Israelite

(Judaic) monarchy is its enforced end by Babylonian interventions between 597 and 587 BCE. Monarchic traditions survived to a certain extent in a climate of despair, disillusionment, and hope for a timely restoration of the Davidic dynasty.

From biblical and archaeological evidence, as well as from comparative features in ancient Israel's neighborhood, it is possible to reconstruct the religious significance of the Judaic kingdom. As customary in the ancient Near East, the monarch channeled God's will and authority to the people. He represented, in one way or another, the divine order, the question of his biological descent being rather unimportant in this context. The temple in Jerusalem was a royal institution, serving the interests of the dynasty and the state as a whole. Ritual activities included daily sacrifices, coronation ceremonies, and perhaps an annual New Year festival with or without (Mesopotamian) sacred marriage rites.

Psalmic remnants of the monarchic period certainly are tinged by later experiences of sorrow and nostalgia, as well as ancient Near Eastern notions of universalism and eschatology. Thus Yahweh's promises to David (2 Sam 7; Ps 89) have been transmitted in a cultic context, not without critical reflections as to the trustworthiness of Israel's God. Coronation texts (cf. Ps 2 and 110) assume a world-dominion posture, which is probably messianic in character, and are therefore to be considered as later reworkings. There is a unique psalm celebrating a royal wedding (Ps 45)—the king being addressed by the title "God," "Divine Being" (v. 7, NRSV 6)—which is difficult to locate. Intercessions for the king (cf. Pss 20; 21), thanksgivings by the king (cf. Ps 18; 2 Sam 22), and stipulations and blessings for the king (cf. Ps 72) quite likely are dealing with the royal figure in retrospect and hoping for a final renewal of the dynasty. In any case, possible older texts have been used and reworked through exilic/post-exilic times, thus also carrying the meanings of these later periods. Their origins in court rituals, however, are by no means insignificant. Therefore, we have to consider real court life as the origin of royal hymns, and take into account subsequent royalist memories and longings within the emerging community of Yahweh faith, in order to do justice to this *Sitz im Leben*.

## The Post-Exilic Community

The most important life setting of extant psalms, above all those mentioned, are the worship services or similar liturgical enactments of the post-exilic community. We have to understand the general situation of post-monarchic Judahite communities in their homeland as well as abroad. Lacking an autonomous state-structure the survivors of the Babylonian wars and ensuing deportations organized themselves along ethnic and religious identities. The latter proved to be very strong symbols of cohesion, and the Babylonian policy of letting deportees live in their own, closed settlements favored the formation of Yahweh communities. Similar social agglomerations can be studied in many immigrant groups in modern history, including those in the US: defense of homeland traditions, of language, culture, and customs also implies a high valuation on religious beliefs. Quite often, immigrants, in reaction to a foreign and distrusted environment, overdo their zeal for homeland traditions, becoming modern zealots.

Be that as it may, we can be sure that the remnants of Judeans everywhere, numbering tens of thousands, constituted local faith communities, seeking, however, to maintain cohesion among each other by a common orientation to Jerusalem, the reconstructed temple, and by strong adherence to the word of Yahweh, which began to be assembled in various places. The torah of Moses already plays a distinct role in the Ezra–Nehemiah literary complex, which we have to date to the second half of the fifth century BCE. The gathering of sacred literature became a prime occupation of community leaders, it seems. The process itself, however, must not be considered a mere academic endeavor. Rather, the holy texts grew out of and in context with regular meetings and worship services. They were largely composed to serve in community discourses, not as literary profusions for distant generations.

The psalms, as it were, obviously continued to belong to situations of joy and jubilation, or sorrow and danger of those groups which existed under such circumstances. Families still were strong, but the main social body of Judeans in their process of becoming Jews was the religious community built on torah, Shabbat, circumcision, seasonal festivals, and so on. The psalms composed or heavily redacted in this period[2] echo the specific needs and the new social body created to be the "people of Yahweh" in contrast to all other nations. Post-exilic psalms are full of instruction as to the goals of life, from the individual's perspective, and the right ways to live. They remember the great deeds of Yahweh in the past and incite hymnic praise. They muse about transience, untimely death, justice (goodness and

---

2. In my commentary on the Psalms, I define at least 80 Psalms as belonging to that group, e.g., Pss 1; 8; 9/10; 12; 14; 15; 16; 19; 28; 29; 33; 34; 37; 39; 44; 46; 47; 48; 49; 50; 52; 53; 58; 60; 61; 62; 66; 67; 68; 71; 73; 74; 75; 76; 77; 78; 79; 80; 81; 82; 83; 84; 85; 86; 87; 89; 90; 91; 93; 94; 95; 96; 97; 98; 99; 100; 101; 103; 104; 105; 106; 108; 111; 112; 113; 114; 115; 117; 118; 119; 121; 122; 124; 126; 129; 130; 131; 132; 135; 137; 139; 144; 145; 146; 147; 148; 149; 150. Of course, some of the above cited psalms are re-editions of older prayers and songs. See Gerstenberger, *Psalms, Part 1*.

its rewards), theodicy, sin and forgiveness, the godless people, and so on. In short, the variety of late psalm-compositions in the Psalter reflects life and communication within that special association of Yahweh-believers.

I should like to focus for a moment on one of the very typical communal features of extant psalms: the collective use of the personal pronoun in the first person plural—the "we" voice. There are fifty-three examples of different genres in the Psalter that present this ostentatious "we," so seldom extant in the large amount of ancient Near Eastern psalmic compositions. To my knowledge, there have been very few scholars so far who have directed their attention to "we" psalms. Those who have[3] unanimously confirm the impression that communal "we" psalms are genuinely linked with worship situations of the early Jewish community. The "we" passages either contain authentic responses of the worshiping congregation or else they constitute speech figures articulated by the leaders of the ceremony in the name of the assembled people. We may briefly look at some examples. A collective refrain opens and closes a hymnic prayer (Ps 8:2, 10; NRSV vv. 1, 9):

> O Yahweh, our Sovereign,
> > how majestic is your name in all the earth!

A similar closing line is found in Ps 21:14 (NRSV v. 13), a prayer for the king:

> Be exalted, O Yahweh, in your strength!
> We will sing and praise your power!

In some psalms, passages using the first-person singular alternate with those stylized in the first-person plural (cf. Pss 44; 60; 66; 74; 75; 85; 103; 106; 108; 118; 122; 123; 144). "We" in these cases may refer to distinct groups of the congregation, but in general the whole assembly seems to be the subject. Apparently, the changing voices are indicative of alternating liturgical proceedings. Last, not least, there are those psalms that employ the first-person plural throughout (cf. Pss 46; 47; 48; 79; 80; 90; 95; 100; 115; 124; 136; 147). They indeed belong to different genres and thus may be counted as especially weighty arguments in favor of their true and intimate connection with ancient community life and worship. Many of them, in fact, have entered our own hymn books and still serve today as communal songs in worship. See, for example, the words of Ps 100 and the way it is creating a religious, confessional identity:

---

3. Scharbert, "Das 'Wir' in den Psalmen"; and Seybold, "Das 'Wir' in den Asaph-Psalmen."

> Make a joyful noise to Yahweh all the earth.
>> Worship Yahweh with gladness;
>> come into his presence with singing.
> Know that Yahweh is God.
>> It is he that made us, and we are his;
>> we are his people, and the sheep of his pasture.
> Enter his gates with thanksgivings,
>> and his courts with praise.
>> Give thanks to him, bless his name.
> For Yahweh is good;
>> his steadfast love endures forever,
>> and his faithfulness to all generations.

The subject matters of all of these communal hymns in the first-person plural are typical of the newly emerging community of Yahweh believers. They deal, for example, with the promulgation of torah (Ps 95), the central role of Mt Zion (Pss 46; 48; 79), the election of the people by God (Pss 66:1–13; 80), and his wonderful care for them even in calamities (Ps 124). Enemies are being scorned at and their idols condemned (Ps 115), and the transitoriness of human life (because of God's scorn!) is being focalized (Ps 90; cf. 39). Interestingly enough, the three great torah psalms (Pss 1; 19; 119) are all tuned to the individual meditator, thus placing a decisive emphasis on personal decision for Yahweh and on joining the community of worshipers. We may deduce, however, from practical worship customs, that the praying "I" in reality was also incorporated into congregational worship.

Descriptions of worship (e.g., Deut 29–31; Neh 8) and seasonal assemblies (cf. 2 Chr 6; 29–30; 35), prophetic references to communal cult (cf. Amos 5:21–24), and remnants of congregational liturgies (cf. Joel 1–2; Jer 14; Isa 63:7—64:11),[4] as well as other vestiges of congregational activities, for instance homiletical and pedagogical endeavors behind the biblical texts, certainly may be further adduced. To cut short a line of argumentation that I personally keep using, especially in the exegesis of the psalms: To my mind, the prayers and songs, even at the latest stages of redaction, have been used consistently in and for worship ceremonies of various kinds. The mere reading of psalmic poetry for individual edification, it seems to me, has been only an invention of monastic orders like that of Saint Benedict.

---

4. Note, in the last passage, the three repetitions of the emphatic, communal "Yahweh, you are our father" (Isa 63:16; 64:7).

## The Tradition Process

In sketching four basic social groups or levels of organization with their distinct rituals and psalmic texts I have only arrived at a first, general goal: It is possible to point to likely areas of social life in the biblical period as origins for specific texts. But the psalms collected into the Psalter (excepting temporarily, of course, the fourth group) did not remain fixed to their original social locations. They antedate the period of the Psalter's collection and composition. By being selected for use in the post-exilic faith community they moved into the social sphere of that new type of assembly, stamped by confession of faith and individual decision for Yahweh. But the prehistory of texts is far from being unimportant. It has to be considered and still sheds light on meanings when the text becomes rooted in a new social and liturgical context. Yet the new emphases also have to be observed and taken into account. Only those psalms that originated in the new social grouping and its ritual life need not be analyzed according to their previous shape and meaning. Since, however, the first two life situations (family and neighborhood) continued into the community area there may exist quite close affinities between older and newer texts, and the properties of the faith community organization are not so easily discernible. The third life setting (monarchy and royal cult) definitely was no longer in existence when the Psalter was collected and composed. In this case, we have to heed a slightly different set of precautions whenever we proceed to analyze extant psalms of the Psalter.

The problem we face, therefore, is that of transmission: Individual texts have been used over a longer period of time serving different social and religious aggregations of people. Texts in constant use, especially sacred readings, all share this feature of changeability. One may compare it with the process of recycling materials. Only archival writings remain fixed in their genre positions and meanings. Sacred Scriptures, however, are living organisms prone to be adapted to new environments. What are the consequences for our exegetical task? It is perhaps a matter of agreement that exegetical ethos requires an in-depth study of any ancient text. The traditio-historical dimensions of the biblical words have to be recognized as deeply as possible. In the case of our psalms and their original life settings: The confluence of different materials from different social moorings into the liturgical treasure of post-exilic Judaic faith communities, it seems to me, is an established fact. (Older historical-critical investigators spoke of the Psalter as the "Prayer book of the Second Temple community.") Just how much collectors and redactors really modified older texts (or rather, how the new community shaped songs and prayers by its use), especially in regard to their theological outlooks and affirmations, remains a matter of debate.

In my opinion, the sheer literary processes of selecting, collecting, and composing psalms for the Yahweh community of the Second Temple all have been geared to the needs of cultic communication with the Divine within their various groupings and interests. Thus, the theological concepts of individual authors presumably were of secondary importance. Furthermore, given the complex social structure of the community (families, neighborhoods, confessing group, deviant factions, international brotherhood, etc.), we may not expect a uniform theology reigning over emergent Judaism. My proposition is this: Let us regard the specific life situations in which psalms have been used. As I said before, family affairs continued as ever in post-exilic times. The need for healing and rehabilitating stricken individuals naturally was present. The community, it is to be surmised, offered rituals along the line of former shamanistic ceremonies, now under the auspices of Yahweh faith and in parochial solidarity. Were they led by Levites, scribal experts, priests? We do not know. But it is important, to my mind, to stick to that vision of psalms of individual complaint having been used in living liturgies, also after the Psalter had been composed. Individual headlines for most of the psalms, literary structure, and theological contents all speak in favor of this assumption.

As to the second original life setting, the agrarian village neighborhood, it also persisted into post-exilic times and onward. According to the new theological orientation of the Yahweh community, original hymns of praise to weather and fertility gods now were amplified to include emphatically the deeds of Yahweh for his people, especially his giving of torah. Communal complaints and acts of penitence increasingly were articulated under the overarching rubric of the "guilt of the fathers," who had disobeyed the ordinances of the Lord (cf. Ezra 9; Neh 9; Ps 106; Dan 9). It is very likely that this "Yahwehization" of local cult rituals started before the exile, when the state god slowly infiltrated socially lower levels of worship. But religious affiliation of shrines was not regulated (contrary to Deuteronomistic claims) during the time of the monarchies. Only when the Yahweh community really took shape in the post-exilic Persian area did the exclusivity of Israel's God and his salvific torah become a firm guideline. This development is clearly represented in the hymns and prayers of neighborhood concerns, now being administered by the parochial community of Judahites throughout the ancient world (with variations, e.g., in Elephantine).

The third group of psalms coming from monarchic backgrounds already has been referred to: its life base had totally passed away with the loss of statehood. But David and his dynasty kept holding on in the minds and hopes of many Judeans, and this mental base gave rise to a teaming psalmody of messianic hope. Zion theology and Yahweh kingship celebrations may have been tied into the royal expectations in one way or another, although they seem relatively devoid of direct allusions to the Davidic king.

## Theology and the Social Sciences

A final remark may be in order. Why do I emphasize so strongly the social origin and conditioning of biblical texts? How can I possibly consider social stratification as a basis for different theological concepts? Am I, as some dear colleagues suggest, walking on the bad path of surrendering unconditionally to social sciences, making theology a slave to empirical research and the precarious knowledge of social structures and processes? On the contrary, I would claim that my efforts to approach the Bible consistently from its human side, to tie texts to their social (and liturgical) roots, to admit social conditionings of biblical authors and modern exegetes, of theological conceptualizations and ethical judgments, does serve a thoroughly theological purpose. The word of God is known to us and communicated to us only by way of contextual events and sayings, narrations and confessions. Thus it is able to really interact with our limited human minds. The small change of God's love and forbearing can be recognized only in detailed studies of life's reality. From the different life situations of old, then, we may make inferences as to our social and personal situations today, and God speaks to us within exactly these rather earthly configurations. The Word which turned flesh really incorporated (and still incorporates) the conditions of our existence and our personal acting therein.

To my mind, the differentiation of social layers, pertinent specific modes of communication, and "god-talk" in biblical and other ancient societies[5] is helpful (or even necessary) for the biblical exegete to overcome historical and cultural distances. Changes of social structures over the millennia, such as those that occur in family, neighborhood, and state, are more easily grasped and bridged than totalizing worldviews would admit. Instead of dealing wholesale with "clashes of civilizations" and all-round, one-dimensional creeds, as Christian theologians we may dedicate ourselves to this fragmentary, contradictory life and faith of our spiritual ancestors. To read the Bible is a piecemeal happening. To study the multilayered Psalter is a wondrous experience in climbing hills and mountains, which allow for quite different perspectives on God and the world. After all, we should be aware of the fact that we are inhabitants of

---

5. Cf. Gerstenberger, *Theologies*.

a dust particle in an unknown universe, whose dimensions in time and space must escape our minds. The concept of all-embracing Oneness is far too big for our poor little brains and short lifespans. That is the reason why we should content ourselves as theologians to deal with the small and fragmented things that do concern us—and in which God's untiring love is working day and night—not with the grand schemes of everlasting order and happiness. God is speaking to us—says Dom Pedro Casaldáliga, former bishop of São Félix do Araguaia, Mato Grosso—not in a divine, eternal language, but only in the vernacular of our own environments. The prayers and songs of the Psalter are wonderful responses to God by people who accepted the limitations of their human existence.

# 4

# Theologies in the Book of Psalms

### Points of Departure

How can Biblical Theology, the very goal of our work, be approached? In this purview focusing on the Psalter as a prime example for theological reasoning in liturgical contexts, I am starting from several assumptions.

One simply says that God-talk or theology can hardly be uniform, universal, and valid through the ages. Rather, God-talk, for deeply divine and human reasons, for the very heart of faith must be contextual, temporary, unfinished and in a certain concordance with changing customs, cultures, social conditions.[1] Our theological discourse must not be taken as eternal truth. We think and talk as transitory beings, firmly tied to the textures of our socialization and cultural identities.

Secondly, since there are great varieties of cultural and social patterns—in coexistence as well as in conflict with each other—we certainly have to count on quite different modes of talking about God, with different experiences and conceptualizations of the Divine. Living side by side, nowadays, with many other god-fearing or god-ignoring people, intensely feeling the challenges of our pluralistic societies, we have the unique opportunity to test our own theological affirmations and learn of their richness and deficiencies, and their precious, human relativity—that is, affinity—to our own cultural settings.

What rarely has been recognized, however, is that pluralism (to a certain degree this always has been the case) has invaded even the stronghold of individual being. Each of us lives at the same time in very different social contexts. We are on the one hand members of small, intimate

---

1. Cf. Gerstenberger, *Theologien* (ET *Theologies*); and Gerstenberger and Schoenborn, eds., *Hermeneutik—sozialgeschichtlich*.

groups of family and friends, and on the other of various economic, political, and religious associations. In both kinds of social conglomeration we play our roles according to different tunes. Personal experience may tell us that theological concepts and argumentations are distinctly different in either context. God is perceived on the one hand in terms of personal relations, in I–Thou terms, and on the other as an ordering power with increasingly superpersonal authority. God, the companion who exercises solidarity with his (or her) people, cannot easily be reconciled with that divine being who speaks through thunderstorms, smites the enemies, and administers justice to all mankind.

The Psalter is a uniquely opportune work to test out the manifold and multilayered theological discourse I have tried to suggest above. Most biblical "books" do have some cohesion, plot, or structure. The "book of Psalms," however, seems to be a much more loosely-knit compilation of liturgical texts, used for different kinds of interactions, rites, ceremonies, gatherings.[2] In any case, the broad confluence of texts from greatly different sources in the Psalter provides a very colorful picture of human conditions and longings. This makes the biblical Psalms an unmatched treasure of diverse theological concepts.

## Life Settings

The early masters of form-critical analysis, Hermann Gunkel and Sigmund Mowinckel,[3] emphasized social and communicative settings in establishing their genre-classifications of the psalms. They traced complaints, hymns, royal songs, and wisdom poems back to determined groups of people interacting with each other and with their God at different "recurring" opportunities. Although large differences exist among form-critics, in detailed evaluations the basic human associations producing and using those principal genres emerge clearly enough in socio-historical and form-critical research.[4] We may identify four main types of human association, not precluding sub-divisions and overlappings, with each of these basic social conditions producing its proper psalm types.

---

2. Naturally, not all experts will agree at this point. Many defend a well thought-out organization of the material at hand. But there is a good deal of consensus as to the various fountain-heads of individual psalms and genres.

3. Their classical studies are: Gunkel and Begrich, *An Introduction to Psalms*; and Mowinckel, *The Psalms in Israel's Worship*.

4. Overviews of research offer, e.g., Buss, *Biblical Form-Criticism*; Reventlow, *Gebet*; Müller, "Formgeschichte/Formenkritik I"; and see also Chapter 2 above.

(1) The first type is the small intimate family cluster, the age-old economic and religious nucleus of humankind, resorted to cultic means, whenever one member fell seriously ill or was threatened by demonic powers. Petitionary rituals were held, often in the precincts of the patient's home, as may be learned from hundreds of Akkadian (Assyrian-Babylonian) incantations. A ritual expert would lead the ceremony and let the endangered person recite the decisive prayer of complaint, confession, and petition.[5] This pattern of ceremonial healing is common in most tribal societies to this very day. Even modern religions maintain some of those archaic proceedings; for example, prayer-services for the sick, last unctions, exorcisms, and secularized remnants may be discovered even in today's medical and psychotherapeutic practices. Exuberant thanksgivings after graces attained and fortunes restored were the counterpart of complaint and petition, also celebrated among intimate circles of family and neighbors. Offerings to God, opulent meals, testimony of the saved one and merriment were characteristic elements of this "private" festivity.

(2) A second layer of religious or cultic action without doubt was the regional aggregation of families in village or township with their own local sanctuary. The Old Testament quite often refers to the *bamah,* the open-air shrine, of a neighborhood, whose existence archaeology has amply confirmed in many Israelite sites. People were united by common interests principally according to the seasonal calendar, with respect to personal *rites de passage,* and in spontaneous cases of common grief and joy. Early victory songs may pertain to this category, led by inspired women (cf. Exod 15:21). The noisy crowd would join in shouting refrains, as cheerleaders intoned the lines: "Yahweh is good," "His loyalty endures forever" (Ps 136:1–26). Appealing to and hailing the God of weather and fertility, protection and victory was the main end of such cults of local and regional dimension. Countless religious activities survive even today in boroughs, clubs, rural centers, etc. destined to support the communitarian life of people not related by blood but tied together by vital interests on a smaller scale, on a person-to-person basis.

(3) Gradually, with growth and diversification of society, cultic activity passes into the larger ambit of tribal and national concerns. Anonymity grows with the sheer number of persons involved in cultic interactions or assemblies. Rules of communication—as well as common interests—change considerably, and with such changes theological concepts also fall into different patterns, gaining a new profile. To complicate matters, state cults in the ancient Near East are dynasty-centered, managed by professionals,

---

5. Cf. Gerstenberger, *Der bittende Mensch.*

and, as a rule, discourage popular responsibility. With the establishment of divine or semidivine monarchies (a switch that causes much concern in Judg 9 and 1 Sam 7–12), state cults become restricted to officially-appointed royal priesthoods. Since the hymnic material of the Davidic court (if anything from that source has survived at all) was used and remodeled by the exilic/post-exilic community (cf. Pss 18; 20; 21; 45; 72; 132; 144) also in terms of messianic expectations (cf. Pss 2; 110), we cannot be sure how much authentic material of the pre-exilic state-cult has been preserved. In any case, the "highest" level of ancient Israelite social organization falls into line with bureaucratic and autocratic forms of government, which reduced the anonymous mass of citizens to a subservient state, while permitting freely, as it were, all kinds of family, local, and regional cults on their respective social levels and with their specific theological interests. In addition, ancient Near Eastern monarchies always purported to truly serve—in the name of highest deities—the needs of the weakest elements of society (cf. Psalm 72 and Hammurapi's prologue to his law-edicts).

(4) After Israel's final defeat of 587 BCE and the loss of monarchic structures, a complete reorganization of the people of Yahweh was inevitable. National ambitions could only survive underground. Local communities, apparently, soon rallied around old family and tribal traditions. In retrospect, monarchy, temple, and prophecy all became unifying factors for a new Israel—which identified herself with *torah*, sabbath, circumcision, temple, and the holy land—as the people elected by Yahweh, creator of heaven and earth and supreme king over all nations.

This new, unheard of community of faith,[6] without state government, was the decisive social group shaping the sacred traditions and handing them down to the Jewish, Christian, and even Muslim communities. Exclusive adoration of Yahweh—much later erroneously designated as "monotheism"—is the hallmark of this religious body of local congregations. In many ways the book of Psalms carries the stamp of this latest period in Old Testament history.[7] As far as contemporary songs and prayers are concerned, we should consider the so-called "wisdom" poems as products of that early Jewish community. The main spiritual need of the congregation was for divine guidance in a pluriform religious environment and under foreign domination. *Torah-psalms* such as 1, 19, and 119 occupy important positions in the Psalter. Reflections about life, death, and the ups and downs

---

6. Possibly, the followers of Zoroaster in ancient Persia had earlier formed communities of faith transcending family ties. See Boyce, *History of Zoroastrianism*.

7. While working on a two-volume form-critical commentary (*Psalms, Part 1* and *Part 2*), I became more and more convinced that much reworking of older Psalms is evident in the canonical text: e.g., in meditative, homiletical, and late hymnic genres.

of faith (cf. Pss 9/10; 23; 37; 39; 49; 73; 90; 139) in the midst of internal strife about true righteousness and fidelity are typical for the latest layer in Old Testament psalmody. Theological wrestling with historical developments leading to a loss of national and religious independence (cf. Pss 44; 89; 106; 137) are sure signs of the communities' state of mind in those crucial sixth/fifth centuries BCE. Of course, the community of faith was not a homogeneous social block. Different liturgical needs of varying groups persisted, such as attendance to the sick, ostracism of pilgrims on their way to distant Jerusalem, members of a congregation stricken by poverty, or priestly groups particularly attached to a Zionist theology. These groups maintained specific songs and liturgies, as still extant in the Psalter.

In summary, the different genres of psalms reflect specific social and cultic groupings, consisting always of real flesh and blood people, in Israel's long history of faith. The trajectory of psalmodic expressions runs from small-group, domestic services to regional assemblies and royal state rituals back to parochial community worship related to our Christian Sunday-morning gatherings. Moreover, to remind us of our presuppositions, these modes of religious expression were and are tied to determined social bodies that do not simply form a historical chain or sequence, but may exist contemporaneously, side by side, at any given time. Many of the theological problems and blessings connected with the book of Psalms have their origin in this fundamental, at least four-part social setup experienced by the early Jewish fathers and mothers. In sociological terms we are dealing with psalm theology coming out of: (a) family and clan milieux; (b) regional neighborhoods; (c) royal state cults; and (d) the newly-founded religious community of faith, representing a quite new kind of communal organization somewhere between family and state structures and conceptions.[8]

The exilic/post-exilic community of faith thus left us with its powerful heritage of spiritual and theological patterns of contemporary social moldings, together with its own complexities and confusions. We should now inquire after the specific religious experiences and conceptualizations of the Divine, that is, for the contextual theologies on each level of social organization. For practical purposes I am drawing together stages (a) and (b), since they are close to each other in featuring organic face-to-face relationships between members.

---

8. Cf. Gerstenberger, "Conflicting Theologies."

## Personal God, Family, and Neighborhood Religion

For millennia, before taking the step towards sedentary life and organized communities of a larger scope, humankind existed in isolated bands structured according to kinship lines. Even the Israelites, latecomers in the Near Eastern theatre, visualized a prehistoric stage occupied by patriarchal and sometimes perhaps matriarchal families with their specific customs and beliefs. Modern research from Albrecht Alt to Karel van der Toorn and Leo G. Perdue, etc., acknowledges this particular religious setting that brings forth a distinct mode of theological conceptualization. It is interesting to note that researchers in modern small-group sociology tend to confirm the existence of a specific kind of religious faith within primary social clusters. This means that the original structuring of faith has not been lost over the ages. And the Psalms, having one of their ancient roots in family environment, can give us a vivid impression of how family-religion has come about and is still in operation.

The principal deity of the family, primarily aligned to the male or female leader—in my opinion, more to the latter; house-cults of old were probably administered by chief women[9]—of the small unit, was more or less considered a member of the group, even if a prominent or supreme one. Affinities with ancestor worship probably existed.[10] The "God of my father" (although not attested, we should expect also "of my mother"!) becomes the deity of every member of the group, a helper and savior in daily troubles from birth to grave. God—committed to a particular group—was (and still is!) a defender of his or her client's interest (cf. Jacob's conditional vow to serve the deity he finds at Bethel, Gen 28:20–21). From this very intimate relationship between God and small group arise dimension and atmosphere of family faith down to our own days:

> It was you who took me from the womb;
> 
>> you kept me safe on my mother's breast.
> 
> On you I was cast from my birth,
> 
>> and since my mother bore me you have been my God.
> 
> (Ps 22:9–10 NRSV [MT vv. 10–11])

> O God, from my youth you have taught me,
> 
>> and I still proclaim your wondrous deeds.

---

9. Cf. Gerstenberger, *Yahweh the Patriarch*, 55–66.

10. Cf. Tropper, *Nekromantie*; Loretz, "Die Teraphim"; Loretz, "Nekromantie und Totenevokation."

> So even to old age and gray hairs,
>
> O God, do not forsake me,
>
> until I proclaim your might
>
> to all the generations to come. (Ps 71:17–18a, NRSV)

Personal faith is embedded in family-relationships, the most horrible experience being abandonment by close kinsfolk and becoming the object of naked aggression on their part (cf. Pss 27:10; 41:5–9 [MT vv. 6–10]; 88:8, 18 [MT 9, 19]).[11]

God is experienced totally in personal categories, not as an abstract power. The I–Thou relationship, so influential and precious in our whole religious heritage, has grown out of ancient family faith. Some of the highest values of Jewish-Christian theology—childlike trust in God, personalized hope for divine solidarity and help, courage to argue with the divine protector, expectation that he or she may heal aberrations, broken relationships, illnesses, social disruptions—all these familiar features of personal faith do have their beginnings with family religion. Faith is grounded in belongingness, and belongingness generates the deepest kind of trust. Therefore, formulas of "kinship" and expressions of confidence abound in individual psalms of complaint or thanksgiving.[12] "You are [he is] my God (helper, shield, shepherd, castle; rock, refuge, etc.)" is a very concise statement of this basic relationship of trust (for example, Pss 22:10 [MT v. 11]; 31:14 [MT v. 15]; 63:1 [MT v. 2]; 118:28; 140:6 [MT v. 7]; 7:10 [MT v. 11]; 54:4 [MT v. 6]; 71:3, etc.). Some psalms may be classified as "songs of confidence," because trust is their dominant mood (cf. Pss 4; 11; 16; 23; 27; 56; 62; 131).

The vocabulary in the Psalter expressing confidence in and nearness to God is large, and the form-element, as already indicated, propels prayer to the personal, familiar God. Interestingly, these individual petitions and thanksgivings do not need the notions of exodus, covenant, torah, king, or Zion. They are more directly related to the deity, being independent of secondary institutions. God belongs to their social group. God is dwelling in the midst of the faithful. We may again refer to domestic cults in Israel, clearly attested in Gen 31:34; Exod 21:6; Judg 17:1–5; 1 Sam 19:13, 16. The "household idols" actually were personal, familial deities represented by figurines. Perhaps they were identical with those clay models found by the hundreds in Israelite homes of monarchic times, for the most part of

---

11. For all psalm expositions in this essay, cf. also "Introduction to Cultic Poetry" and interpretations of individual texts in Gerstenberger, *Psalms, Part 1* and *Part 2*.

12. The motif or form-element expressing confidence in God is an essential item in individual complaints; see Gerstenberger, *Psalms, Part 1* and *Part 2*, glossaries under "Affirmation of Confidence"; Miller, *They Cried to the Lord*, 127–30.

nude female deities.¹³ We need not, in my opinion, shun away from this testimony to "alien" Gods in Israel. On the contrary, if the above line of argumentation is at all sustainable, we find household religion an incredible enrichment of theological experience within the Bible.¹⁴ Encountering the divine on the lowest social level, experiencing inclusively the female side of the deity, is basic for faith and theological insight. We should be grateful for the width and depth of biblical tradition. The Yahweh-alone theology is to be understood inclusively, not exclusively: God offers contacts and revelations on all levels of human social organization, in each and every cultural sphere, for all kinds of people.

The point just made is underlined by another piece of evidence. A host of personal names in the Hebrew Scriptures testifies most clearly to the prevalence of well-defined family-outlooks on life, kinship, blessing, salvation from evils, etc.,¹⁵ to the exclusion of national religious concerns. In personal names, "individual relationships to God are put on the same foundation as in individual complaints and salvation oracles: they do imply an archaic, creational state of affairs."¹⁶ God assists the mother to give birth (cf. *Yiftah*, "[God] opened [the womb]"; *Elnatan*, "God gave [a child]"; *Amminadab*, "my uncle [= God] promotes [birth?]," sustains and saves the child,¹⁷ and indeed is his or her "Father" (*Abihu*, "my father is he"). "A trustful relationship of individuals to their gods antedates their existence; it is anchored in being created by the deity. Trust is not initiated by a human decision . . . Personal ties to God are in a way unalienable, just like the relationship between parents and children normally is not liable ever to be cancelled."¹⁸ We may conclude, therefore, that familial faith has been thoroughly routed, as far as the psalmic literature of Israel and her neighbors is concerned, in the ambit of small-group structures and outlooks. The psalmists, at this level,

---

13. Cf. Winter, *Frau und Göttin*; and Schroer, *In Israel gab es Bilder*.

14. Like many other exegetes, Karel van der Toorn judges that state religion eventually supersedes family faith (*Family Religion*, 181–82, 218–25, 373–79). In my opinion, family experiences of God never have ceded to any superior influences, but maintained their autonomy into our own times.

15. Cf. Albertz, *Persönliche Frömmigkeit*, 49–77. Albertz points out that: (a) personal names in the Old Testament are all but lacking references to "national" creeds in Yahweh's salvific deeds; and (b) these names rather refer to familial experiences of divine benevolence, sustenance, and help in regard to birth, illness, threats, dangers, upkeep, blessing, etc.

16. Albertz, *Persönliche Frömmigkeit*, 59.

17. Albertz lists fifty-eight names attributing to the personal deity all sorts of care, protection, help, salvation, vindication etc. (*Persönliche Frömmigkeit*, 61–65).

18. Albertz, *Persönliche Frömmigkeit*, 75.

are taking over the role the deity's children: "I have calmed and quieted my soul, like a child quieted at its mother's breast" (Ps 131:2).

From this infant's perspective there is a thread to expressions of confidence even in the majestic deity portrayed in many psalms: "hide me under the shadows of your wings" (Ps 17:8; cf. similar expressions in Pss 36:8; 57:2; 63:8; 91:4), if "wings"[19] really is referring to the guardians of the ark and not—as in the famous Jesus saying—the protection of a roosting hen (Matt 23:37). Language of confidence has also been drawn from the imagery of war and protection, that is, from the realm of larger social structures (God is "my king," "my shield," "my castle," etc.). For millennia families lived within widespread organizations and experienced the pressures and opportunities of such more ample and anonymous contexts. They were certainly familiarized with the language and metaphors of a wider society. But apparently the real roots of personal trust are age-old experiences: to be sheltered within the intimate kinship group and the neighborhood in village and small townships, which partially function on kinship ties. In distinction to mere family bounds, ancient neighborhoods as a rule operated according to common interests in agricultural and seasonal tasks, defense against hostile outsiders, and internal peace-keeping. Anthropological insights help us to differentiate between family and village life. The latter have to build on custom and law that already exists, while families live on the solidarity of "natural" kinsfolk. In consequence, faith and theology in a village community, although partly prolonging family-attitudes towards the larger group, reach out for a God who is less tied to micro-groups but rather deals with seasonal and political affairs. This local deity was venerated in early Israel at open-air sanctuaries. The challenge originating from community religion clearly was for all participants to overcome self-centered family interests.[20]

From this perspective it seems fully clear, then, that the material and spiritual interests articulated in expressions of confidence and belongingness are those of the familial group. This means that faith and theology revolve around basic needs of life, health, survival of the individual, and his or her immediate surroundings. Accordingly, God is provider of food, housing, and group-harmony (Ps 133), midwife of the newly born (Ps 22:10), protector against fire and water, disease and bad luck (Ps 91:2–6), healer of all illnesses (Ps 38), and protector against demonic onslaught (Ps 91). Naturally, the personal and familial God takes sides in group conflicts in favor of his adherents. Thus, some of the frequent references to

---

19. Cf. Dommershausen, "כנף *kanap*."

20. For more on village and small-town religion, see in Gerstenberger, *Theologien*, chap. 5 (ET *Theologies*, 93–110).

"enemies and evildoers" in the book of Psalms certainly pertain to the inner circle of familial piety, especially in those prayers which show strictly personal, individual traits of suffering, persecution and defense (e.g., Pss 22; 38; 55), as well as of revenge (Ps 109). On the other hand, the God of the rural community has to take care of weather and soil, herds and plantations, inter-familial relations and customs, evil-minded neighbors, and seasonal feasts (cf. Pss 8; 12; 65; 118, etc.).

One of the most spectacular features of familial theology has always been noted with a certain surprise by those modern Christian theologians who believe the Almighty must be a sovereign of sorts, ruling all the world and therefore not suffering any obstacles to his or her rule. Family religion of old, however, did not visualize God in terms of national or world dominion, nor does a modern family faith do so. That means that familial deities—belonging to the small group and facing competition from other small-group divinities—were accessible for argument and rebuke. Individual complaints in the Bible and in the ancient Near East (much like in tribal societies around the world) have been vehicles of serious censure and violent complaints against God, which is only possible on the basis of that intimate familial relationship. Wherever we meet similar characteristics in communal laments (cf. "city-laments," or "communal complaints" as in Lamentations and Pss 44 and 89) we need to identify the life-settings and consider the possibility that familial forms have been used in a congregational or national service. Originally, direct and aggressive language against God from his own followers most likely arose in the religious family tradition of the kinship-God.

My contention, all in all, is simply this: Kinship theology, both at home in familial groups and to some extent in village communities—realized primarily in house-cults (mostly under direction of women?) and familial pilgrimages to regional shrines as that of Elkanah, Hannah, and Peninnah (1 Samuel 1)—is primeval and the primary theology of all mankind. The faith of the small kinship group forms the basis for all subsequent theological systems, and still is most essential for human existence. It persists into our own time as a distinct type of religious faith. After all, where else than in small groups face-to-face with co-religionists could we exercise our faiths and become human beings? The hallmarks of family religion are intimacy, interpersonal relations, limitations to individual lives and necessities, and struggle for wholesome solidarity, both human and divine. Correspondingly, the features of God in kinship theologies should lack tyrannical, arbitrary, majestic traits, since his or her face is human:

> Yahweh is merciful and gracious,
> > slow to anger and abounding in steadfast love.[21]
>
> He will not always accuse,
> > nor will he keep his anger forever.
>
> He does not deal with us according to our sins,
> > nor repay us according to our iniquities.
>
> For as heavens are high above the earth
> > so great is his steadfast love toward those who fear him;
>
> as far as the east is from the west,
> > so far he removes our transgressions from us.
>
> As a father has compassion for his children,
> > so Yahweh has compassion for those who fear him. (Ps 103:8–13)

Psalm 103 is in my opinion a "communal hymn" that shows typical concerns of a congregation in a tradition-minded and universalistic setting. Nevertheless, the individual member of the group is voicing his or her eulogies to Yahweh, probably in common worship. And the portrayal of the fatherly deity taking care of all believers has certainly been derived from family experiences and traditions.

## Faith in Society at Large

All other kinds of social organizations apart from family and kinship-groups emerged fairly late in cultural or civil development.[22] We may distinguish several such "secondary" or "tertiary" societal arrangements in antiquity and modernity: the tribe, state, ethnic entity, political and trade associations, professional societies, religious and gender alliances, etc. In the present context, however, we are interested only in one common feature: larger associations very soon tend to become anonymous entities in which the individual does function differently from his or her own family environment. In other words, larger and anonymous groupings develop their own set of rules, no longer based on kinship values (no matter how insistently the participants clamor for "brotherhood" and "sisterhood"), but now governed by more "objective," impersonal norms and perspectives. In fact, emergent "law," with its offshoots in village customs, is one prominent indicator of a society's

---

21. The concept of *ḥesed* ("steadfast love," better: "solidarity") is central to the family and kinship ethos. Cf. Otto, *Theologische Ethik des Alten Testaments*, 64–67, 81–94.

22. Cf. Ribeiro, *O Processo Civilisatório* (ET *The Civilization Process*).

growing anonymity. "Bureaucracy" and "loss of solidarity" are others. As far as "law" is concerned, strict impartiality must prevail in the name of justice, while family solidarity, in contrast, is built on individual and group needs. (To "consider the person" is against the law! Compare Exod 23:3; Deut 1:17; 16:19, but this is necessary within the family ethos).

The Psalter also reflects the secondary level of socialization, consisting, as it were, not only of prayers of the small-group type. A good number of texts have their origin in ceremonies or rituals oriented towards military and political organizations of Israel and/or Judah. In modern research these are often named "collective" or "national" psalms, serving distinct opportunities in the life of the nation. Conspicuous are situations of complaint (cf. Pss 44; 89), thanksgiving (cf. Ps 124), victory (cf. Ps 68), hymnic praise (cf. Pss 105; 136; 148), public education (cf. Ps 78), and national mourning and penitence (cf. Ps 106; Neh 9). All these texts were no doubt adapted, used, and reused among the exilic and post-exilic communities, thus serving the ends of a group of worshippers that was markedly different from either family or state organization.[23] But sociologically speaking, these texts also preserve sufficient traces of that anonymous larger body of people that outgrew the limits of kinship structures.

Would anyone doubt that in larger associations, with their different ways of life, a different type of faith and theology needs to emerge? In other words, the concepts of God (by necessity?) have to be different, when they emerge from so disparate a social setting as anonymous organizations. The main characteristics of these theological models are:

- God assumes hierarchical leadership, which is mirrored in monarchic structures.
- The city, state, or ethnic group, with its peculiar organization and interests, also becomes the matrix of theological thinking.
- The state economy and contemporary ideas about property, commerce, and political associations play a significant role.

One prominent realm—attributed by some scholars along the lines of Julius Wellhausen as the decisive influence on Old Testament theological thought—is the "military camp," where war-rituals were celebrated and where Yahweh was envisioned as the Lord of battle. The image of God was one of a terrifying hero, wielding superhuman powers in favor of his followers and against their enemies:

---

23. See the following section, "The Only God of the Exclusive Congregation."

Then the earth reeled and rocked;
> the foundation of the mountains trembled
> and quaked, because he was angry.

Smoke went up from his nostrils,
> and devouring fire from his mouth;
> glowing coals flamed forth from him.

He bowed the heavens, and came down;
> thick darkness was under his feet.

He rode on the cherub, and flew;
> he came swiftly upon the wings of the wind.

He made darkness his covering around him,
> his canopy thick clouds dark with water.

Out of the brightness before him
> there broke through his clouds,
> hailstones and coals of fire.

Yahweh also thundered in the heavens,
> and the Most High uttered his voice.

And he sent out his arrows, and scattered them;
> he flashed forth lightnings, and routed them.

Then the channels of the sea were seen,
> and the foundations of the world were laid bare
> at your rebuke, O Yahweh,
> at the blast of the breath of your nostrils.

> (Ps 18:7–15 NRSV; MT vv. 8–16)

The "theophany report" occurs frequently in the Hebrew Scriptures (cf. Pss 68:7–10 [MT vv. 8–11]; 77:16–19 [MT vv. 17–20]; 97:2–5; Hab 3:3–15, etc.).[24] The inherent concept of God here has nothing to do with mercy and care, or the individual's well-being and daily concerns. It is instead oriented towards the crises of a threatened larger entity, a political body of sorts, which has to fight back in order to survive. Unconditional confrontation—war until the enemy's annihilation—is the order of the day. God is consequently pictured as warrior,[25] with his anger (more literally, his "nostrils") raging, and nature reeling with anxiety. God's armament is

---

24. Cf. J. Jeremias, *Theophanie*.
25. Cf. Miller, *Divine Warrior*.

superior, and nobody can resist his fierce onslaught.[26] Thus he intervenes in favor of Israel, saving his clients from extreme dangers. Should this frightening picture of Yahweh really be fundamental to Israel's faith? We must at least admit that a deity like the warrior-god did play an important role in certain contexts of biblical times.

There are other models of God that belong to different situations in the life of Yahweh's people. Suffice it to point out a few of the resulting portrayals of the deity.

- Any larger association of people wants its own God to be first in power and authority. Psalm 29 challenges other deities by using elements of Canaanite myth to acknowledge the supremacy to Israel's God: "Ascribe to Yahweh, O heavenly beings, ascribe to Yahweh glory and strength . . ." (v. 1).

- Psalm 104, apparently following Egyptian hymnic tradition, lauds the heavenly constructor of the world in a theological effort to show his creative capacities: "O Yahweh, my God, you are very great, you are clothed with honor and majesty . . . !" (v. 1; cf. the mythical narration of the chaos battle in vv. 2–9).

- The sustenance of the world-order in which Israel has been living is guaranteed by the divine judge over all law-enforcing powers that exist: "God has taken his place in the divine council; in the midst of the gods he holds judgment . . ." (Ps 82:1).

- The supreme authority of Yahweh over nature, kingdoms and powers is majestically expressed in Psalms 95–99, which belong to the Yahweh-Kingship type. These Psalms also demonstrate the adamant will of the people "called by his name" to be recognized, probably in marked contrast to their actual state of destitution, as a valid part of humankind and possibly as the leading one.

On the side of human macro-organizations the most important issues are these: (1) How can we establish and maintain a solid identity over against other political, ethnic, and religious entities? (2) In what ways may internal administration of justice be guaranteed?

Leaving aside for the time being traces of tribal religion centering on the war-god Yahweh, we now briefly turn to Israel's statehood. The book of Psalms, although composed pretty much in exilic and post-exilic times,

---

26. The Pentateuch and the Prophets quite frequently touch on Yahweh's battles for his people; cf., for example, Exod 14–15; 17:8–16; Deut 20; Judg 4–5. A terrible description of the blood-splashed warrior-god appears in Isa 63:1–6.

retains some valuable information on the theological workings of monarchy (e.g., in Pss 45; 89; 110) and on ancient Zionism (cf. Pss 46; 48; 76; 132). These memories—be they authentic or modified by exilic and eschatological concerns—demonstrate to what degree hierarchic theological thinking superseded older kinship and tribal outlooks and values. The will and help of God is now channeled by way of dynasty and national symbols of invincibility. Yahweh—who had come into the early tradition as a fierce warrior-god fighting for his tribal clients—becomes, in a way, a state official who is cultically manipulated by the royal government in Samaria or Jerusalem (cf., for example, 2 Kgs 22). As such, he is the Lord of internal order and potentially of dominion over less powerful neighbors. Needless to say, kinship religion and local cults that cannot be identified with official state ideology persisted side by side with royal Yahwism, perhaps borrowing here and there concepts and names from the "superior" cult.

Theologically speaking, the Psalms represent a full measure of state-supporting theology around Davidic kingship and Zion-mythology but do not provide many hints of the prophetic critique so well-known from the second part of the canon. Psalms 18; 20; 21; 72; and 144, for example, paint the picture of a victorious monarch, while only a few (later?) exhortations alert to the dangers of human pride, stubbornness, and abuse of power (cf. Pss 78; 95:7-11; 106; 144:3-4; 147:10). The individual supplicant is subsumed under society at large, for society's very well-being is at stake. The state God does not live in solidarity with small groups; his or her face is not the parent-type image, but he or she governs or runs—with equity and justice—a large company of human beings. In spite of all criticism within the Bible itself (e.g., by prophets) we have to admit that theology in the context of larger and anonymous societies is legitimate and necessary to a certain degree. General principles must take a certain precedence over individual needs. Royal Judaean theology, with its hierarchical state-order, is an attempt to do justice to that particular social context. But to build all theological reflection on a macro-organism such as this, together with its governing deity, would be disastrous. Sadly enough, it was not long before Christian theologies indulged in such error.

## The Only God of the Exclusive Congregation

We have already pointed out[27] the changes that came about during the sixth and 5th centuries within the exilic Judaean communities. A new type of organization, sociologically speaking to be located between kinship group and

27. See the section "Life Settings" above.

macro-society, emerged among the deportees in Babylonia and afterwards with the returnees to Judaea. A decapitated nation turned into a community of faith, existing, as it were, as a separate entity within the pluralistic empires of Babylonian and Persian provenance.[28]

From a sociological perspective, the newly emerging Jewish faith, which was dissected into several creative centers, lacked political unity, hierarchical (monarchic) order. It had, therefore, to build a new identity by utilizing traditions of family, tribal past, priestly extract, etc. In contrast to many displaced peoples and emigrants of various epochs, the emerging Jewish community succeeded in organizing itself in congregations that rallied around religious symbols such as Torah, Sabbath, and circumcision. The only and exclusive deity became Yahweh, who had proven sufficiently independent of state authorities to remain the God of the religious community. The new structures of life and faith of the Judean groups in Palestine, Babylonia, Egypt, and possibly other countries were characterized by several focal points:

- Identification via confessing Yahweh as the exclusive personal and communal God.
- Experience of pluralistic and globalizing societies.
- Submission under foreign rule with concomitant economic exploitation.
- Internal strife in order to assert exclusivist positions.
- Most important, communal life was at one and the same time oriented towards the believing individual and his autonomous decision to adhere to Yahweh alone, and towards the needs and wellbeing of the local communities—in more modern terms, towards the parochial entity, and towards the world-wide Jewish community as symbolized in Temple and Torah.

These focal points of spiritual life became the generative matrixes of theological thinking.

The Psalter, more than most other Hebrew writings, is a treasury of early Jewish theologies. Since the Psalms focus on the exemplaric needs of congregations and their theological solutions, but always with the members as persons in view, several features may be highlighted:

---

28. For a more detailed analysis and synthesis, cf. Gerstenberger, *Theologien*, 166–216 (ET *Theologies*, 207–72).

- The importance of individual prayers within the context of congregational worship (cf. the great number of individual psalms in the Psalter).
- The astonishingly strong motivation to draw conclusions from prior salvation history (cf. the so-called history-psalms such as 78; 105; 106; 136).
- The endeavor to concentrate on the Mosaic Torah as the backbone of Jewish identity.
- Numerous examples of psalmic homilies or teachings.[29]

The image of Yahweh that emerges is of a supreme God, creator and maintainer of the world order, yet also an exclusive, zealous Overlord of his religious community, and the consoler, teacher, and provider of each individual adherent.

Yahweh is teacher, wise man, counselor. He himself gives vital instruction to the younger generation, through his precepts (which are probably written: each block of eight acrostic verses features up to ten synonyms for *torah*). Psalm 119 addresses throughout this Instructor-God of the Torah-community:

> Blessed are you, O Yahweh;
>   teach me your statutes.
> With my lips I declare
>   all the ordinances of your mouth. (vv. 12–13)

> I rise before dawn and cry for help;
>   I put my hope in your words.
> My eyes are awake before each watch of the night,
>   that I may meditate on your promise. (vv. 147–48)

> Yet you are near, O Yahweh,
>   and all your commandments are true.
> Long ago I learned from your decrees,
>   that you have established them forever. (vv. 151–152)

The vocabulary of "teaching," "making understand," and "open the eyes" is prominent in the entire, extensive text. Torah implies salvation, grace, and

---

29. For the latter item, cf. Gerstenberger, "Höre, mein Volk, lass mich reden!"

shalom ("all-round well-being, bliss," cf. Ps 1), and Torah is synchronized with the cosmic order:

> The heavens are telling the glory of God;
>> and the firmament proclaims his handiwork...
>
> In the heavens he has set a tent for the sun,
>> which comes out like a bridegroom from his wedding canopy...
>
> The law [*torah*] of Yahweh is perfect,
>> reviving the soul;
>
> Yahweh's decrees are sure,
>> making wise the simple... (Ps 19:1, 4c, 5a, 7)

In consonance with the universalistic worldviews of Babylonian and Persian cultures, and in sheer defense against spiritual subjugation by the ruling powers, Judeans claimed the absolute sovereignty of Yahweh over all the earth (Ps 24:1), without forgetting the response of individual persons (Ps 24:2–4). Thus in their temple rituals they elevated their God to the top position:

> Lift up your heads, O gates!
>> and be lifted up, O ancient doors!
>> that the King of glory may come in.
>
> Who is the King of glory?
>> Yahweh, strong and mighty,
>> Yahweh, mighty in battle.
>
> Lift up your heads, O gates!
>> And be lifted up, O ancient doors!
>> that the King of glory may come in.
>
> Who is this King of glory?
>> Yahweh of hosts,
>> he is the King of glory. (Ps 24:7–10)

The ancient war traditions of the Yahweh tribes come to the fore in order to give expression to the new, universal theology. Yahweh-Kingship hymns and eschatological songs in the Psalter sometimes underscore more aggressively the quest for Yahweh's world dominion (cf. Pss 47; 93; 95–99; and Pss 2; 110, etc.). Reminiscences of past statehood-structures linger in the minds of post-exilic Judeans; they are worked over and partially condensed in feverish expectations of a new reign of David or of the final kingdom of God.

To my mind, this plurality of divine functions in the emerging Jewish community points to a segmentation of theology in different discourses, subject to social groupings within the whole entity of the faithful all over the world—a situation that is also familiar in our churches today. We may consider this a kind of fragmentation of reality, and consequently a breaking up of the Divine. Which do we really prefer: the illusion of wholeness and uniformity, or the stark reality of disquieting, piecemeal theological insight and practice of faith? Ancient communities called upon the personal God with respect to individual and familial necessities. The God of state-order and general ethos played a role in legal administration and in the preaching of equity among the congregation. Yahweh, the God of heaven and earth, was finally the supreme guarantee in all questions of one's larger identity and all instances of conflict with the universalizing ideologies of the time. Naturally, the borderlines between different groups and discourses also allowed for a good amount of fluctuation in terms of language, metaphors, and contents.

From this perspective, the book of Psalms neither diachronically nor synchronically represents a uniform theology. To the contrary, it exhibits multilayered conceptions of God. We may also suggest possible differences between laypersons' models of God and learned reflections, between wealthy congregants and poor ones, perhaps even between male and female adherents, to the all-embracing Yahweh-faith.[30]

## Conclusions for Our World

Recognizing layers of theological thinking and conceptualizations within the Psalter does not mean abandoning the basic idea of one world and one all-inclusive God. But it does presuppose the hiddenness of this concept. In our limited theological discourse we are dealing only with contextual models of God; affirmations about an ultimate and exclusivistic Oneness are left to God him/her/itself, but with hope for and belief in a firm foundation of this world and a final convergence of all the centrifugal forces of life.

On the other hand, our own lives according to day-to-day experience are partitioned and dissociated into several levels of existence. The witness of the Psalter, it seems to me, is thus of utmost importance to us. Its depth and theological diversity stimulates an ecumenical chorus of singers and supplicants,

---

30. Cf. Gerstenberger, "Weibliche Spiritualität in Psalmen und Hauskult."

mediators and confessors.[31] Just as the early Jewish community in its prayers and songs treasured texts for various groups and occasions—admitting distinctly different models of God side by side (Pentateuch, prophetic canon and wisdom literature still contribute more to these variations)—we also are allowed (better: commissioned) to preach differently in various social contexts. My own experience as a pastor tells me this: The Christian message becomes flesh in particular ways with small groups (for example, in personal counselling and family celebrations), with communal worship and interfaith dialogue, or with national and international discourse on the burning issues of humankind. God today is at one and the same time—and these models are not reconcilable, nor to be smoothed over theologically—the personal partner, the guarantor of justice and equity, and the hidden principle and critical yardstick of evolution, science and the world economy.

The quest for unity remains alive in our thinking, because we can hardly exist without a vision of coherence and belongingness. After all, we feel like one determined person with respect to defined groups and entities. Our identity seeks to be one and the same in different walks of life. If this is correct, we should remind ourselves that this desired unity does not reside in our own existence. It is not given into our hands, but we are pilgrims on the way toward such a peaceful state of affairs (cf. Ps 39). We must not claim that unity in order to coerce others to receive it from our hands and be subdued to our whims. The unity of God, the world and humankind—unity of our own individual existence—is a goal, a gift, and a future glory:

> O Yahweh, you have searched me and known me.
> You know when I sit down and when I rise up;
>     you discern my thoughts from far away.
> You search out my path and my lying down,
>     and are acquainted with all my ways.
> Even before a word is on my tongue,
>     O Yahweh, you know it completely.
> You hem me in, behind and before,
>     and lay your hand upon me.
> Such knowledge is too wonderful for me;
>     it is so high that I cannot attain it. (Ps 139:1–4)

---

31. Cf., e.g., Gerstenberger, "Singing a New Song."

# 5

# Modes of Communication with the Divine in the Hebrew Psalter

"COMMUNICATION" IS A WIDE-RANGING concept today just as it was in antiquity.[1] While everyday connotations revolve around the parameters of "personal dialogue," "interactive group exchange," or "direct medial contact" (always implying human verbal intercourse) the ancient (biblical and Near Eastern) ideas encompass a much wider range of possible participants, including forces and entities of nature, demonic and semidivine figures and, most notably, a great variety of non-verbal means of signification (musical, ceremonial, gestural, emotional and others). On the other hand, modern conceptualizations of "communication" may easily extend into the life-sciences and into chemistry and physics with their particular modes of systemic exchanges.[2] In this essay I will stay on a middle road, without losing awareness of the broader debate. I hope to gain insight into the ancient means of entering into contact with the gods and thereby gain additional information about our forebears' theological conceptualizations.

The task at hand is the analysis of some basic patterns of communication with the divine in the Hebrew Bible.[3] To narrow down the choice of examples: no other biblical book offers such a wealth of emotions, thoughts, or arguments in relation to the divine as the Hebrew Psalter. (In spite of its impressive questioning of divine justice, the book of Job is much more

---

1. Within the humanities there is a great variety of theoretical aspects; see, e.g., Griffin, *A First Look at Communication Theory*. There is special emphasis on reader-reception theories; see, e.g., Iser, *How to Do Theory*.

2. See von Bertalanffy, *General Systems Theory*.

3. The Hebrew Bible, not to mention other ancient Near Eastern literature, offers a wide field for research in all kinds of dialogue structures; see, e.g., Welke-Holtmann, *Die Kommunikation zwischen Frau und Mann*; and U. Schmidt, *Zentrale Randfiguren*.

thematically monotonous, engrossed in a single topic and adhering to limited models of argumentation.) Due to the nature of the texts collected in the Psalter we find diverse forms of communication with the divine in these old songs and prayers, deriving from a variety of different life situations.[4] Accordingly, the Psalter provides an ideal place to begin searching for parameters of human–divine communication.

By drawing on older studies of the Psalter and applying some common sense we may surmise that, in spite of the great diversity of communications with the divine in the psalms, we may identify a limited number of basic forms of communication.[5] This assumption rests mainly on insights into psalm categories or genres, developed by Hermann Gunkel, Sigmund Mowinckel and others. If the categorization of psalm texts according to genre (and their implied *Sitz im Leben*) is valid, then modes of communicating with the divine seem likely to fall into similar patterns.

It should be clear from the beginning, however, that communication is ritualized almost everywhere in the world, and the means of encountering deities are especially perceived as needing a high level of standardization, that is, the cultic ceremony. This holds true also in the Psalter. The poems collected there very likely come from or are part of a variety of liturgies, rituals, or ceremonies, in distinction to the spontaneous prose prayers that sometimes appear in narrative contexts, although even these much less formal supplications adhere to some basic structure of petition, reflecting the fundamental elements of the liturgical pieces in the Psalter.[6] There is a great deal of internal and external evidence for the regular psalms in the Hebrew Bible being genuine ceremonial poems, composed by expert singers for general use in diverse worship or meditative rituals, even if the life situations of determined categories of psalms may have changed over time from a domestic to sanctuary environment or vice versa.[7]

---

4. A careful form-critical and genre-oriented analysis of the individual psalms and their life situations is still, despite some opinions, very useful for recognizing the variations of exchange with the divine; see Gerstenberger, *Psalms*, 2 vols.; Gerstenberger, Chapter 2 above; and Gerstenberger, "The Psalter."

5. See Gerstenberger, *Der bittende Mensch*; and Gerstenberger, *Psalms*, 2 vols.

6. Patrick D. Miller has a list of such "prose prayers," which (correctly) leaves out actual psalms quoted in the text (e.g., 2 Sam 22; Isa 38; Jonah 2); see Miller, *They Cried to the Lord*, 337–57.

7. Mowinckel defended this idea, taking exception only for the "private sapiential poems"; see Mowinckel, *The Psalms in Israel's Worship*, 2:104–24 ("Learned Psalmography"). His notion of "cultic use," however, is too much aligned to temple worship only (*The Psalms in Israel's Worship*, 202–6; cf. also Mowinckel, *Religion und Kultus*). On subsequent developments in research, see Brueggemann, *The Psalms and the Life of Faith*. Against Mowinckel, Gunkel considered many psalms "second-hand spiritual

Be this as it may, I propose to look more closely at three of the very basic patterns that form means of communication in the Psalter. The first is connected with prayers of lament, complaint, or supplication. Clearly, the conditions of misery, anxiety, and sickness that bring about a ritual prayer of this sort under the guidance of a shamanistic expert constitute a very special situation, opportune for developing distinct forms of communication. Secondly, there is the large group of psalms that breathes praise and thanksgiving, a very particular mood and attitude concerning divine beings and divine order. Lastly, the Psalter contains a number of didactic poems, also called wisdom psalms. These are usually attributed to the last stage of psalm collecting and editing and reflect the life and institutions of the post-exilic community. These categories form three principal modes of communication with the divine (whether the number of matrices is sufficient to serve all the extant genres of psalms we will evaluate at the end). For our limited purposes they constitute examples of differentiated ways of approaching the divine realm.

## Crying Out from Below

Communication, according to our own conceptualization, always involves two or more parties. The divine being is one active participant whose specific role we must search for: are there special rules and parameters for talking to a deity or listening to his or her voice? We may dismiss this question as insignificant insofar as the discourse of the miserable extant in complaint psalms is pretty much modelled after secular human imprecatory patterns.[8] The problems of communication in the relevant psalms

---

poetry," modelled along the line of older worship specimens; see Gunkel and Begrich, *Einleitung*, 93–94, 261–65, 415–33 (ET *Introduction*, 63–64, 195–98, 319–32). "Detachment from any cultic performance" is the main development for him. The strongest arguments for continued cultic use of the psalms can be adduced from the individual complaint genre; aside from the formal liturgical structures, the analogy of Babylonian incantation prayers embedded in extensive ritual prescriptions ought not to be disregarded (cf. Gerstenberger, *Der bittende Mensch*; Maul, *Zukunftsbewältigung*; Miller, *They Cried to the Lord*, 5–31, 55–134; Cunningham, "Deliver Me from Evil").

8. Cf. Gerstenberger, *Der bittende Mensch*, 17–63 ("Das alltägliche Bittschema"): customary behavior and words (i.e. ordinary ritual patterns) determine the behavior of any person who needs to approach someone else for help. Differences of psalm procedure are principally due to the liturgical framework for which they were made and not to any metaphysical otherness of the divine sphere. Annette Zgoll has very ably drawn on Babylonian audience etiquette to explain prayer postures ("Audienz"); and Hartenstein refers similarly to royal practices (*Das Angesicht JHWHs*).

rather lie in the extreme gap (not of the qualitative kind) between sufferer and helper: "Why are you so far from helping me . . . ?" (Ps 22:1[2]) is a reproachful question often used in complaints.[9] The distance in horizontal or vertical ("From the depths I am calling"; cf. Ps 130:1) terms is distressing, as it implies physical and spiritual dimensions and impedes contact with the potential helper. The normal and wholesome relation between supplicant and Yahweh would be that of closeness, trust solidarity as is easily recognizable in "affirmations of confidence": the salvific attributes given to Yahweh.[10] One outstanding appellation (invocation) of the deity sought suggests a very personal, familial relationship: "My god" ("god of my strength," "refuge," etc.; cf. Pss 22:1[2]; 40:5[6]; 71:3–6).[11] To what extent a willful absence of a god from the downtrodden may be understood as a divine castigation on account of committed sins or some unaccounted for estrangement, possibly caused by mischievous enemies, was a matter to be resolved in each individual case by proper diagnostic analysis.[12] On the whole, we may take the note of complaint—abysmal distance!—to have been the main obstacle to communication in this category of psalms. Yet this distance was considered an anomaly; it had to be overcome in personal confrontation with the protective deity via proper entreaty, possibly accompanied by ablutions, exorcisms, small sacrifices, vows, confessions of guilt or other means of atonement and rehabilitation.

Plaintive, reproachful communication in the Psalter is thus not neutral, but an intentional, partisan affair. It does not purport mere dialogue, exchange of opinions or assertions. In particular, the "cry from below" arises from despair; the communication in such situations aims first of all

---

9. Verse numbering is according to NRSV, with MT enumeration in square brackets where applicable.

10. The formal "expression of trust" element in complaint psalms is important; it signals the basis of the mutual reliance between the supplicant and the deity; see the discussions in Gunkel and Begrich, *Einleitung*, 232–36 (ET *Introduction*, 170–73); and Gerstenberger, *Der bittende Mensch*, 127–30; Miller, *They Cried to the Lord*, 178–232.

11. Cf. Gerstenberger, *Theologies*, 25–91. The familial affiliation of this personal God is the decisive theological feature. Phenomenologically, faith in a familial deity constitutes a particular type of religion, as already Alt, *Der Gott der Väter* (ET "The God of the Fathers"). See also Albertz, *Persönliche Frömmigkeit*; and Vorländer, *Mein Gott*.

12. The problem of enemies or evildoers is a very serious one in the complaint genre. See Gerstenberger, "Enemies and Evildoers"; Mowinckel, *Psalmenstudien I* (ET *Psalm Studies* 1:1–173); Keel, *Feinde und Gottesleugner*; Bauks, *Die Feinde des Psalmisten und die Freunde Ijobs*; Riede, *Im Netz des Jägers*; and van der Velden, *Psalm 109*. Proper diagnosis as an issue in communication with the divine powers sometimes shows up in narratives in the Hebrew Bible (cf. 1 Kgs 14:1–3; 2 Kgs 1:1–2; Num 5:11–31). More extensive procedures are known from ancient Near Eastern sources; see Heeßel, *Babylonisch-assyrische Diagnostik*.

to overcome the barrier of distance—sometimes due to guilt or misunderstanding—and in the second place targets the power in the divine realm that is handled by a deity potentially willing to step in and save and restore the wretched person.[13] The real aim of supplicants is to regain power and life; psalms of complaint are intended to reach the deity, secure a benevolent ruling about their misery and thus tap the resources of their god in order to fill the vacuum on the human side. Supplication is a balancing act of power, wrestled from a superior divine being (cf. Gen 32:23–33) who is nevertheless considered responsible for his or her familial clients. It asks for a transfer of divine power to the human end of the spectrum, where there is extreme need of it. In this sense, the cries from below aim to produce a participatory action involving both deity and petitioner and resulting in the wellbeing of the supplicant.

Viewed through the concept of power regulation, we may try to sketch the mechanism of complaint and petition in the Psalter as one of the main types of communication with the divine. There are many variants in the complaint psalms, of course, and due to space we can only look at some basic issues here.[14] First, professional communication with the divine power in the case of a patient fearing for his life would have been no easy task, with intricate and conventionally fixed procedures to be followed. The overall bundle of rites is complex; just like today, the experts needed to clarify causes and consequences of the calamity at hand, determine the powers responsible for sending remedies, prepare proper means and rituals to counteract the evil and so on. All these operations belong to this type of lament-communication, although they are only rarely considered in the context of our topic. Studies on Mesopotamian diagnostics and related subjects already illuminate the general situation.[15] The trajectory of complaint rituals from preparatory rites to thanksgiving conclusion has been outlined and analyzed by a number of scholars.[16] Communication, we may learn, does not go without preparation, nor can it avoid the professional help that

---

13. In his classic study, C. Barth, *Die Errettung vom Tode*, maintained that the supplicants experienced their precarious situation already as a real death predicament (cf. Ps 88). The supplicant thus requires rescue from this death zone.

14. A fairly exhaustive enumeration of the internal structure of complaint may be found in Gunkel and Begrich, *Einleitung*, 240–50 (ET *Introduction*, 177–84); and Mowinckel, *The Psalms in Israel's Worship*, 2:1–25, esp. 9–11; my own summary is in *Psalms: Part 1*, 11–14.

15. Cf. Heeßel, *Babylonisch-assyrische Diagnostik*; Mayer, *Untersuchungen*; Cunningham, *Deliver Me from Evil*; Gerstenberger, *Der bittende Mensch*.

16. Cf. Mayer, *Untersuchungen*; Gerstenberger, *Der bittende Mensch*, 113–60; Maul, *Zukunftsbewältigung*, 29–113; Cunningham, *Deliver Me from Evil*; and Frechette, *Mesopotamian Ritual-Prayers*.

itself makes the subjects of communication uncertain: Is it the practitioner or the patient who communicates with the divine?[17]

Such verbal acts relating to the divine helper are at least partially transmitted in the psalms. The formulation leaves open the possibility that other words besides the psalms were spoken in healing ceremonies and the possibility that concomitant gestures, movements and interactions may have played a considerable role in complaint ceremonies. Putting all the paraphernalia aside for the moment, however, the complaint psalms reveal a great deal about communication under stressful conditions. Formulas of petition normally begin with an invocation of the deity by name, often connected to an initial plea to be heard. Afterwards follow several elements, mostly in support of the supplication: complaints (including descriptions of sufferings, misdeeds of enemies), affirmations of confidence and maledictions (imprecations) on evildoers. The final supplication is often already implicit in these other elements, but as a rule it is spelled out before Yahweh or other gods in the plea for their intervention. The wordings of these prayers are artfully composed to achieve their ends and they are time-honoured by long and efficient use in ceremony.

With regard to communication in the opposite direction, from the deity to the petitioner, psalm interpreters have long asked whether or not the ceremonies allowed room for exchange, or, more precisely, whether the deity was called upon to answer the petition.

This is a major issue in psalm research and is perhaps decisive for our recognition of the dialogical framework of communication. Research on this question of "arguing with the deity" also opens up windows towards wisdom literature in the ancient Near East and related compositions in the Hebrew Bible, such as Job and Ecclesiastes. Even within the psalms, however, we have a considerable amount of impatient, challenging questions, reproachful complaints and protestations of innocence, all directed against the deity who is supposedly leading the investigation into the petitioner's maladies. There are also faint signs that the supplication ceremony could (and would) have been interrupted or concluded by a divine oracle of assurance: "You have been heard" or similar. Psalm 35:3 asks verbatim for such an affirmation—"speak to me: 'I am your salvation'"—while Ps 5:3(4) "watches" for a positive reaction of Yahweh and the last word of Ps 22:21(22) may be understood as "you have answered me." Together with the deliverance formula elsewhere in the Hebrew Bible ("Do not fear . . . ," frequently occurring in Deutero-Isaiah) a case may be made for verbal exchange within the complaint ceremony, although the particularities of how the deity would communicate him or

17. See Brown, "The Psalms and 'I.'"

herself are hardly verifiable.[18] The divine partner in this situation is the personal, familial, client-oriented deity, as presupposed in family religion, and the basic theological concept in the background is that of familial solidarity.[19] The personal god, possibly inherited from ancestor worship, belongs to the family group; he or she is accessible to personal entreaty and can change his or her mind, because all parameters and connotations of this helpfully close god are oriented to social group ties.

The other question still pending is that of the real subjects in this type of communication. We assume that the ritual expert, a shamanistic healer or conjurer, was the actual performer of functions and the author of the liturgical words. They reflected his expertise and experience and guaranteed, to a certain extent (as these professional guarantees go), the effectiveness of the rites. Yet the supplication ceremony is being executed in the name of the patient. Babylonian prayers that resemble the Hebrew Bible's complaint psalms put an Akkadian N.N.-sign at the beginning of an incantation prayer where the cantor-patient has to insert his own personal name, and the ritual prescriptions in the same texts occasionally advise the performing priest: "Let the patient speak . . ."[20] This plainly means that communication may occur on concomitant or doubled levels, with the healing experts (diviner, diagnostician, incantation priest, curer) identifying with the person in distress and his intimate group. They take up the advocacy of the endangered supplicants in their professional capacity and co-perform with their paying clients in an effort to win back attention and support from the personal god.[21]

For us, the final query must be: How does this kind of communication from the depths come to an end? On the basis of shamanistic activities in more modern times we may conclude that rituals of healing performed by seasoned experts are usually successful; one can find "success rates" in the range of 60 to 80 percent, sometimes equaling the rates of modern medical doctors. When ancient Israelite and Judahite clients were delivered they were obliged to bring a thanksgiving sacrifice or service to Yahweh (cf.

---

18. The pioneer study was that of Begrich, "Das priesterliche Heilsorakel." The debate about the oracular response in healing rituals has continued ever since; cf. VanGemeren, "Oracles of Salvation."

19. Cf. Gerstenberger, *Der bittende Mensch*, 113–60; Gerstenberger, *Theologies*, 25–91; van der Toorn, *Family Religion*.

20. Cf. Gerstenberger, *Der bittende Mensch*, 64–112; Miller, *They Cried to the Lord*, 55–134.

21. Maul's thesis that the priest in certain moments takes upon himself the identity and the ill-fate of his client the supplicant may, however, be overdrawn (Maul, *Zukunftsbewältigung*, 67–71).

Ps 107). Returning to the imagery of power transfer, we may notice desolation and weakness. The supplicant receives a new chance for (normal, wholesome, un-afflicted) life and a small return in gratitude is in order; part of the blessing is thus reverted to the donor of these good gifts and the balance of energies returns to normal.

Our first basic form for relating to a (personal) deity in situations of danger to life is conceived as a dramatic appeal to the loyal god along well-known lines of human social behavior (law-suit, argumentative contestation, confession of guilt, plea for mercy). Though the enactment of Yahweh's own part in the dialogue may have posed liturgical problems, the idea was that the supplicant—with the help of an expert advocate and ritual performer—approached the deity asking for deliverance and rehabilitation and ready to offer up thanks to a helpful, merciful deity. We may term this model of communication "personal interaction."

## Praising from on High

The second type of communication in the Psalter is connected with praise contexts. Naturally, variants of this eulogy type are numerous, but a basic context is discernable for many of them. Praise, as a rule, does not start out from dire need and despair (though there are some thin moorings of hymnic poetry even in petitionary situations).[22] Rather, praise of a god from the human side usually presupposes divine power and plenty, as imaginable in the context of yearly seasonal harvest festivities realized on a local or regional basis (cf. Exod 23; 34; Lev 23; Deut 16). The social and ideological context, as a rule, is also different from individual complaint discourse. We may safely imply that hymns were (and are) used usually by collective entities, not by individuals—larger organized groups of some political standing, not isolated families.

Correspondingly, the concept of the divine in these communications reflects regional or national interests and is couched in the imagery of royalty and hierarchy and deals with a different power structure than those of individual lament. The worldview and the theological horizon that emerge from the praise psalms are those of ancient Near Eastern social organizations; hymns celebrate a god for his or her great deeds and gifts to communities,

---

22. Cf. Gerstenberger, "Praise in the Realm of Death." Many researchers have marveled that eulogies of the gods addressed in Mesopotamian complaints can be quite strong, in contrast to the Hebrew use of laudatory language with individual supplication; some have gone so far as to denounce the mean, cajoling mind on the side of Babylonian supplicants. See Begrich, "Die Vertrauensäußerungen"; Widengren, *Accadian and Hebrew Psalms of Lamentation*; Miller, *They Cried to the Lord*, 14–15.

dynasties and nations. If they involve sentiments of gratitude directly, then the thank-offerings discussed under the first paradigm of communication may take place in analogous manners, but praise is more than offering a god thanks: it means further activating and preserving the power of a benign deity in favour of a determined social group or association.

Again thinking of power balances, there may be a certain lack of equilibrium between a deity's potentialities and human capacities; these latter were, according to ancient Near Eastern conceptions, only a small (but real) fraction of the divine powers. At festive gatherings (e.g., harvest, commemorations of victories, sheep-shearing, building dedications) the worshipping crowd praises the gracious provider, probably led by priest or other cultic functionaries. What happens in this process? The act of praising is a dynamic performance, understood to help produce and sustain the goods for which thanks are given. Praise helps to create and maintain the majesty of Yahweh imagined as a flow of power from the human to the divine side.

Instances in the psalms alert us to this idea that the gods need the supportive attention of humans. The old Canaanite hymn Ps 29 advises the "sons of god" to bring to Yahweh "glory and strength" (v. 1). Rivers and other natural powers are instructed to hail Yahweh of the universe (cf. Pss 93 and 96) to stabilize his supreme authority further, and cosmic forces have to sing his ethereal praise (Pss 19; 148). One rather cryptic verse in Ps 22 declares Yahweh to be "enthroned over the 'praises of Israel'" (v. 3[4]). The existence of creative power and its workings in the world provokes jubilant outbursts of praise, periodically refreshed and reiterated: "O sing to Yahweh a new song, sing to Yahweh all the earth" (Ps 96:1); "Declare his glory among the nations, his marvelous works among all the peoples" (v. 3); "Ascribe to Yahweh, O families of the peoples, ascribe to Yahweh glory and strength" (v. 7). All humanity is called to sing out to Yahweh, with all creation participating:

> Say among the nations, "Yahweh is king!
> The world is firmly established;
>    it shall never be moved.
> He will judge the peoples with equity."
> Let the heavens be glad, and let the earth rejoice;
>    let the sea roar, and all that fills it;
>    let the field exult, and everything in it.
> Then shall all the trees of the forest sing for joy
>    before the Lord; for he is coming,
>    for he is coming to judge the earth.

> He will judge the world with righteousness,
>> and the peoples with his truth. (Ps 96:10–13; cf. Ps 98:7–9)

On a truly grandiose scale, Ps 148 enacts an all-encompassing eulogy of the creator by enumerating all those who are to join into this great concert of voices:

> Praise Yahweh!
> Praise Yahweh from the heavens;
>> praise him in the heights!
>
> Praise him, all his angels;
>> praise him, all his host!
>
> Praise him, sun and moon;
>> praise him, all you shining stars!
>
> Praise him, you highest heavens,
>> and you waters above the heavens!
>
> Let them praise the name of Yahweh,
>> for he commanded and they were created.
>
> He established them forever and ever;
>> he fixed the bounds, which cannot be passed.
>
> Praise Yahweh from the earth,
>> you sea monsters and all deeps,
>
> Fire and hail, snow and frost,
>> stormy wind fulfilling his command.
>
> Mountains and all hills,
>> fruit trees and all cedars!
>
> Wild animals and all cattle,
>> creeping things and flying birds!
>
> Kings of the earth and all peoples,
>> princes and all rulers of the earth!
>
> Young men and women alike,
>> old and young together!
>
> Let them praise the name of Yahweh,
>> for his name alone is exalted;
>>> his glory is above earth and heaven.

> He has raised up a horn for his people,
>> praise for all his faithful,
>> for the people of Israel who are close to him.
>
> Praise Yahweh! (Ps 148:1–14)

These two psalms are impressive in their conception of the divine world as also created by the deity responsible for all existence. They compare thematically to the great speeches of Yahweh demonstrating to the rebellious Job what real wisdom and power are like (Job 28; 38–41). This power is real, effective and does not suffer counterargument. The advice of hymn-singers to a congregation of adorers is to join into the chorus of praise from around the world and in the midst of all existence.

Yet what are the concepts of this praise, the perceptive horizons in this almost universal painting? Certainly we are not facing a dreamy, enthusiastic, artful and exuberant admiration of curious bystanders as in some romantic glorification of nature. There is communal and personal involvement discernable in every phrase. Furthermore, because Yahweh and other ancient Near Eastern deities are strengthened by the praise of their worshippers in this way, they are not the unmovable mover of Greek philosophy, the absolute good or the overall principle of truth and beauty. The world Yahweh created is far from being an utterly harmonious entity, even though it is credited with stability, truth and justice. Behind the scenes there loom forces of destruction, corruptions of order and deviations from the plans of the creator. Psalm 96 pinpoints the defaults in saying that Yahweh will "judge" (שפט) the earth, applying "righteousness" (צדק) and "truth" (אמונה; all v. 13).[23] Psalm 148 also has a somewhat hidden reference to the powers of destruction that have been overcome by the good creator: "He has raised up a horn for his people" (v. 14). Within the chorus of jubilant voices who join in praise of the creator there is the necessity of supplying refuge and power (the "horn") to the minority people of Yahweh in an oppressive and violent world.[24] The general concept of an ordered world, opposed by destructive chaos powers, pervades ancient Near Eastern mythology and other literature; vestiges of primordial and ongoing

---

23. The concept of judging in the Hebrew Bible implies the responsibility of right governance in accordance with the good world order; cf. Niehr, "שפט šapaṭ." "Righteousness" and "truth" are the foundational pillars of the universe; they speak to the pervasive concepts of world order in the ancient Near East; cf. Ringgren and B. Johnson, "צדק ṣedeq"; H. H. Schmid, *Gerechtigkeit als Weltordnung*.

24. The symbolism of the bull or sheep/goat horn is very ancient in the Near East; see Kedar-Kopfstein, "קרן qrn." It stands for power, authority, and protection. For a form-critical analysis of Ps 148, see Gerstenberger, *Psalms, Part 2*, 447–52.

battle for the good order are found frequently in the Hebrew Scriptures (cf. Gen 1:1–5; Pss 18:7–15 [8–16]; 74:13–15; 77:16–19 [17–20]; 89:6–11 [7–12]; 93:1–4; 97:1–5; 104:1–9; 114:3–8; etc.).[25] Praise is badly needed to counteract these antagonistic forces of disorder and injustice.

In analogous iconographical material from the human political sphere, iconographic representations show scenes of adoration with the king seated and jubilants standing in awe before him. This same motif can depict the veneration of a deity by a client.[26] This praise is normally combined with song and instrumental music to lend it force. Since the first half of the third millennium instruments were used to accompany praise of the gods, including drums, stringed instruments, pipes, horns, and brass. Their common effect was to enhance the acoustic power of eulogy and make a "loud noise to Yahweh" (cf. Ezra 3:10–13; 1 Chr 15:16; 2 Chr 20:19, etc.). Singing and instruments are an important part in collective praise.

Collective praises are indeed the rule, not the exception. Sometimes an individual articulating jubilations all by him- or herself seems to be in the forefront of eulogy (cf. Pss 78; 103), but as a rule even such first-person hymns serve the community. Likewise, a hymn to the glory of an individual person such as Ps 8 (perhaps celebrating his coming of age) is framed by the collective eulogy: "O Yahweh, our sovereign, how majestic is your name in all the earth!" (vv. 1, 9 [2, 10]). In the same vein, Pss 103 and 104 begin in the first person singular, with a self-exhortation of the singer ("Bless Yahweh, O my soul … ," Ps 103:1–2; 104:1), only to continue explicitly in the first person plural. This is the predominant form for (collective) hymns. The personal laudation of the individual on account of an experienced salvation (thanksgiving song and sacrifice) is quite a different matter.[27] There are numerous poems in the Psalter that testify to their origin in community circles or parochial worship by employing first person plural discourse.[28] This is a strong indication of collective action organized by professional leadership, whether in the temple or other community institutions.

Verbal articulations (presumably accompanied by gestures, mime or corporal enactments like dance) underline the impersonal power aspect of praise. I have elsewhere sketched the verbs used in elevating rituals and

---

25 Cf. Ortlund, *Theophany and Chaoskampf*; and Watson, *Chaos Uncreated*. There is also a counter-current subjacent in biblical tradition, ably portrayed in Brueggemann, *Theology of the Old Testament*.

26 For examples of both forms of adoration, see Keel, *Die Welt der altorientalischen Bildsymbolik* (ET *The Symbolism of the Biblical World*)

27 Psalm 107 calls for a thanksgiving service for four particular salvific events; see Crüsemann, *Studien*, 210–84.

28. Cf. Gerstenberger, "Psalms," 86–89.

the frequent use of magnifying, uplifting, strengthening and empowering language.[29] Suffice it to add that all verbal and corporal expressions in hymnic performance were tuned to the task of strengthening praise. We often misunderstand praise language as mere admiration of what is at hand or in sight in terms of obvious glamour and majesty. This is too short-sighted an interpretation of eulogy. The words, phrases and enactments aim to achieve what they are pronouncing. Hymn singing, as much as any conjuring type of speech, is performative in essence. This quality of discourse has to be taken into account when discussing psalmic praise communication.

There is not much importance to be attributed to the different areas of life and thematic specifications of the hymns that appear in the Psalter. Even the object of praise may alternate from Yahweh himself to his city, Mount Zion, Torah, commandments, and blessings. Praises are enacted in grand processions (cf. Pss 24; 68; 48; 132; 2 Sam 6:14–15) or theophanic events (cf. Pss 18; 47; 98; Hab 3). The topics touched on in the hymns of the Hebrew Bible vary among victories over enemies, creation and subjugation of primeval chaos forces, deliverance of Israel and the promise of the holy land, the gift of Torah and seasonal abundance in crops. Important for us is the underlying scheme, of the people (through its hymnic experts?) reacting to the general benevolence of their god. They offer back some of the power and glory granted them by their deity in order to strengthen his or her potency in every respect and to secure future well-being. From a position of relative strength and happiness, the sung praises initiate a flow of energy towards the deity of all destinies and sustenance.

The crucial question, however, concerns the significance of the aforementioned observations for the praise-model of communication. We ought to be wary of our own understandings of praise, which may be object-centered and fixed on dialogical structures. According to the evidence above, there is no dialogue at all in these eulogies of the beneficial divine presence and action. The creator may withhold his blessings with (or without) understandable reason, but there is no way to negotiate the resumption of grace (cf. Ps 104:27–30). The only means of attempting to secure good life is to sing Yahweh's praise and thus ward off the "wicked" (Ps 104:31–35; cf. 139:19–22). Even the imagined interlocution of Job and Yahweh (Job 38–42) is based on the presupposition that Yahweh's creation and wisdom must not be contested but extolled. We hear frequently the voice of the liturgist summoning the worshippers to praise the great god of creation and sustenance. The praise itself goes on with great noise, not only with words but with music, movements, processions, clapping of hands and shouting, probably

---

29. Cf. Gerstenberger, "Psalms," 123–24.

including endless repetitions of short formulae like "halleluyah," "God is great," "majestic are you," and so on. The liturgical action seems one-sided, with no response of the deity expected at all. Rather, the words and gestures start on the human side, trying to reach the divine font of all good gifts and centralized power. The concept of god that transpires from these hymns has little in common with a dialogue. The creator is a remote figure dedicated to ruling a region, a state or the whole universe. He relates to humans, to be sure, but like a distant king working for his subjects, providing necessities of life and keeping up the overall order of the world for the benefit of creation. The whole praising mechanisms are set up because of these background regulations. Many scholars—including Gerhard von Rad, Patrick D. Miller, and Walter Brueggemann—have posited that divine action is an essential presupposition of praise. They do not sufficiently emphasize, however, the inherent mechanisms of the *do ut des* model, that is, the obligatory paying back of some of the gifts received.[30] In fact, the emphasis of praise hymns seems not to be entering into an exchange of words with the eulogized one(s), but to return support in exchange for the received gifts and thus to strengthen the position of the benefactor in the future.

The second type of communication with the divine in the Psalter, then, is distinct from the personal encounter type found in complaints. It arises from a collective setting of worship and is aimed at a distant creator and sustainer. The underlying theological assumption is that the good and just order must be supported by the human recipients of existing fortunes and must be perpetually strengthened against the disruptive forces that are rampant in the world. Praise communication, consequently, enters directly and with powerful performance into the battle for the sustenance of the righteous world, building up the power of the supreme deity him or herself. Eulogy may thus be identified as the flow of energy from humankind to the divine. Functionally, it compares to fans singing their chants in sport arenas: those praised welcome the support they receive, and in the same vein the deity accepts the empowerment without immediate response.

## Musings over the Word

A third sharply distinguished mode of communication with the divine in the Psalter is paid little attention in regular psalm exegeses. This is the large and heterogeneous group of poems called "wisdom" or "didactic"

---

30. The classical study on receiving and giving back is Mauss, "Essai sur le don" (ET *The Gift*).

psalms in most modern treatments.[31] Form-critically, it is true we cannot identify a uniform genre among these, but the diverse poems demonstrate a common mental pattern and a way of approaching problems that make them likely products of one and the same social and/or religious group. Their self-reflective attitude is typical for a faith community concerned with the will of Yahweh and the destiny of his followers and their opponents (the "just" and "wicked").

It is clear enough that the Yahweh-communities of the exilic and postexilic periods focused on the written and oral transmission of divine revelation through Moses. Torah (and other writings) being the backbone for this kind of new religious organization (unheard of in pre-exilic times), the life and worship of emerging Judaism really revolved around the "word" of Yahweh.[32] Without doubt, this involved extensive studying and memorizing of scripture, institutionalized instruction in the divine will must be presupposed of Jewish congregations in the Persian period.[33] The didactic psalms may have been part of these communal educational efforts in which individuals (in classrooms?) meditated aloud the (written) word of God in order to acquire the holiness and righteousness prescribed by Yahweh.

The mode of communication with the divine in these didactic psalms is quite characteristic and particular. It does not fit into the aforementioned schemes of praying from below directly to a personal god nor extolling and strengthening the god of order and creation from above. Rather, the supplicant here is practicing a very quiet soliloquy, meant to be overheard only by the god of wisdom. He or she is meditating, perhaps remembering, reading (?), or listening to the divine words of the Torah. "To meditate the Torah day and night, from sheer joy in the will of the Lord" (paraphrase of Ps 1:2) seems to be not only the acknowledged life situation of Pss 1; 19; and 119 but also of musings like those in Pss 9/10; 37; 39; 49; 73; 90; 95; 139; and so on. The contemplator ponders over diverse subjects connected to his or her attempt to be a faithful adept of Yahweh, the universal and merciful god of Israel and source of all knowledge, without entering into a demanding and exacting mood. Thus the transience of human existence is a problem (cf. Pss 39; 90), as is the quest for the impeccable righteousness of God himself (the theodicy problem; cf. Pss 9/10; 33; 37; 49; 94). Personal

---

31. Mowinckel, *The Psalms*, 2:104-25; Gunkel and Begrich, *Einleitung*, 381-97 (ET *Introduction*, 293-305); Crenshaw, *Old Testament Wisdom*, 187-94, with further references. For a paradigmatic study of a wisdom psalm, see Casetti, *Gibt es ein Leben vor dem Tod?*

32. Gerstenberger, *Theologies*, 207-72.

33. Gerstenberger, *Israel in der Perserzeit*, 292-322, 328-53 (ET *Israel in the Persian Period*).

sin may pose a question but more so from the positive side: How can the righteous live up to the exigencies of the commandments (cf. Pss 1; 19; 119)? The past history of Yahweh with his elect people may also be a topic of meditation (cf. Pss 78; 105; 106). In short, there is no lack of themes in the rich tradition of the Yahwistic faith community that may be mused over in individual or collective reflection. But how can we evaluate this particular mode of communication against the previous two?

The heart of the matter in these sapiential musings seems to be the exercise of a special spirituality, which grew out of the faith community itself. Allegiance to the Torah implied a complete trust in Yahweh's revelation and a firm determination to adhere to the rulings and orientations of this god's benevolently revealed words. Means of reflection on and digestion of the divine will have sprung up together with the public reading of Torah (Neh 8). Reflective exercises, possibly in private but more likely in community gatherings or worship, were probably designed to foster familiarity with and allegiance to the covenant stipulations. Meditation on and in response to written or recited texts thus becomes a new vehicle of communication with the divine. It constructs and maintains a creedal identity and a workable spirituality. The conceptions of god underlying this internal communication are remarkable. We can understand this relationship as a mystical one cultivated by the contemplator of Yahweh's ways and human nature. Yahweh is not approached directly and personally nor is enhanced as the great creational power but experienced through the inherited traditional revelation; all kinds of spontaneous prophecy has either ceased (cf. Zech 13:2–3) or been transformed into Torah interpretation (cf. Jer 11). Faith in the deity starts to be communicated by the text (continuing down to the present in the Jewish, Christian and Islamic traditions) and, by necessity, the reader's reaction to the divine is channeled through a dialogue with the book rather than confrontations with the divinity directly.

The formal address to Yahweh is, as a rule, maintained in the relevant psalms: "Yahweh, you have been our dwelling place in all generations . . ." (Ps 90:1); "O Yahweh, you have searched me and known me . . ." (Ps 139:1); "Yahweh, let me know my end . . ." (Ps 39:4[5]). Yet these appellations or invocations sound abstract and seem more rhetorical than real, at least insofar as they lack the urgency of petition or praise addresses. Even more neutral are the descriptive openings of meditative or exhortative psalms (cf. Pss 14; 37; 49); in these the real partner in dialogue often seems to be the speaker's own self: "I said, 'I will guard my ways . . .'" (Ps 39:1[2]); "Do not fret because of the wicked . . ." (Ps 37:1); "How can young people keep their way pure?" (Ps 119:9). Yahweh is listening in, eventually giving his opinion via the reflective process, and will ultimately decide the cases requiring decision.

The arguments, brought forth by the members of the faith community who composed these psalms, however, are usually not of a controversial type. They re-affirm only that which has been age-old praxis in nature and human society. Yahweh appears to be the sovereign, little riled lord of wisdom who administers a stable world with revealed, immovable guidelines (the Torah). His age is measured in eons (Ps 90), his articulate presence is the written Torah (Pss 1; 19; 119) or the radiating holiness inside the temple (cf. Lev 16). His fame reverberates through the universe in a non-verbal language (Ps 19:1–4 [MT 2–5]), and it is the general destiny of all mortals that is the burning question (Pss 39:4–6, 11 [MT 5–7, 12]; 90:9–12). The futility of all human endeavor is frustrating ("Mortals cannot abide in their pomp; they are like the animals that perish"; Ps 49:12, 20 [MT 13, 21]). How could communication with the deity be possible in this world? It occurs by way of the murmuring of Scriptures and attempting an inner dialogue with oneself and the sages—and thereby with Yahweh of the book.

The third mode of communication in the Psalter is a novelty, unprecedented in the history of spirituality of the ancient Near East. Personal exchange with Yahweh is by immersion in an inner dialogue via the comparison of passages, addressing the deity by confessing loyalty to and identifying with his revealed will, with all this being done in continuous, permanent meditation and prayer. We may call this communication the "mystical immersion" type, prompted by the spirituality of the post-exilic Jewish community and facilitated by the written tradition.

## Communication

The Psalter is the foremost example within the Hebrew Bible of the multi-layered theological conceptions that have grown from diverse spiritual situations in the long history of Israelite religion. Because of this, a uniform "theology of the Old Testament" cannot be expected, nor can there be a homogeneous means of communication with the divine.[34] Participants in the dialogue or discourse of heterogeneous social, cultural and religious situations will, by necessity, employ diverse models of communication. The Psalter illustrates the wide range of possibilities in an unsurpassable and superb manner, containing as it does the richest collection of spiritual texts available from Israel's heritage.

The final question to address is whether it is legitimate to single out, as the present study does, only three models of communication to represent

---

34. Cf. Gerstenberger, "Theologies in the Book of Psalms"; and Gerstenberger, *Theologies*.

an unknown number of ancient parameters. The selection of three exemplary types is arbitrary and restrictive, meant to illuminate the situation but by no means conclude the analysis. Complaint and praise have been long recognized to constitute fundamental means of approaching the different deities—for some redactors exclusively Yahweh—in the psalms.[35] Yet there are clear differences in the forms of communication in the laments of individuals and those of larger social entities; there are also a great number of variations in the thanksgivings (of which this essay does not consider any) and many diverse praise situations (e.g., victory, seasonal blessings, rites de passage etc.). Finally, there is a considerable spectrum of meditative modes of communication, with some musings directly involved with scriptures and others impacted by life problems. Given all these variants, the three selected models may only serve as (prominent) examples of the communicative patterns extant in the Psalter.

Communication is exchange, involvement, and discourse with a real partner. In trying to grasp the processes of communication we, unavoidably, start from our own societal experiences: one friend talks to another in vivid interlocution; group interaction proceeds according to specific conventionalized rules. As to the divine, we are confronted with some dimensions that go beyond human experience; the divine transcends human limits of time and space to include larger and extremely large extensions up to the whole of the universe. Yet according to the ancient understanding, as visible in psalmic literature, there is no fundamental difference between inter-human and human–divine communication. The formulaic language used in lament-discourse, for example, is quite congruent in both areas.[36] Praise language in the psalms also resembles and has roots in complementary speech forms in the human realm; the musings of the self in relation to Yahweh are intimately intertwined with the human capacity for self-conscious internal dialogue.[37] Thus we must leave behind what

---

35. There are a large number of studies portraying laments and eulogy as basic attitudes and ceremonies in the Psalter; see, e.g., Westermann, *Praise and Lament*; Brueggemann, *Psalms and the Life of Faith*.

36. Cf. Gerstenberger, *Der bittende Mensch*. There I make the point that the rhetoric of supplication in the psalms is derived from the everyday discourse between the needy and the potential helper.

37. Cf. Brueggemann, *Israel's Praise*; and Miller, *They Cried to the Lord*, 178–232. Miller emphasizes the absolute divine quality of Yahweh's actions that solicit praise but explicitly rejects any degradation of human praise. Rather, "[t]he rule of the Lord . . . is confirmed in the praises of the people" as "praise is fundamentally a social or communal experience" (Miller, *They Cried to the Lord*, 225, 227). Cf. Brown, *Psalms*. There are literary works from the ancient world that already testify to human internal dialogues; see Baumgarten et al., eds., *Self, Soul, and Body in Religious Experience*.

philosophers call transcendence and immanence in our evaluation of the forms of communication with the divine in the Hebrew Bible: everything in the Psalter happens on the same plane of reality, not in a world divided between human and divine existences.

In our present parameters of thinking, exchange with the divine is a "fictitious" as well as a real affair. Indeed, all our thinking and imagining is fictitious in contrast to historical positivism of the nineteenth century: it occurs according to how we conceptualize the world we are dealing with. That is, we are dealing with the constructs of world rather than with autonomous facts. There is no way of objectively portraying the reality as it "really is in itself" (*das Ding an sich*).[38] We are leading all the way with conventionalized visions and interpretations of the world and of the divine. Thus, logically, all our interactions with the world and with the larger-than-human reality of the divine also occur within these established parameters (usually religious or confessional creeds). This means that the reality we are describing is a construed one, although as such it is real reality for us. We are, in any case, actively involved in the very formation of the world; we are by no means neutral and outside spectators of developments.

Modern worldviews and analytical tools fit in this general picture. There is a host of theories and methods employed to understand and practice "communication": May the insights gained from these be helpful in the analysis of ancient patterns of communicative exchange?[39]

Within the humanities we may distinguish between empirical research—anthropological, sociological, socio-psychological, ritual studies as well as behavioral investigations—and more virtual, theoretical reconstructions (nature of language, discourse, apperception, performance etc.).[40] Keeping in mind that all modern theories and techniques have been achieved on the basis of modern evidence (e.g., anthropological field work, analysis of actual literature) and contemporary philosophies, we realize that they may not be directly usable in relation to ancient literary and ceremonial sources. Still, we may legitimately and cautiously use modern instruments of analysis. Thus, speech act theories, reader response models, ritual studies as well as more virtual constructivist approaches may contribute a good deal of insight to understand better what is going on in human–divine

---

38. Cf. Kant, *Kritik der reinen Vernunft* (ET *Critique of Pure Reason*). Kant argues that the "real things-of-themselves" are inaccessible to empirical knowledge.

39. Numerous fields of study, ranging from the humanities to the natural sciences, contribute to communication research today; see von Bertalanffy, *General Systems Theory*.

40. Cf., e.g., Austin, *How to Do Things with Words*; Searle, *Speech Acts*; and Iser, *How to Do Theory*.

communication within the Psalter. Thus we may realize that the three models of exchange presented above represent typical patterns of human–divine relations in determined social and cultural contexts. The concomitant theological as well as anthropological concepts vary greatly according to the basic set-ups of encountering the world.

Looking at the Psalter in this fashion, the very idea of communication in the Bible and the ancient Near East gains new dimensions, strange as it may seem given that traditional patterns of analysis tend to overshadow and hide ancient conceptualizations. Modern plurality of views and approaches is thus able to liberate even archaic patterns of thinking. These liberated perspectives will undoubtedly also bounce back on the petrified models of communication that may remain in our imagination of divine–human relations.

# 6

# The Psalms and Ritual Praxis[1]

## The Question

AT LEAST SINCE THE beginning of form-critical research, the question of how far the current text of the Psalter reveals the roots of individual genres in practiced rites has been hotly debated. While Hermann Gunkel viewed the texts that were now available as "spiritual revisions" of old liturgical compositions,[2] Sigmund Mowinckel searched intensively for the cultic events to which he could assign the Psalms. He determined that the so-called "Enthronement of Yahweh" was the central point of connection for many genres of psalms. Only the so-called "wisdom or didactic psalms" could not be accommodated in this dramatic framework because of their apparently non-cultic nature.[3] A chronological succession of "cultic" and "non-cultic" psalm texts has been used by some experts; it has even been used as a fixed criterion for differentiation and speaking of late "psalms in the post-cultic sphere."[4]

## Explanation of Terms

The brief references make it clear that the ideas of "cult" and "rite" in Old Testament research are inconsistent and require clarification. In the Protestant

---

1. Translated by K. C. Hanson.
2. Gunkel and Begrich, *Einleitung*, 180–83, 260–65 (ET *Introduction*, 127–28, 195–98), for example, on the complaint song of the individual.
3. Mowinckel, *Psalmenstudien* II (ET *Psalm Studies*, vol. 1:175–494); Mowinckel, *The Psalms*, 1:42–78. Because of the assumed "corporate identity," the priority of social over individual consciousness, Mowinckel can say: "The royal psalms . . . are thus really congregational psalms" (*Psalms in Israel's Worship* 1:76).
4. Stolz, *Psalmen*.

sense, "cult" cannot simply be regarded as an act of sacrifice; "rite" is more than a soulless ceremony. It might be advisable to approach the usage of anthropology and ritual studies in Old Testament research, which deal "full-time" with the phenomena mentioned.[5] Here we find quite neutral descriptions of the facts in question. "Rites" are any repeatable, ceremonial act that takes place interactively in a group.[6] With their interpretations of ritualization in the animal kingdom, behavioral researchers add the moment of imprinting into genetic memory.[7] Up to this point, we cannot understand the term "rite" in the human sphere, but a look at the phylogenesis of ceremonial activities can increase our understanding of their depth, intrinsic dynamics, and effectiveness. On the other hand, we must not restrict the term "cult" to the performance of sacrifices. Anything that is part of worshipping a superhuman being or a superior power is cultic. The cult includes a group of people; recognized, effective sacred acts and words; often also special places, times, clothing, equipment, hierarchies, functionaries, officeholders, etc.; and the collective attunement to the superpersonal.

When it comes to the relationship between ritual practices and the texts that show us their existence or give us an inkling of their existence then it must be clear from the start: texts are in themselves neither rituals nor cult. At most, they can give more or less clear ideas of the processes to which they have organically belonged or belong. However, because the texts in question are by no means intended to be narrative or descriptive, and as a rule cannot even be, we—in contrast to empirical field researchers—are dependent in every case upon reconstructions for rites or cultic actions. The psalms to be considered are at best parts or reflexes of rituals and cultic practices. On the other hand, however, all biblical texts (this is my personal conviction) are the results of communicative actions. Without a human, interactive community, they are purely dead and meaningless. Psalms (prayers, songs,

---

5. Specialized ritual research has only recently organized itself as an offshoot of religious studies and anthropology; see Grimes, "Ritual Studies." However, groundbreaking studies were made much earlier; see van Gennep, *Rites of Passage*.

6. One can lament the expansion of the concept of ritual to include secular sequences of actions: it is of great use in view of the actual comparability of events and their meanings, see Lang, "Ritual/Ritus." Grimes, *Beginnings in Ritual Studies*, for example, distinguishes five stages of ritualization: Decorum = social regulation of face-to-face interaction (39); Ceremony = more intentionally fashioned behavior (41); Liturgy = reaching into realms beyond ourselves (43); "Liturgy is a full emptiness, a monotony without boredom, a reverent waiting without expectation ..." (44); Magic = "Ritual which not only has meaning but also 'works'" (45); Celebration = "highest form ... includes play, drama, comic" (47).

7. Eibl-Eibesfeldt, *Grundriss*, 19–34, 250–70: heredity (instincts), habituation, and learning behavior come together in animal ritual acts.

and meditations) require the soundboard of religious communities to be realized. A purely individual use in a private setting is difficult to imagine for biblical antiquity. It requires a distinctive reading and writing culture and a certain degree of individualism, as can be expected at the earliest in educated, economically privileged layers of Hellenistic society.[8]

The central question now is to what extent the Psalter in its current form shows traces of past and contemporaneous ritual practice. Complete protocols of religious acts are hardly to be hoped for, and are rarely found in the rest of Hebrew literature either. As examples of more or less preserved, descriptive or normative ritual texts,[9] we can reckon: Num 5:11–31, the so-called jealousy ordeal; Lev 8–9, the form of the high priest's ordination; Lev 16, the scapegoat ritual; possibly some more sacrificial and purity regulations in Lev 1–7; 11–15). Many other passages stop at mere descriptions or declarations of intent to perform a (festival) ritual, without revealing any details about the ritual structure.[10] The Psalter itself appears to have preserved only a few ritual instructions, descriptions, or ritual text compositions. Rudiments of instructions could be, for example, the superscriptions to Pss 92 and 102 or the invocations in Ps 47:2 (as well as other hymnic introductions) and 48:13. Descriptions of cultic acts are, for example, Pss 26:6; 35:13–14; 68:25–28; 73:13; 122, while remnants of ritual compositions are perhaps in Pss 91; 132; and 136.

Be that as it may, it would be too wasteful for us to trace every reference to rituals through the Psalter. Under the working hypothesis that social grouping and text production belong closely together, we want to concentrate on two specific religious forms of community and their possible cultic psalm texts, the familial and the parochial group. They represent the beginning and end of the Israelite cult history, clearly recognizable in

---

8. Hengel, *Judentum und Hellenismus*, 191–95, 202–4 (ET *Judaism and Hellenism*); Davies, *Scribes and Schools*, 17–19, 28–30. The development of the book and reading culture had two roots: the traditions of ancient Near Eastern archives and Greek libraries.

9. Descriptions of rites or injunctions to perform them are sometimes found in sung or recited passages of a ceremonial act, e.g., Pss 24:7–10; 26:6; 48:13; 68:25–26; 118:27; 122:1–2; 132:6–7; etc. The so-called ritual instructions, which may be added to the recitation text and are intended to control the ritual events, must be distinguished from these inner-textual references to what is happening. Babylonian incantations, for example, are composed of distinctly different recitation and instruction parts, see Gerstenberger, *Der bittende Mensch*; Maul, *Zukunftsbewältigung*.

10. In the narrative literature it then says succinctly: "Abraham built an altar to Yahweh" (Gen 12:7), or "Josiah commanded all the people to keep the Passover to Yahweh your God, as prescribed in this book of the covenant" (2 Kgs 23:21).

the Psalter.[11] The other social structures—tribe; monarchically organized people; village and town districts are also represented in the Psalter, but for reasons of tradition they play a lesser role. Family rituals go back a long way into the prehistory of the Psalter, because the small family who lives, works, and forms a community of faith is clearly the oldest and most stable social institution of all, with far-reaching consequences for theology and ritual practice in every period.[12] And because that is the case, family rites continue to have an effect even within "higher" organizational levels,[13] often under drastically changed environmental conditions.

## Cult in a Small Circle (House or Family Cult)

Researchers of form and genre have always pointed out the relatively large number of "complaints and thanksgiving songs of the individual" in the Psalter. Up to sixty individual texts belong to this genre. Is the assumption to substantiate in the texts[14] that these are prayers originally derived from the family milieu, which may also later serve the cultic and social rehabilitation of needy supplicants (the sick, socially marginalized, those frightened by evil omens)? What criteria can we find for the actual ritual use of these individual prayers? It is helpful to differentiate between the original use of the individual texts and the use that has been adapted to changing social circumstances.

The structure of the individual psalms and their recognizable formal elements provide a first, important argument for the fact that they are real "complaints or supplications" from the routine practice of ancient priests or healers. As form critics have repeatedly emphasized, the most important building blocks are "invocation" (often with a request to be heard), "expressions of confidence," "complaints," "supplications," and "vows."[15] They occur relatively regularly and in a well-suited liturgical order, so they do not form

---

11. Cf. Gerstenberger, *Theologien*, 21–25 (ET *Theologies*, 19–24).

12. Cf. Gerstenberger, *Theologien*, 26–77 (ET *Theologies*, 25–91).

13. Cf. Ribeiro, *O Processo Civilisatório* (ET *The Civilzation Process*).

14. As an initial suspicion and working hypothesis, the thought is appealing because similar prayers of complaint and supplication were and are needed—verifiable in ancient cultures and today's tribal societies in the context of healing and rehabilitation of the suffering and endangered people (see below). Lastly, van der Toorn worked up extensive material on the religion of the small group (*Family Religion*).

15. For more on structural issues, see Gunkel and Begrich, *Einleitung*, 212–50 (ET *Introduction*, 152–84); Mowinckel, *The Psalms*, 2:1–25; Gerstenberger, *Der bittende Mensch*, 118–34; Gerstenberger, *Psalms, Part 1*, 11–14. The individual elements use many formulas, but still show a certain range of expressive possibilities.

a rigid, one-line form, as is sometimes expected. That would not even be possible in the face of the multitude of reported emergency situations. If necessary—presumably depending on the result of a previous diagnosis[16]— an express confession of guilt or plea of innocence must be inserted. The religious service measures required in cases of illness and rehabilitation can therefore only be flexible and also come from different individual sources in Israel (cf. Korah and Asaph traditions). The basic pattern of personal complaint, supplication, and thanksgiving is clearly recognizable, at least for the Near Eastern region in which ancient Israel existed. Then the patient or the person suffering from misfortune recites a prayer that corresponds to his or her plight and overcomes it, probably under the guidance of a ritual specialist. It follows the everyday pleading scheme:[17] a needy person tries to attract the attention of the higher-ranking patron, to induce him to provide help by presenting his need and pointing out the relationship of solidarity between the supplicant and the one supplicated. Depending on the diagnosed cause of suffering, the standard components of the prayer are designed, emphasized, and arranged differently. The large arc from the invocation to the request and the vow of thanks can, however, usually be recognized; it corresponds with a high degree of probability to the ritual course of a liturgical occasional act. The framework of action, including the musical components (cf. the naming of musical instruments in the corpus of psalms: cf. Pss 7:18; 43:4; 57:8–9; 71:22), can be deduced from allusions.[18]

Second, references to the performance of prayer and framing ritual can be found here and there in the Hebrew Bible and the Psalms themselves. For example, Hezekiah is lying on his sick bed when he says his personal prayer of thanks (Isa 38), and the prophet Isaiah is nearby as a healing expert (vv. 21–22). Elisha performs contact rites over the dead son of the Shunamite woman, which include a prayer (2 Kgs 4:32–35). David is heartbroken over the serious illness of the son of his favorite wife Bathsheba. He subjects himself to harsh penitential rites (2 Sam 12:15–23), similar to those in Ps 35:13–14:

---

16. For the proper treatment of patients, it was also necessary at that time to determine the cause and extent, e.g., of an illness, before the ritual treatment. In some narratives, therefore, the main question addressed to the prophet (diagnostician) is: Does the sick person have a chance of surviving? (cf. 1 Kgs 14:3; 2 Kgs 1:2). And the messenger of Job 33:23–24, who visits the home of the poor, obviously also has diagnostic and advisory functions.

17. Cf. Gerstenberger, *Der bittende Mensch*, 17–63.

18. The Babylonian incantation texts, on the other hand, allow a direct view of the ritual events because of the ritual instructions that have also been handed down; cf. the broad presentation in Maul, *Zukunftsbemligung*, 11–13, 39–106.

> But as for me, when they were sick,
>> I wore sackcloth;
>> I afflicted myself with fasting.
> I prayed with head bowed on my bosom,
>> as though I grieved for a friend or a brother,
>> so I walked around sadly;
> I went about as one who laments for a mother,
>> bowed down and in mourning. (NRSV)

Hannah's prayers in Shiloh (1 Sam 1:10–13; 2:1–10), Jonah's thanks from the fish's belly (Jonah 2), David's song of victory (2 Sam 22), Jeremiah's prayers (Jer 10:17–25; 12:1–6; 15:10–21; 17:12–18; 18:19–23; 20:7–18), etc. hardly contribute anything to the elucidation of the liturgical processes, but at least situate the marked religious speech in profane surroundings.

The sporadic references to the place and circumstances of personal prayer in the Psalter are somewhat more informative. For example, Ps 6:7 ("I flood my bed with tears") or 63:7 ("I think of you in bed at night") indicate a domestic situation. The psalmist shifts prayer to the sanctuary, e.g., in Pss 5:4; 63:3; 84:9, 11; and from a great distance from the homeland it sounds in Ps 42:7; 61:3.[19] Prayer gestures like the "raising of the hand" (Pss 63:5; 77:3; 88:10; 134:2; 142:2) or "prostration" (5:8; 138:2; cf. Pss 95:6; 132:7) are attested quite frequently. Rites such as "handwashing" (Pss 26:6; 73:13), "offering up the sacrifice" (not metaphorical! mostly with personal thanksgiving offerings and ordeal requests: Pss 4:6; 5:4; 22:26–27; 116:17; cf. Ps 51:19, 21), "offering of incense" (Ps 141:2: "My prayer arises like a smoke offering before you"); "fasting" (Pss 35:11; 69:11; 109:24); "penitential rites" (Ps 35:13; cf. Neh 9:6), etc. are incidental and therefore authentic references to ritual acts. Finally, we would like to point out the participants in routine acts that emerge from the psalm texts: the direct address of unfaithful relatives in Pss 4; 11; and 62 is hardly a rhetorical accessory. Rather, it suggests the actual presence of opposing factions at ritual gatherings in which conflicts evidently took place.

None of these phenomena can be explained as characteristics of a "cult-free" poetry or something similar that may be intended for a readership. The language of the individual's complaint and supplication is generally not narrative, epic, or lyrical. It is not intended for solemn monological recitation, and neither is it intended for private reading. Rather, it shows all the characteristics of liturgical use, with changing voices, corresponding and contrasting formal elements, and a dramatic structure.

---

19. Cf. Gerstenberger, "Topographie des Betens," 3–6.

Expressions of cultic action in the texts cannot be considered contrived, spiritualized, metaphorical, or the like.

But the question remains why there are no pronounced ritual instructions in the Psalter, as is the case, for example, in the Babylonian collections of incantations. The answer can only be: such notes were superfluous in the late context of the exilic/post-exilic community because the old rituals were revised through the understanding of prayers and songs in the cultic life of the community. They have apparently been replaced by very sparing comments on the liturgical handling of the psalms in community worship, the so-called "superscriptions" of the individual psalms. We can only understand them in part, but they represent a new type of ritual instruction in thoroughly community-related, stereotypical elements[20] and as such prove the further use of the individual texts in certain religious services, both community and incidental, compare, for example, Ps 102:1: "A prayer of one afflicted, when faint and pleading before Yahweh" (cf. Ps 142:3; 1 Sam 1:15). The section Ps 102:13–23 reveals communal interests. Obviously, only the central prayer—surrounded by a few gestures, activities, and rites—has remained from the formerly extensive petition ceremony in the house of one who is sick or pursued by misfortune. The congregations evidently knew how to perform or recite a *šir, mizmor, mašal, šiggayon, maskil*, a *tepillah*, etc. And if *lamnaṣṣeaḥ*, which often appears in psalm superscriptions (but after Ps 109:1 only in a single complaint: Ps 140:1), means something like "choirmaster," "prayer leader," or the like, then that is the one responsible for the communal liturgies. In the case of an abstract formation, "for liturgical performance," this specialist would be addressed indirectly. Clear instructions for a community can be found in Ps 30:1 ("A song at the dedication of the temple") or Pss 120–134 ("Song of Ascents").

I can only point out in passing the extra-biblical parallels between personal prayers and thanksgivings and their use in the small cult of primary groups. Because, for example, in the large Babylonian–Assyrian collections of incantations ŠU.ÍL.LÁ ("raising the hand") and NAM.BÚR.BI ("its solution") ritual instructions are copiously handed down together

---

20. The primary elements of the superscriptions are: naming of authors or liturgical authorities; musical notations (instruments; text categories for the performance; melody specifications [?] such as "after 'Doe of the Dawn Treader'" [? Ps 22:1] or "according to 'Dove on Distant Terebinths'" [? Ps 56:1]); historical additions from David's biography (Pss 51:2; 54:1; 56:1; 57:1; 59:1; 60:2; etc.): they are intended to present the great king as an exemplary person of prayer. Despite all the lexical uncertainty, the frequent expression *lamnaṣṣeaḥ* is most likely to be understood as an assignment to the liturgical leader of an assembly, contrary to Mowinckel, *Psalm Studies*, 2:603–8 (orig. *Psalmenstudien* IV:17–22); see also Mowinckel, *The Psalms*, 2:212–13, who interprets the infinitive as an impersonal indication of purpose: "On Mercies" (Yahweh's).

with the recitation texts,[21] we have impressive visual aids at hand. The unity of word and action becomes clear: a ritual specialist leads the "petition ceremony." He is responsible for all its parts, from purification of the location, through the offerings of incense and sacrifices, the magical formulas and prayers, to the disposal of contaminated components or materials of the ritual process. At the instruction of the liturgist, the patient has to address praise, complaint, request, confession to the deity. The ritual instructions to the specialist (in Akkadian mostly called *āšipu*) expressly say: "You should allow him to speak." This is followed by the prayer text, which may have been recited word-for-word. The Babylonian complaint and penance prayers that occur in such a ritual framework show a strong structural, terminological, stylistic, and theological relationship with the Old Testament psalms of the individual.[22]

In a broader sense, healing rites of all periods are to be used for comparison, because they too often offer analogous structures and formulations.[23] The anthropologically interesting rule that similar situations can also produce comparable rites and texts seems to be confirmed especially in the area of treatment of the sick. In industrialized societies (i.e. societies shaped by modern science and technology), the handling of patients has been subjected to "more enlightened" rules of the game, which no longer oblige the patient to participate actively in rituals. But the general "supplication scheme" for those in need who seek help from others still follows the age-old pattern of invocation, praise, complaint, confession, plea, vow of thanks, etc.[24]

## Community Cult

A complete description of the ritual practices recognizable in the Psalter would have to investigate, after the treatment of "individual" psalms, the

---

21. Above all, see Maul, *Zukunftsbewältigung*; then also Ebeling, *Die akkadische Gebetsserie "Handerhebung"*; Gerstenberger, *Der bittende Mensch*, 64–112; Mayer, *Untersuchungen*.

22. The agreement as to genre was noticed very early on; see, for example, Widengren, *Psalms of Lamentation*. But no conclusions have ever been drawn regarding the sociological *Sitz im Leben*.

23. Compare, e.g., the field research on the Navajo nation: Reichard, *Prayer*; Reichard, *Navajo Religion*; Wyman, *Beautyway*. Anthropological reports and biographies from many of today's tribal societies contain abundant illustrative material examining ceremonies, festivals, and rites of all kinds; see, e.g., Talayesva and Simmons, *Sun-Chief*; Evans-Pritchard, *Nuer Religion*; Turner, *The Ritual Process*.

24. Cf. Gerstenberger, *Der bittende Mensch*, 17–20.

texts that go back to secondary social formations, for example to the village and small town community, the army camp of the tribal associations, the national cult in the royal capital. The first-named group gathered—according to evidence from 1 Sam 9:12; 20:6, 29—mainly in the rhythm of the agricultural year at the local sanctuary. Their interest was to ensure the fertility of the fields, as shown in Ps 65:10–14. The tribes were primarily defensive alliances. From them old songs of victory will come like Ps 68 and Judg 5. From the environment of the royal temple, whose priesthood was entrusted with the care of the kingdom and dynasty, the archetypes of the royal songs and the Yahweh Enthronement psalms and the psalms of Zion presumably derive. The texts that have come to us from these three socially and historically distinguishable communities have, however, since been handed down in the Psalter, all taken over into the use of the exilic/post-exilic community and adapted to the needs of the new residence. We have it before us in a new guise and presumably as an expression of a community liturgy and theology.

Instead of examining those three psalm sources, let us turn directly to the most important community that brought the collection of the Psalter to a close, the early Jewish local community in Persian times. It absorbed a lot of traditional material, but also produced its own poems and compositions in abundance.[25] This last level of transmission of the Psalms falls at the time when the Yahweh community was constituted around the Torah scroll and its festivals and norms, that is mainly the Persian period between 539 and 333 BCE. In spite of some previous approaches—so it appears—the scriptures are only now fully integrated into the life of the congregation, the worship service and the presumed routine actions. Scripture becomes part of the liturgies, scripture determines the course of ritual actions.

The most striking formal characteristic of the community use of the Psalms is a collective "we" in a number of different texts. A total of fifty-three individual psalms belonging to various genres show this stylistic phenomenon, which is rare in the ancient Near Eastern liturgical material. How can the phenomenon be explained? As Scharbert already established in 1986, the type and position of the "we" passages make it unlikely that a writer or poet has joined forces with an imaginary readership in a virtual community.[26] Much more plausible is the explanation that in each case, real

---

25. The social structure of the exilic/post-exilic religious groups in the province of Judah and in the diaspora has been relatively little researched; however, it is of the highest importance; see Kippenberg, *Religion und Klassenbildung*; various works by Weinberg; Zevit, *Religions of Ancient Israel*. For details on how far the collective songs reflect the post-exilic community, see Gerstenberger, *Psalms, Part 2*, passim.

26. Scharbert, "Das 'Wir' in den Psalmen."

responsories from an assembled worship congregation are available here, in a form designed for practical use. Thus a refrain in Ps 8:2, 10 frames a prayer hymn, which has as its content the astonishing power of humans in the cosmos. The congregation intones:

> O Yahweh, our sovereign,
>> how majestic is your name in all the earth! (NRSV)

Similarly, communal praise closes the prayer for the king:

> Be exalted, O Yahweh, in your strength!
>> We will sing and praise your power.
>> (Ps 21:13, NRSV; see Ps 33:20–22)

In a whole series of texts, passages in the first person singular are interspersed with the first person plural (cf. Pss 44; 60; 66; 74; 75; 85; 103; 106; 108; 118; 122; 123; 144, etc.). The "we" is not entirely clear and may reflect different groupings within a worship congregation. But in the majority of cases the whole congregation seems to be the subject. This is true even if a passage has been recited by a leading liturgist. The change between singular and plural forms most likely signals liturgical alteration. The psalms, which are written exclusively in the "we" style (cf. Pss 46; 47; 48; 79; 80; 90; 95; 100; 115; 124; 136; 147, and others) lead completely into the realm of community worship. These psalms belong to different genres and thus prove that different acts of worship were performed. Some of them are a strong reminder of the congregational songs we are familiar with today:

> Make a joyful noise to Yahweh
>> all the earth!
> Worship Yahweh with gladness.
>> Come into his presence with singing.
> Know that Yahweh is God.
>> It is he who made us, and we are his;
>> we are his people and the sheep of his pasture.
> Enter his gates with thanksgiving!
>> and his courtyards with praise.
>> Give thanks to him, bless his name.
> For Yahweh is good,
>> his love endures forever,
>> and his faithfulness to all generations. (Ps 100:1–5, NRSV)

The themes of the communal psalms are characteristic of the Yahwistic community of the sixth, fifth, and fourth centuries BCE.[27] They revolve around the exclusive veneration of Yahweh in the midst of a religious pluralism lived all around. The exilic/post-exilic cultic community finally had to define itself in the Babylonian and Persian multinational empires. The Torah became the only valid guideline for this life in connection with Yahweh. Interestingly, however, in important psalms of the time, this Torah is related to the individual member of the congregation (Pss 1; 19; 119), although it is entrusted to the people as a whole (cf. Pss 50; 81; 95). The individual is not isolated, however; rather, we see how dominantly the personal sense of responsibility of the individual and how firmly the "I" of the prayer was embedded in the "we" consciousness of the religious community in this phase of Old Testament cultic history.

The Zion psalms also catch the eye (cf. Pss 46; 48; but also 47; 79; 147). The sacred mountain, on which Yahweh himself took up residence, has increasingly become the spiritual center of the scattered Yahweh community from the time of exile. In the songs that have Zion as their main content and extol Yahweh's universal power (cf. Pss 95; 100), the "we" feeling is expressed particularly vividly.

So there are indications for the collective, community origin and use of various psalms. The recognizable liturgical features (responses, congregational singing, focus on Torah-reading, parades, processions, etc.) are to be classified as authentic according to the further understanding of rites recommended at the beginning, even if animal sacrifices would not have been part of the repertoire of the congregational events. With the "we" psalms it is particularly easy to understand that the writing and transmission took place in the service of the community. Presumably, liturgists (Levites?) commissioned by the community took on the care and further training of the liturgical materials. The other explanatory model, that the Psalms were reading material for the pious in the post-exilic congregation following the example of Ps 1, seems less convincing. Above all, one would have to look for an explanation for the "we" phenomenon.

---

27. This judgment presupposes that the formation of the faith in Yahweh did not occur until the so-called late period of the Old Testament; cf. Gerstenberger, *Yahweh the Patriarch* (orig. *Jahweh: Ein patriarchal Gott?*); Gerstenberger, *Theologies*, 207–72 (*Theologien*, 166–216).

## Ritual and "Book"

Ritual research, oriented towards anthropological and religious studies, has examined human behavior patterns in a vast number of individual studies in the last few decades. Sociology and ethology contribute their observations of ceremonial processes in living communities. Theater studies, communication studies, and literary criticism assess the action elements of interpersonal exchange. So it is no wonder that the formation of theories with regard to rituals, ceremonies, and communication would be extremely lively.[28] It is about the weighing of action and word in ritual, about the symbolic power of the whole, the correspondence with the world and order of life, the emergence of rites and ceremonies (prehistoric, going back into the development of life, psychologically, biologically, or socially), about their stabilizing or revolutionizing influence, etc. The progressive, pragmatic investigation of ritual processes in different social and religious contexts and the interpretations that arise from them have produced at least two important results: ritual behavior cannot be dismissed as a childhood disease or an instrument of repression. In ritual events, word and action form an indissoluble unit that encompasses all layers of human existence.[29]

The big question now is whether and how Old Testament research on the Psalms can use the results and perspectives of modern ritual science. Critical self-control is urgently necessary, even after the above considerations and precisely because of them. Because the difficulties are considerable: historical distance, type and assessment of the ancient sources, theoretical (hermeneutic, religious) location possibly create an unbridgeable distance between modern interpretation and ancient practice. Regarding the fundamental concerns, it can be said that the historical gap between antiquity and modernity certainly affects large areas of scientific and technical knowledge, but hardly ritual human behavior. According to everything we know about the processes that are shaped in social events, the tendency towards ceremonial presentations has persisted for thousands of years. Anyone who thinks that humanity today behaves more scientifically or rationally than their Stone Age ancestors will quickly be taught better in reality. From individual courtship and display behavior to the irrationality of today's religious conflicts, the basic patterns of ceremonial behavior seem to have remained consistent over time. One likes to speak of "anthropological constants" in this context, and that is probably the point. The dream of the "education of the human race" and an unstoppable moral

---

28. Cf. Grimes, *Beginnings in Ritual Studies*; Bell, *Ritual Theory, Ritual Practice*; Gill, "No Place to Stand"; cf. Gill, *Native American Religious Action*.

29. Cf. Zuesse, "Ritual."

ascent should be over. This is not meant as bowing to the achievements of the Enlightenment, but a warning against naive trust and an encouragement to soberly judge human nature.

For the basic structures of social existence this means: We can rely with some certainty on the fact that human life at all times and across cultures has been and is, to a high degree, ritualized. Established and socially accepted courses of action or communicative patterns of action enable social interaction in the first place. We cannot want to reinvent the basic reactions of togetherness every day. This is particularly true for living together with divine powers, i.e. for religious rituals. We can assume that the biblical communities in their various organizational forms developed or adapted patterns of behavior, i.e. "liturgies," appropriate to the basic needs of human–divine coexistence. The biblical texts testify to this fact, if not in the desired detail, then at least partially and indirectly. To reiterate the areas envisaged above: In ancient Israel (but also in the New Testament world) there must have been ceremonies of supplication and healing with which the evil that had happened to someone or was threatened could be overcome. Without the help of God and without sufficient knowledge of the cosmic and regional distribution of forces as well as the ritual possibilities and practices, treatment was impossible. Even the individual care required a lot of knowledge, skill, and experience.

To the same extent, ritualized communication processes are to be assumed for communal life, especially again in the religious area. If we can assume that the actual, confessionally determined Yahweh community was only formed during and after the exile,[30] then the state structures were occupied by the imperial powers at that time. Israel had to organize itself on the local as well as on the supraregional level on its own, i.e. preferably by religious strength. The Torah given by Yahweh became the focal point of tradition. The community found its identity in the written will of God. Communication and execution of God's will formed the orientation points for community life, consequently also for rites and festivals. Nehemiah 8; Deut 29–31; Josh 24; Pss 50; 95; 1 Chr 16, and other texts suggest that community meetings took place in which Torah-proclamation, responses from the congregation, and possibly chants formed the focus. The ritual structures therefore developed under the influence of proclamation of

---

30. The assumption that the religious community of Yahweh only came into being after the collapse of the Jewish state with its Yahwistic state religion is finding more and more supporters; see, for example, Lang, *Der einzige Gott*; Gerstenberger, *Theologies*, 207–72 (orig. *Theologien*, 172–201); also Albertz, *Israel in Exile*, 435 (orig., *Exilzeit*, 324): "without the exile experience there would never have been the discovery of monotheism in the strict sense in Israel."

the word, not animal sacrifice. The cult functionaries were interpreters of tradition, not administrators of a holy order without history. This groundbreaking innovation in ritual events had far-reaching consequences for Jewish and Christian worship.

The second objection concerns the assessment of the ancient sources, which do not allow any direct insight into what was happening, but in any case only present a frozen state of the ritual event in a peculiar sense, and which is only conveyed in an always fragmentary, secondary way. We assume that the Hebrew scriptures were mainly collected after the fall of the state of Judah by the Yahweh congregations that were being formed, i.e. by their scribes and leaders. The collection and transcription of older traditions went hand in hand with the creation of new texts. To what end did this literary fixation come about? What were the communication processes that required or stimulated the preservation? From our current perspective, books are intended for individual reading. We live in a book-reading culture, which, for a variety of reasons, we should not simply assume for the ancient world—at least not until the beginning of the Hellenistic period.[31] It seems to me far more likely that the Hebrew scriptures were compiled for collective, ritual use, not for private reading.[32]

The previously mentioned passages Neh 8; 10:1–2; Deut 29; Exod 24:7; 2 Chr 34:29–33 refer to the congregational use of written texts, mainly through reading. Those gathered hear the divine message and respond affirmatively. The writing of the prophet's word in Jer 36 also presupposes congregational use.[33] The first and second versions of the Jeremiah message are clearly intended for public reading. In the Chronicler's account, the "Book of Yahweh's Torah" apparently also serves as an instruction all over the country (2 Chr 17:9). Whenever there is talk of God's will, which has been handed down in writing, the traditionists primarily indicate the communal, collective use of the text. In our context, this means: The Hebrew text collections were created as liturgical commodities and have been used in the new rituals of religious and communicative action that have been taking place since the exile of the Judahite population. The scriptures lived in the context of religious meetings, festivals, collective instruction, and probably also a

---

31. Cf. Davies, *Scribes and Schools*; Posner, *Archives in the Ancient World*; Niditch, *Oral World and Written Word*.

32. Biblical texts that undoubtedly testify to individual reading of Scripture are rare; cf. Acts 8:28: The Ethiopian eunuch uses the prophet Isaiah as reading material on his journey home. Psalm 1:2 speaks of the happy one who immerses himself in the Torah and murmurs it to himself. However, the written original and the isolation from other readers are not expressly mentioned.

33. Cf. the analogous situation of 2 Kgs 22:8–23: Josiah hears the words of the book.

congregational routine practice.[34] The Old Testament is therefore primarily—at least as far as the meaning of *torah* extends—a collection of reading texts for congregational gatherings. How and where writings outside the Torah were used must be examined on a case-by-case basis.

With regard to the Psalter, this is urgently needed and at the same time highly controversial. Against the background of the development of the Torah based on the ritual practice of the early Jewish community, we ask: For what purpose and in what life situations were the Psalms compiled and written? The above-mentioned aspects—structure, style, superscription, etc. of the individual psalms, plus extra-biblical analogies—are good references to the liturgical-ritual origin and use of the texts. Can this assessment also be retained for the final state, the biblical Psalter as a written document? Has written fixation of the Psalms led to a relocation of them into the private sphere or the scribal academy?[35] How do the individual texts, which are clearly separated from one another, even in the final canonical state, relate to clearly editorial notes (cf. 41:14; 72:18–20; 89:53; 106:48) and to the total Psalter? Does the Hebrew, possibly the Greek, book title reveal anything about the purpose of the collection? To go straight to this last point: The text collection is usually called *tehillim* in Hebrew, *psalmoi* in Greek, or *sefer tehillim* or *biblos psalmon*. The consequent use of the plural in view of the "book-like" combined individual texts immediately shows the weight of these small units, which is also expressed by the many separating superscriptions for the psalms. A collective purpose of the book suggests itself.

Yet questions upon questions remain that are still in great flux. This much can be said for the time being: Direct evidence of a non-ritual use of the Psalter, i.e. for purely private reading, cannot be produced. Its existence as a book is already secured by the genuine colophon in Ps 72:20: "The prayers of David the Son of Jesse are ended." But even in the Hellenistic period, a "book" was not initially used for private edification, even if the individual reading of scriptures began in this period, but rather for communal use. In the ancient Near East, especially religious text collections had orienting functions for the expert many centuries before Israel; compare

---

34. Cf. Gerstenberger, "Psalm 12."

35. The thesis of the transition of the Psalms into private prayer life and thus the non-ritual use is astute and imaginative in Germany, especially by Notker Füglister, Erich Zenger, Frank-Lothar Hossfeld, Norbert Lohfink, Rolf Rendtorff, and Matthias Millard; and represented in the US, with different accents, by Gerald H. Wilson, Gerald T. Shepard; J. Clinton McCann; et al. Because the debate is far from over, two statements may be considered representative: Gerstenberger, "Der Psalter," 3–13; Zenger, "Provocation."

the so-called incantation series.³⁶ Collections, writings, or "books" were used directly for the preparation and implementation of ritual acts in the broadest sense, viz. communitarian ceremonies of groups, led by experts, to whom the written texts were also available as a handout. The Old Persian Avesta seems to have had similar functions,³⁷ as well as parts of the Qumran literature,³⁸ and important Mandaean written corpora.³⁹ Hermetic writings, on the other hand, are more likely to be found in schools because of their literary form (e.g., dialogues).⁴⁰ To sum up: In the ancient world, hymns and prayers were written down mainly by experts in the service of community events. They were recorded out of ritual needs and have therefore retained the ritual functions stemming from oral tradition, even if the routine practice in particular may have adapted to the new circumstances. Presumably the rites that inspired the creation and use of the texts on a pre-literary level were changed by the reading technique. It may also be that, for example, hymn texts were used to teach and admonish the congregation (cf. Deut 31:30; 32:44–47; Ps 78; etc.). Even so, they remain part of lived ceremonies, which we cannot deny the designation "rituals."

The preliminary conclusion: The Psalter not only contains open and cryptic messages of all sorts of traditional ritual acts in Israel, it is itself a collection of thoroughly liturgical documents. We can ascertain the time-related and society-related ritual structures by reconstructing communicative courses of action from the texts. This will only succeed if we recognize questions, criteria, and patterns for ritual action from descriptive analogue texts from the ancient world and observable ritual practices of our time and use them as auxiliary constructions in the recovery of Old Testament rituals.

---

36. The best publicized and commented upon example is the *nam-bur-bi* series; cf. Maul, *Zukunftsbewältigung*; also Zimmern, *Beiträge zur Kenntnis der babylonischen Religion*.

37. Cf. Lanczkowski, "Iranische Religionen"; Boyce, *History of Zoroastrianism*.

38. Stegemann, *Essener*, 116–23, assigns some scriptures to liturgical use, but above all he emphasizes the collective study of the Bible and community regulations. Private use of the scrolls was permitted only for senior priests.

39. Especially the compilations called *genizah* (treasure) and *qolasta* (praise) contain a great deal of liturgical material.

40. Cf. Tröger, "Hermetica."

# 7

# Non-Temple Psalms

*Their Cultic*
*Setting Revisited*

BASIC CLASSIFICATIONS AND DEFINITIONS in Psalms research have been in constant flux: "Genre," "form," "cultus," "life situation," to name a few, have received quite different interpretations over time and across cultural regions. Without presupposing fixed traditional theories, we can profitably start by assuming some basic affinity between psalms and ancient Israel's cult and agreeing that there are four main dimensions of "cult": place, time, act, and person.[1] Old Testament research in the past few decades has heavily emphasized central and uniform Israelite institutions, ignoring social and religious plurality.[2] Only slowly have new avenues in Old Testament cult studies fostered a broader view of multilayered religious developments in Israel,[3] which has also opened up new perspectives on the genesis and use of Psalm poetry.

Consequently, we should add a fifth parameter to the concept of "cult": social setting (*Sitz im Leben*). After all, different groups of people bring forth religious rituals, including supplications and hymns, meditations and teachings. Neither words nor rituals generate themselves, nor are they the exclusive property of individuals. Rather, they are the creation of people in communication and interaction, given a determined social structure, even if a gifted person should shape and transmit established discourses. And within any particular community, most certainly

---

1. See Haran, *Temple and Temple Service*. For a critical overview, see Diebner, "Gottesdienst II: Altes Testament."

2. Kraus, *Gottesdienst in Israel* (ET *Worship in Israel*); Rowley, *Worship in Ancient Israel*; Haran, *Temple and Temple Service*.

3. Van der Toorn, *Family Religion*; Gerstenberger, *Theologien* (ET *Theologies*).

in regard to its religious ceremonialism, certain idiosyncratic patterns of speech and ritual inevitably develop.[4]

The Second Temple was, indeed, a focal point of ritual (liturgical) development in ancient Israel. Many psalms focusing on Zion, Jerusalem, the Ark, and the Davidic dynasty are clearly aligned to worship in this unique temple. The Deuteronomic centralization law (Deut 12) looms behind the spiritual significance of the holy site, where Yahweh or Yahweh's "name" has been imagined to "dwell" among the people of Judah. Without a political "corset" (a socio-religious novelty!), the confessing faith-community rebuilt, by permission of the Persian overlords, the sanctuary, which had served primarily dynastic purposes in monarchic times. Congregational needs and interests handled by leaders such as Torah-experts, Levites, priests, and prophets helped organize worship, feasts, and pilgrimages, Sabbaths, customs, and—as far as possible—civil life. First Kings 8:23–53 refers to worship (prayer-) programs for Jews scattered through the known world. The "house of prayer," Yahweh's temple, was supposed to be open "for all the people" (Isa 56:7), which certainly implies not only sacrificing but also hymn-singing and supplication.

Yet making temple liturgies the exclusive ground for the cultivation of psalms is, admittedly, one-sided. There have been other settings for diverse genres of psalms outside temple precincts, because the religious life of emerging Judaism was by no means limited to temple worship. One need only point to the emergence of synagogal meetings, precisely because the temple was so distant to many believers; they were also much more opportune for Torah-based communities. On another point: There always had been in ancient Israel, just like in other religious bodies, rites of passage and healing, which were naturally independent of larger-scale public worship at a regional or state sanctuary. Furthermore, given different "life-settings" for various communications with the divine world, we have to allow for a certain interchange of motifs and texts among the distinct ceremonies and places of worship. Only logical rigidity, untouched by real-life procedures, would strictly, and therefore artificially, limit particular genres to only one and the same type of worship agenda. Each category of psalms originating from non-temple situations may have had phases or occasions that were also included in temple worship, the contours of which we do not really perceive very clearly. Still, we may be certain that some genres of psalms at some stages of their tradition were not part of temple rituals. Such is the focus of this essay.

---

4. Gunkel and Begrich, *Einleitung*, 1–7 (ET *Introduction*, 1–4).

## Individual Complaints and Thanksgivings

The long history of biblical psalm traditions can be illuminated by comparison with ancient Mesopotamian genres of sacred songs. Most notably, there have been prayers of supplication and thanksgiving, originally tuned to the suffering and eventually to the saved individual and his or her small group (family, neighborhood). They were part of healing and rehabilitation rituals as known from many cultures and historical epochs.[5] The Psalter has preserved a large group (thirty to forty specimens) of such "individual complaints" slightly varying in composition, style, emotional involvement, and thematic outlook.[6] A basic thread and a specific situation, however, are easy to recognize in this poetic genre: Some anonymous patient in danger of perishing is pleading with God to be saved from illness, false accusations, and bad luck.[7] The sufferer may hint at his domestic environment (e.g., "bed" in 6:7[6]; 41:4[3] and "visitors at home" in 41:7[6]), or express his longing for the holy city (e.g., 5:8[7]; 42:5[4], 7[6]). Abhorrent physical conditions may have made him or her incapable of visiting a shrine and, at the same time, because of cultic uncleanness, prohibited him or her from attending (22:7–9[6–8]; 38; 88).

Although there may have been occasional supplications in personal affairs at local, regional, and even central sanctuaries (e.g., Hannah at Shiloh in 1 Sam 2:1–10), these probably were exceptional cases or retrospective narrative constructions. At least terminally sick people would not be able to travel to a distant shrine. And evidence for house calls made by shamanistic healers abounds from antiquity to the present. The Old Testament reports of Elijah's successful ritual over the deceased boy of the poor widow (1 Kgs 17:24), and Elisha does the same to the son of the Shunammite woman (2 Kgs 4:18–37). The Aramean general Naaman is, of course, able to move himself to the prophet's house (2 Kgs 5), but he expects healing right there, not at a local sanctuary. Other instances of "house-calls" by the healer (i.e., man of God, incantation specialist, shaman) include the prophet Isaiah (Isa 38:1, 2, 21) and the messenger of Yahweh in Job 33:23–28. If there is a need, however, to involve a temple priest for any reason (e.g., diagnosis, purification, exorcism, etc.), the burdened person has to be taken to a shrine (e.g., Num 5:11–31; Lev 13:2–8).

---

5. Cunningham, *Deliver Me from Evil*; Gerstenberger, *Der bittende Mensch*.

6. Lists of individual complaints and thanksgiving vary; Gerstenberger, *Psalms, Part 1*, 11–16.

7. See Gunkel and Begrich, *Einleitung*, 220–21 (ET *Introduction*, 157–62); Gerstenberger, *Psalms, Part 1*, 88; Gerstenberger, *Psalms, Part 2*; Miller, *They Cried to the Lord*, 55–134.

More explicit testimony to the role of the healer, to the forms of discourse, and to the efficacious words used on such occasions is found in numerous Mesopotamian "incantation" texts. They contain, for example, supplications very similar to the Old Testament "individual complaints." Sometimes those are explicitly marked as "to be recited by the patient."[8] This is to say, the formulaic compositions with invocation, hymnic trust, complaint, supplication, and vow were in the possession of the healer who "makes his client recite them," probably line by line. But not only does this structural parallelism with Hebrew complaint psalms call for attention—Babylonian incantations also offer precise descriptions as to how to stage the supplication ceremony.[9] Ritual ordinances begin with the diagnosis of the patient and his surroundings by the expert (Akkadian *āšipu*, Sumerian *mašmaššu*). Nils Heeßel has edited and discussed the extensive cuneiform diagnostic texts.[10] The Mesopotamian specialist had to observe painstakingly every ominous phenomenon while going to and visiting with his patient; every person was considered an integral part of his or her environment. The collections of incantations proper, which orient the ceremony of supplication, describe the preparation of the place (on or near the living quarter, next to the river, etc.), offerings of incense, foodstuffs, purification rites, and, as mentioned above, the recitation of a personal prayer, which was so important for the ceremony as a whole.[11] Hebrew psalmists certainly never copied Babylonian supplications, but we may safely assume that—if the traces of healing rituals in the Old Testament are true indicators of the actual proceedings—ancient Israel practiced similar rites outside any temple precincts and other sacred institutions. The original social setting of individual complaints in the Psalter thus becomes the backdrop for that genre's scholarly and kerygmatic interpretation.[12]

Some further support for this view on the generative force of "life settings" may come from worldwide anthropological observations. Healing and rehabilitation rituals are usually kept separate from important holy places. The locale of such prayer and exorcist ceremonies in a small circle of family members is quite private. Shamanistic experts prepare ad hoc an

---

8. Gerstenberger, *Der bittende Mensch*.

9. Cunningham, *Deliver Me from Evil*; Maul, *Zukunftsbewältigung*, 37–113.

10. Heeßel, *Babylonisch-Assyrische Diagnostik*.

11. Take, for example, the great prayer to Ishtar in *ANET*, 384–85. It includes all the essential form-elements of a Mesopotamian supplication—hymnic appellation, petition, complaint, praising vow—all in repetitive, liturgical arrangement. Many similar prayers are attested in the vast cuneiform literature.

12. Gerstenberger, "Canon Criticism"; Gerstenberger, "Social Sciences and Form Criticism"; Gerstenberger, "The Psalms: Genres."

adequate sacred space due to circumstances and possibly due to lack of wider public or priestly interest. They determine proper times, offerings, prayers, ablutions, and all the paraphernalia needed for the cure of the sick. Two examples include Navajo medicine men or women performing varied rituals for ailing people in their proper *hogans* (log cabins) with the patient sitting on a sacred sand painting,[13] and Afro-Brazilian religious communities such as Macumba or Candomblé often incorporating consultation and treatment of mental sufferers into the ecstatic dance performances of their mediums.[14] In the latter, the benevolent saints (*orixás*) speak directly through the spirit-possessed dancer, who also performs purifying and invigorating acts. Healing rituals all over the world from time immemorial follow similar patterns.

Ancient Israel was not excluded from such elementary procedures to save the seriously ill and those who suffer from bad luck, divine punishment, human discrimination, demonic possession, or any other calamity on the personal level. American Indians and African ghost healers practice some healing ceremonials of this sort just as Asian shamans. We may legitimately regard such rites designed for personal survival as some of the oldest prehistoric and enduring expressions of religious faith. While the numina approached for salvation from threatening death changed in history and across cultural boundaries, the basic pattern of supplication persisted over millennia. A central part of the ritual for desperate people was the personal prayer. Even today, for example, in casual pastoral care for the sick, biblical complaint psalms for the individual or modern equivalents can serve as the liberating and comforting prayer in personal crises. Dogmatic statements and sweeping collective confessions usually cannot help in times of danger. Only the deepest strand of personal faith—quite distinct from official religion—existing apart from "temple" and other large-scale religious institutions is able to provide spiritual sustenance. Personal prayer is the core of all religious practice.

In the course of Israelite history, the old individual complaints, administered by healing experts, became stripped of much of their ritualistic wrappings. Supplications (and their attendant form elements), along with scarce commenting superscriptions (e.g., authors, melodies, performing notes, etc.), were incorporated into the psalm texts and the final Psalter. One phrase in a psalm heading recalls an earlier life setting: "Prayer of one

---

13. Kluckhohn, "Myths and Rituals"; Reichard, *Prayer*; Spencer, *Mythology and Values*; Griffin-Pierce, *Earth Is My Mother*.

14. The rites of Candomblé, Macumba, and Umbanda religions are discussed, e.g., by Berkenbrock, *A experiência dos Orixás*; Bastide, *O Candomblé da Bahia*; Pröschild, *Das Heilige in der Umbanda*; Capone, *Search for Africa in Brazil*.

afflicted, when faint and pleading before Yahweh" (Ps 102). Without a doubt, the setting of supplicatory prayers was changed in the faith community after the exile. Quite probably, though, some kind of concern for the individual survived in the new congregation. We do not know about specific ceremonies for the suffering, however, in early Jewish congregations. May we surmise prayer sessions of a patient with his rabbi or elder? Some adaptation of old individual texts to new communal structures transformed personal prayers into congregational laments (e.g., Pss 12; 102). Whether or not the Second Temple was made the locale of healing is hard to determine. The temple program for supplications (1 Kgs 8:31–53) does serve mostly collective concerns. Only the foreigner is mentioned in the singular (vv. 41–43). Individual sufferings such as ill-health are not mentioned in this text. Jesus is depicted in the gospels as pursuing his healing office everywhere but in the temple. The Passion reports draw on complaint psalms, but the way to the cross does not touch the temple precincts. It is a relief to learn from the Psalms that faith retains its own niches of cultic action that must remain unadulterated by large, anonymous organizations.

Much the same social configurations valid for individual complaints we could elaborate for individual thanksgivings. They are portrayed already in Pss 22:23–32 and 107:4–32 as private affairs, not bound to the temple, although the "paying of vows" with attendant sacrifice was a sacred matter, requiring a linkage between the family-cult and local sanctuary (see 2 Sam 15:7). Some personal thanksgivings seem to be embedded in a larger congregational setting from the beginning (e.g., Pss 32; 116; 118). We may not be too sure about these allocations, though. Private feasting certainly was part of the ceremonial duties of a person saved from death. In the same vein, we could perhaps trace "individual psalms of confidence/trust" to original family settings (e.g., Pss 16; 23; 62). On the whole, careful analysis has to be done in order to determine each text's tradition through the centuries. All of the psalms in the Psalter, to be sure, ended up in that final collection that we now have, and the whole mixed composition of prayers, songs, and teachings certainly served the Judean faith community of the Second Temple Period, albeit in different functions, that is, in multiple life-settings. Psalms destined to be used in temple worship must be distinguished from those earmarked for synagogue assemblies, which we find portrayed first in Neh 8. Both communal affairs, however, are distinct from family-oriented, casual rites for individual persons.

## Didactic Psalms

Another large group of biblical psalms hardly has any affinities to temple worship and its sacrificial system. Neither do the pertinent exemplars of this group betray any vestiges of priestly thinking (e.g., purity, sin, ablutions, atonement, etc.). I am referring to the so-called "wisdom" or "didactic" poems of the Psalter.[15] There are about thirty to thirty-five of them, all showing a reflective mood, a pedagogical impetus, even though the subject matters are very diverse: human conditions (e.g., transience, anxieties, piety), Torah orientation and praise, historical education, and ethical instruction. Prominent examples of this wide-ranging category are Pss 1; 9/10; 19; 25; 33; 34; 37; 39; 49; 73; 78; 90; 111; 112; 119; and 139. The common denominator of these very variable compositions is, indeed, their setting in educational communication. Intellectually, didactic psalms are connected with the overarching phenomenon of ancient Near Eastern wisdom literature.[16] Some scholars see them rooted in scribal schools or in the academies of their specific cultural environments. Some also consider popular wisdom to be a possible fountainhead of proverbs, fables, contest literature, skepticism, and so on. Hebrew wisdom psalms have largely remained an unsolved riddle as far as their origin and use are concerned.[17]

Spirituality, theology, and didactic intent of the relevant psalms befit a religious community that had neither the chance nor the political ambition of concurring with worldly powers on a state level. Personal and collective faith in the sole and sovereign God was the backbone of the Israelite community, which developed only after the loss of Judean statehood. Babylonian armies had overrun the tiny territory of Judah, burned the city and temple of Jerusalem, done away with monarchy and state religion, and driven several thousands of the Judean elite into captivity. There, on foreign territory, the deportees were able to reorganize themselves, now under the exclusive leadership of their God and God's Torah. As political autochthony vanished, religious authority became the paramount organizational principle. "No human being is governing over us, God is our ruler" (cf. Judg 8:22–23; 9:8–15; 1 Sam 8:1–18). A theocratic zeal emerged in the new congregation. Scribes, Levites, and priests—that is, the religious elite—came to constitute the leadership of that downtrodden people. The

---

15. See also Jacobson, "Wisdom Language in the Psalms."
16. Crenshaw, *Old Testament Wisdom*.
17. Cf. Mowinckel, *The Psalms*, 2:104–25 ("The Learned Psalmography"). Any connections between didactic poems and worship practices have been largely denied. Exceptions include Perdue, *Wisdom and Cult*; Dell, "A Cultic Setting"; Gerstenberger, *Psalms, Part 1*, 86–89.

exiled Judeans invented, so to speak, a congregational or "ecclesiastical" form of social organization, apparently for the first time in human history. The Zoroastrian community, which is transparent in the oldest parts of the Avesta, probably took a similar development.[18]

The Torah psalms (1; 19; 119) fit particularly well into this picture. Torah proved to be the foremost visible instrument of unification. Forming their identity as a people of the revealed word of God (Sinai event), the emerging Jewish community adhered to that very foundation of their faith. One of the most powerful theological metaphors was the "covenant" between Yahweh and representatives of the people of God—Abraham, Jacob, Moses, David—or with the people themselves. Everyone able to understand is visualized to listen to the stipulations of that covenant, and Yahweh in person is understood to proclaim to them (through the liturgical speaker):

> "Gather to me my faithful ones,
>
> who made a covenant with me by sacrifice!" . . .
>
> "Hear, O my people, and I will speak,
>
> O Israel, I will testify against you.
>
> I am God, your God." (Ps 50:5, 7)

Righteous and wicked ones are reprimanded because of their conduct and admonished to do better (vv. 8–23). Torah is instruction in the ways of God (see Ps 119),[19] and therefore the essential knowledge in personal and communal ethics. The historical narratives of the Pentateuch would give depth to Israel's longstanding traditions and, at the same time, exemplify life under Torah. Historical psalms do the same thing to the community; they can be sung in worship (cf. Pss 78; 105; 106; 136; Deut 32). Seasonal feast days, all in commemoration of historical salvific events instead of mere agricultural blessings (cf. Exod 23; 34; Deut 16; Lev 23; 25), and Torah-ordained circumcision would fortify the sense of unity, identity, and election.

A whole group of didactic psalms is concerned with personal piety and questions of righteous life, human destiny, sin and forgiveness, and transience of existence (Pss 8; 37; 39; 49; 71; 73; 90; 139). Yahweh believers who took on their faith by conscious decision in favor of Israel's unique God and against concurring deities[20] lived under surveillance of the ever-present deity and had to account for their everyday behavior. Their faithfulness was measured by their actions, and their welfare depended on their ethical and

---

18. Gerstenberger, *Israel in the Persian Period*, 427–68.

19. Reynolds, *Torah as Teacher*.

20. Deut 29–31; Josh 24:14–18; Isa 63:7—64:11; Pss 5:3[2]; 71:4–6; 84:4[3]; 115:4–7; 135:15–18.

cultic performance. Small wonder that the social order of the community and human relations were also at stake, in particular the problems of justice, discrimination, and oppression of the weak ones (cf. Pss 9/10; 37; 71; 73). Concerns for justice, equity (even within the parameters of a specific class society over predominant patriarchal and hierarchic structures), and world order permeated all ancient Near Eastern cultures and religions. They were entrenched in social teachings at all social levels and consequently also deeply impressed on all conceptions of royal leadership.

Furthermore, there was a strong longing in the dispersed communities to go home to Judah and Jerusalem. City and temple became great symbols of common history (Pss 46; 48; 74; 87; 132) without necessarily including the sacrificial system of temple service. Pilgrimages to Jerusalem and its sacred space to celebrate annual or tri-annual festivities became common (Pss 120–134). The pertinent psalms betray a community not in direct contact with the temple in Jerusalem but centered on local life and its personal and congregational hopes and anxieties. Individual correctness ("righteousness") and corporate obedience to Yahweh ("cultic orthodoxy") were the goals of the community's aspiration. The sacrificial cult at the central sanctuary meant little to distant congregations as far as their daily affairs were concerned. More and more, the revealed ordinances of God, written on scrolls, became the visible center of weekly worship and private study (Ps 1:2). A truly literate piety and concomitant exegetical discourse among leaders and members of the confessional community slowly emerged. Didactic psalms played an important role in teaching situations (see Deut 31:19–22, 30). They became equal to the words of Torah (Deut 31:24–27).

All the different categories of psalms just mentioned may have grown from pedagogical enterprises in the newly formed congregations. If we accept the notion that the main worship service in the Jewish diaspora was a Torah-centered ceremony, as in Neh 8:1–8 (Torah-reading, praise of God, interpretation of Torah, responses and prayers of the congregation), we recognize a clear emphasis on catechetical instruction. Torah, the prime orientation for Jewish communities, was read aloud for hours, and the audience endorsed the leader's effort with a solemn "Amen, amen" and with prostration (v. 6). Besides the main worship service, there may have been specific occasions of the "Sunday-school" type, which served the education of young people and the fortification of adult faith. After all, later Jewish tradition witnesses not only to synagogue worship but also to a family instruction and the "house of study" (*beth midrash*), a religious school predecessor of today's *yeshivah*. We may surmise, also on account of biblical testimony (see below), that some sorts of Torah-instruction were practiced outside regular services already in post-exilic Judaism. The Sabbath became a common symbol of faith as laid down in the Decalogue and other important Pentateuchal texts. Weekly meetings of learning and fraternization on the Sabbath-day apparently started in the Persian period; they would build up and strengthen Jewish identity. To teach and memorize Torah, in order to make it ever present (Deut 5:1; 6:4-9; 11:18-21; 17:18-19; Josh 1:8; Ezra 7:25) and, for that matter, sacred songs, as in Deut 31:19-22, was the main ingredient of religious education at the time. This meant that, for the assemblies of Jews from the beginning, learning about Torah and Israel's history (i.e., memorizing sacred texts) was an essential part of their religious obligation. They constantly had to know more about and penetrate deeper into the spirituality of their ancestors and the ways of Yahweh. In this fashion, pedagogical features of propagating Torah were inherent in all meetings and worship services of the faith-congregation. The holy alliance between Yahweh and the people had to be borne in mind and practiced without ceasing! Contact with the Jerusalem temple was important, but it was subordinated to synagogue assemblies and Torah instruction. Didactic psalms surely played an important role at many occasions in this religious, confessing community. Confession to Yahweh and studying Yahweh's will, therefore, were not limited to just the main Torah worship services.

One could well argue that in the emerging Jewish worldwide community, synagogue life became paramount, in most cases, for sheer reasons of distance from the Jerusalem temple. But, at the same time, there is quite a noticeable shift in the community away from the sacrificial cult toward a Word-oriented, decision-marked, ethically founded spirituality, which had been developed principally by those Judeans living in close contact with Mesopotamian and Old Persian cultures and religions.[21] Torah itself, at crucial points in the history of the people, particularly in the Deuteronomic/Deuteronomistic view, seems to have led toward ultimate confidence in Word and obedience rather than sacrifice (Deut 5:1; 6:4-9; 11:18-21; 17:18-19; Josh 1:8). This attitude reverberates explicitly in the didactic psalms. "I will not accept a bull from your house . . . If I were hungry, I would not tell you . . . Offer to God a sacrifice of thanksgiving" (Ps 50:9, 12, 14).

The great speeches and interventions of leaders like Moses (Deut 29-31), Joshua (Josh 24), Elijah (1 Kgs 18:21-40), Ezra and Nehemiah (Ezra 9; 10:10-11; Neh 13:15-31), all calling for an unambiguous turn to Yahweh, the Lord of chosen Israel, were decisive in this regard. They glorified the exclusive God; they demanded an unshaken decision for him and a full reliance on his promises. Obligation to exclusive veneration of

---

21. Gerstenberger, *Israel in der Perserzeit* (ET *Israel in the Persian Period*).

the unique God and full commitment to his ordinances of truth, justice, and social responsibility are also visible in the oldest parts of the Avesta, the Zoroastrian holy tradition, which came into being simultaneously during the Persian period on the basis of contemporary patterns of thought. Thus synagogue worship (Neh 8:2-8) was geared toward listening to and learning Torah. The didactic psalms ostensibly fell into line. They show a remarkable affinity with the new spirituality of emerging Jewish diaspora life, centered in Torah synagogue worship. Other psalms, notably general hymns and glorifications, were biblical tradition ties to temple settings (cf. Neh 9:5-15; Ps 106; 1 Chr 16:7-36), which seemingly did not preclude their use in synagogue meetings.[22] Prophetic traditions fell in line with this appreciation of the Word of Yahweh being the only guide for a just life. The messengers of Yahweh became preachers and interpreters of covenant and Torah (e.g., Deut 18:15; 34:10; Jer 11:1-8).

Of course, we would like to know much more about the real-life situation of those psalms, which most clearly reflect the mentality, anxieties, and hopes of the early Jewish congregations. The papyri of the Jewish Elephantine community, for example, do not offer much insight into its own spiritual life, nor that of Jewish congregations in Jerusalem, Samaria, or Babylon,[23] nor do the contemporaneous Babylonian/Persian archives of Nippur and Babylon, containing only business and legal documents. They give testimony to the relationship between Mesopotamian Jews, descendants of deportees, and native businessmen. We do not have explicit descriptions of schools, worship services, casual liturgies, and their pedagogical elements or practices outside the Hebrew Scriptures. And within the canonical writings, as we have seen, they remain dim.

Beyond the scarce vestiges mentioned already, we may add a few observations. Parents in their homes certainly had a hand in education from the beginnings of the confessional faith community. "When your son asks you . . ." is a frequent question reported in the Old Testament (Exod 13:14; Deut 6:20; Josh 4:6, 21; cf. Exod 13:8-9). Parents have to communicate the divine ordinances, in particular the exodus tradition, which to this very day is told and dramatized in Jewish homes (Exod 5-15). Educational responsibilities for the parents are basic (e.g., Prov 1-9), pertaining to ethical instruction rather than salvation history. Scribal schools, not explicitly mentioned in the Old Testament, took care of literate and literary skills as

---

22. Asaph and Korah, prominent in Chronicles as temple-singers, allegedly left groups of their songs to the redactors of the Psalter (Pss 50; 42-49; 73-83; 84-85; 87-88). These collections are a mixture of temple-related, family-oriented, and didactic psalms.

23. See Porten, *The Elephantine Papyri in English*.

well as the transmission of sacred texts. They operated, in all likelihood, near the temple and in "academic" schools, whenever they started to function among early Jewish settlements. Ezra, the "scribe of the law of the God of Heaven" (cf. Ezra 7:6, 10, 21; Neh 8:1, 4, 13; 12:36) is the prototype of the learned rabbi, and he must have studied his profession. The narrators of Ezra/Nehemiah presuppose some educational institution. The synagogue service of Neh 8, already pointed out, reflects reading, interpretation, and acclamation of Torah. That is as far as we go, but details of particular instructional processes or institutions are unattainable.

## Psalms, Cult, and Temple

The spiritual life of ancient Israel as witnessed by biblical writings throughout its age-long and multifaceted formation (from about the tenth to fourth centuries BCE) is very rich and complex indeed. There has never been a uniform and fixed code of faith or ethics, because social stratification (family, village, tribe, states, parochial organizations) was so diversified. To declare one determined stratum of ancient Israelite traditions the "center" or "normative thread" of the canon reflects the modern desire for uniformity of faith and doctrine but does not do justice to the pluriform testimony of the Hebrew writings.[24] Songs and prayers have been present in each and all of these literary layers and conglomerations. They were always "cultic" in the sense of pertaining to some religious ritual. Psalms, we may suggest, are by their very nature dependent on their ceremonial wrappings. Whoever even reads the Psalms puts them into some context of attitudes, concepts, gestures that promote human approach to the divine. The temple service, originally dedicated to paving regular sacrificial avenues to God, pretending to keep up the order of society, if not the world, in all likelihood drew on traditions of psalm-singing and playing music.[25]

But large and central sanctuaries with their cultic performances were not the sole possessors of songs and prayers. On the contrary, one of the most powerful streams of psalmic tradition, the individual complaints and thanksgiving, unfolded outside the temple of Jerusalem, namely inside or close to private homes with the aid of shamanistic practitioners (e.g., "men of God," "seers," "prophets," etc.) in ancient times. The ritual of supplication for the suffering person performed by a healer, preserved, so to speak, the original theology of "primitive" man: that of an intimate relationship with a personal deity to whom small groups of humans were

---

24. Gerstenberger, *Theologies*. See also Brettler, "Jewish Theology of the Psalms."
25. Shehata, *Musiker und ihr vokales Repertoire*; Mowinckel, *The Psalms*.

allied in a parental relationship. This original theology survived, thanks be to God, despite all the superimposed constructs of state and imperial theologies with their anonymous structures and ideological premises, which could not wipe out living faith in a direct relationship with the divine. Although personal, familial religion reached out toward local and regional shrines and, finally, found a refuge within the faith community of emerging Judaism and later in Christian and Muslim religions, it did preserve the freedom of personal faith.

The second breakaway from overarching temple theologies in Israelite history was the formation of an entirely new model of religious community, which though quite different from archaic familial beliefs was largely dependent on them. To establish and stabilize their existence in a foreign and often hostile environment, the early Jews created a Holy Scripture on which to build their community. Their belief and mentality was intimately connected to and impressed by the parochial structures of a strictly confessional association of a religious minority in a vast empire of Persian provenance. Connection to the central sanctuary at Jerusalem was maintained as if by an umbilical cord. But preeminent in all problems of daily life was divine guidance through learned rabbinic interpretation of written sources. The tensions between temple and synagogue have always been felt. Yet the people of God moved on, as a rule, along the commandments of the revealed Word. The new genre of Psalms that we call "didactic" gives clear witness as to the new type of religion that was born in those years of discovering Torah. They testify to a faith based on strict norms of ethical behavior, placing human relations into the center of concern, vanquishing chauvinisms, and, to a certain extent, priestly bigotry.[26] A liberated synagogue community led the way into modern times of separation of church and state and the autonomous growth of confessional religion. The didactic psalms signal that new era.

---

26. The continuing attachment to sacrificial purification theologies is apparent in the priestly layers of the Old Testament, generating sustained tensions in Jewish-Christian traditions. See the essentially "Western" enlightened treatment of Psalms with, e.g., Brueggemann, *Worship in Ancient Israel*; and Brown, *Psalms*.

# 8

# The Psalter as Book and as Collection[1]

## Holistic Reading, Canonical Criticism, and Tradition History

THE INTEGRATED, HOLISTIC READING of biblical texts is on the rise, there is no doubt about it. It has the merit of taking seriously the long underappreciated editorial and compositional efforts of the tradents to achieve a "final text" (however we would like to define it). It is not only the alleged "initial stages" of the tradition, those authentic original words that fascinated our spiritual forebearers, that are of significance to the exegete, but also the numerous stages and rivulets of tradition leading up to the literary end-product, the "canonical text" as we have it in our Hebrew editions. In contrast to all models based on tradition history, the "canonical" interpretation puts the predominant to even exclusive emphasis on the "final form" of the biblical texts, knowing full well—but firmly ignoring this insight—that there is no more a definitive "final text" than there is a clear canon decision (cf. MT <—> LXX). Its imaginary value is set by "canonical" exegetes somewhere between 51% and 100%. Using the Psalms as an example, it is worth reflecting on this supreme appreciation of the whole text and its relationship to the preceding individual texts. In doing so, their own basic ideas of canonization, canonical authority, text application, etc. are constantly in play. For example: Every text, large or small, derives from specific communication processes and has a specific social context. We should also be aware of some fundamental problems:

   a. Whoever emphasizes the final canonical form of the biblical writings more or less devalues the historical genesis of our faith tradition. He or she will then also be inclined to put aside the historicality of the Word

1. Translated by K. C. Hanson.

of God in general in favor of a permanent substance and unchanging authority of revelation that is fixed once and for all.

b. Words—even sacred "canonical" words—are always thoroughly human and dependent on a human *Sitz im Leben*. No word lives by itself; every word—even one with a long and varied tradition—has a speaker, an addressee, and a concrete communicative context. The myth of the unbound word or the intrinsically dynamic text is wrong; it also only appears to facilitate the difficult task of biblical exegesis.

c. The final canonical form of the Hebrew Scriptures is thoroughly connected with the particular, historically unique sufferings, joys, and ideas of the post-exilic Jewish communities in Palestine and in the Diaspora. All parts of the canon have been collected and edited there during centuries of active and very tension-filled use. At no time was there a unified plan, a uniform theological orientation, or an authoritative selection of the texts. The restless, contradictory social and spiritual life of the Jewish communities, the competition and the coexistence of different social classes, professions, estates, clans, genders are reflected in the texts. They are the unmistakable product of happenstance of the very pluralistic faith experiences of our spiritual forefathers and foremothers.

## The Book Most Resistant to an Integrated Reading

The Psalter is possibly the book in the Old Testament that most resists an integrated reading. It comes as a collection of relatively firmly numbered individual texts (cf. Qumran variants), most of which are separated from one another by unique superscriptions and the vast majority have a recognizable, special infrastructure, also secured by ancient Near Eastern and other analogous formations. How a "book" that is constructed from such specific texts can be read in a uniform way is an intriguing question.

Proponents of integrated usage employ a variety of techniques to demonstrate the unity of the Psalter as a book of prayer and meditation for the Jewish and Christian communities. These procedures would have to be examined in detail and critically assessed. There is insufficient time for that here. We can only engage in suggestions and samples:

At the level of words and sentences, for example, keyword cross-connections mainly exist between adjacent psalms.[2] Patrick Miller and

---

2. The first influential study in this regard was C. Barth, "Concatenatio." It was taken up again and continued by Lohfink, "Psalmengebet und Psalterredaktion," 7–13; and

Erich Zenger have provided examples.[3] It is interesting that the question of intentional concatenation is not clearly answered. While Gerald H. Wilson in 1985 cited a single genuine example of "catchword-connection":[4] Ps 7:18 [ET 17]: "I will give to Yahweh the thanks due to his righteousness and sing praise to the name of Yahweh, the Most High," is to be taken up again—skipping over Ps 8—in Ps 9:2 [ET 1]: "I will give thanks to Yahweh with my whole heart; I will tell of all your wonderful deeds"—the number of concatenations "rediscovered" today is much larger. It is very difficult, however, to prove the intentionality of the alleged textual connections. The fact, then, that the identical and synonymous words, formulas, and phrases appear in related psalms is indisputable. The question remains wide open, however, as to whether this consonance from psalm to psalm represents a deliberate connection between the texts or is merely an accidental result of related texts being lined up in one writing.

Given the undeniable character of the Psalms as a collection, at least one should be careful not to be too quick to regard verbal echoes as evidence for the composition and integrated treatment of the Psalter. The same applies to form and structural elements that may correspond to each other compositionally. Each individual case would have to be carefully examined to determine whether the terms and phrases quoted belong to an original text of the surviving text or to a reformulation or new formulation by the later redactors.

In this last case one can speak of a genuine connection, and I suspect that the cases of conscious editing of existing texts for the purpose of allowing a continuous meditative text are few in number.[5] This does not mean, however, that there has been no recognizable editorial—better, collection—work on the Psalter. On the contrary: While I worked on my commentary on the first sixty Psalms, I realized more and more how powerful the creative process of psalm composition and reinterpretation was up until the late phase of the Old Testament.[6] The reflective, wisdom, Torah-related, and psalms favorable to the poor (e.g., Pss 1; 9/10; 37; 39; 49; 73; 90; 119; 139, etc.) are new

---

Zenger, "Was wird anders," 399–403.

3. Miller, "Kingship, Torah Obedience, and Prayer"; and Zenger, "Zur redaktionsgeschichtlichen Bedeutung der Korachpsalmen."

4. Wilson, *The Editing of the Hebrew Psalter*. But apparently Wilson did not use C. Barth, "Concatenatio."

5. Cf. Lohfink's very justified questions of doubt about the actual course of the postulated linking work: Did the redaction "insert additions, replace words, perhaps even rewrite individual psalms? Or did they just skillfully exploit existing content and word correspondences?" Lohfink, "Psalmengebet und Psalterredaktion," 8.

6. Similar to Becker, *Israel deutet seine Psalmen*.

formations. They do not serve to create a coherent reading text, but are geared towards new, contemporary problems and expectations of the community in which they arose. Torah loyalty and joy, the transience of life, exploitation of poor communities by rich landowners (cf. Neh 5)—these are burning, topical issues that must be articulated in the life of believers. In some cases it was "sufficient" to update older prayer and song texts, perhaps to verbalize the messianic hope (cf. Pss 2; 45; 110), or to repurpose older prayer rituals dealing with illness and impoverishment for communal use.[7]

## Psalm Clusters

Spiritual and theological interpretations can already be deduced from the keyword combinations mentioned above. Each psalm that is sewn together with the neighboring texts can make completely new statements in the context of its surroundings. Suffering is related to rejoicing, the individual is transformed into a collective, the present leads to the eschatological future, monarchy is replaced by community—there are hardly any limits to the transformations through joint interpretation. Individual texts become new material with transformed expressiveness through accumulation and connection comparable to nuclear fusion, which can reach directly into the Christian community.[8] Even if one does not deny the individual psalms a certain independence, canonical interpreters rather rely on compositional techniques instead of the editorial revisions of the collector(s). These new paths can be taken in the direction of the integrated reading of the Psalter and new horizons of interpretation opened up.

Obviously, the songs and prayers, admonitions and reflections collected in the Psalter did not all arrive purely by accident to the place where we find them now.[9] There are texts that are related to one another in form or content or that have a certain complementary relationship to each other. Psalms 111 and 112 or 105 and 106 are probably designed to go together, whether from the text's original composition or only in the course of the collection remains to be seen. Walther Zimmerli, following Heinrich

---

7. The prayer ritual for individual sufferers, which was used in primary groups, can be reconstructed in particular using the analogy of Akkadian incantations. In Ps 12, for example, it is characteristically converted to a plurality of those in need!

8. Cf. Lohfink, "Was wird anders": The change of meaning is important for our approach to the Psalter! It is achieved by detaching the Psalms from the original (cultic) basis of attachment.

9. The different order of the texts in 11QPs, however, is proof of a certain arbitrariness. Cf. Sanders, *Dead Sea Psalms Scroll*, 261–71.

Herkenne, calls them "twin psalms."[10] Psalms 96–99; 3–7; 146–150; 120–134, etc. form easily recognizable "psalm clusters" that stand out from their surroundings because of similarities in form and/or content. These are well-known facts, and any introduction to the Old Testament tells us that the Psalter in general gradually grew together over long periods of time from older collections. In the end, the editors brought together Pss 1 and 2 and probably the hymn-like conclusion Ps 150 or Pss 146–150 to create a "complete" collection of the most diverse psalm texts.

Of course, the new, integrated interpretation of the Psalter does not stop with the previous analyses. From a holistic perspective and with a good deal of theological knowledge behind you, it is possible to put together groups of psalms that have not been related to one another and to hear a common meaning from them. Erich Zenger, our host and *spiritus rex*, is one of the most successful discoverers of such "psalm clusters" (galaxies). For him, Pss 15–24 belong together spiritually and theologically; they revolve around the center of Ps 19, the text that brings the Torah and the sun (cosmos) into balance.[11] Likewise, in his opinion, Pss 3–14; 25–34;[12] 35–41;[13] and the Korah Psalms 42–49; 84–85; 87–88 have clear connections intended by the collectors, a theological center and overarching theological statement. It should be expressly emphasized that he does not ignore the historical origin of these newly discovered conglomerations: He recognizes stages of growth and outlines the development of the final canonical form; of course, in the current discussions, the overall interpretation is extraordinarily and primarily important to him.[14]

## Accounting for the Differences of Time and Social Context

From what we have indicated so far, it cannot be denied that the long process of collection, arrangement, composition, and editing the Psalter went on from the sixth century BCE at the earliest until the second century BCE (some even think until the first century CE).[15] And I do not hesitate

---

10. Zimmerli, "Zwillingpsalmen"; see Herkenne, *Das Buch der Psalmen*.

11. Zenger, "Was wird anders," 403–4. The heading for this section is his "Thesis 2: In the case of canonical interpretation, the position of a psalm in the respective compositional unit (intended by the editors) is to be observed" (403).

12. Zenger, "Was wird anders," 405–6.

13. Hossfeld and Zenger, "Selig," 23–34.

14. Cf. Hossfeld and Zenger, "Selig," 49–50: He starts from "pre-exilic lay prayers" that were collected and edited in three batches with the sense of a theology of the poor. Cf. also Hossfeld and Zenger, *Die Psalmen I*.

15. Cf. Wilson, "Shape," 137–38.

to explain that the theological significance of this process of collecting and shaping has not been adequately appreciated in previous research, including in the first volume of my form-critical commentary on the Psalms. In the field of contextual reading, as practiced at least in part in the Jewish and then also in the Christian communities, I am happy to be taught further, and we still have a lot to learn together. However, this does not exclude critical queries, but actually includes them.

For me, the basic question is whether the paths taken—keyword concatenation, juxtaposition of poems, and a theologically homogeneous overall concept—create that unity of meaning in the Psalter that is the prerequisite for the unified interpretation of such a very mixed body of literary pieces. I find it difficult to see this in the concatenation of keywords in the Psalms, because in my opinion it cannot be proven to have been consciously, newly created or skillfully composed in a collage-like manner.[16] The collection of formerly completely independent Psalm poetry certainly offers opportunities for the realization of an overall idea. On the other hand, on closer inspection, the successive accumulation and rearrangement of texts, including completely new compositions, proves to be unsuitable for introducing guidelines into the colorful diversity. In any case, the individual psalms very tenaciously retain their original situation-related structure—according to the analogous ancient Near Eastern texts—so it is difficult to force them to make new comprehensive statements;[17] and the entire process of creating the collections is fractured in so many ways, not coherent and one-dimensional, that we absolutely cannot speak of achieving a theological level of unity. Even if all the small and special collections of psalms within the Psalter have come about as they appear from the point of view of integrated interpretation, the various agglomerations necessarily lie on quite different theological levels, having been drawn from different eras of different communities at different times with starkly diverging interests and ideas.

Furthermore, the final editing cannot claim any special dignity compared to the previous editing, and the closeness of the final version to

---

16. The careful work of Wilson, *Editing*, does not, in my opinion, prove the theological amalgamation of the Psalms, but, on the contrary, the persistence of individual texts in a utilitarian collection. "The [superscriptions], regardless of their secondary nature, have no explicit concern with the larger question of structure or organization of the whole Psalter. Each [superscription] refers only to the single composition it heads. Its purpose is 'descriptive' and not organizational" (139–40).

17. The literary-critical work on the Psalms, which has also experienced a strong upswing in recent years—in no small measure due to Walter Beyerlin's keen research activity—should be dealt with separately.

Christian beliefs,[18] which is sometimes stated, reveals above all the—quite legitimate—interests and theological concepts of *contemporary interpreters*. It seems to me that this is where the real foundation of the unity of the Psalter lies: Our backward-projecting theological interest separates the individual texts and the complete Psalter from their time-bound and conflict-ridden original situations and turns them into well-tempered, also socially critical, theological frameworks that we can relate directly to ourselves.[19] With this, however, the variety of life situations, the strange, different rootedness in the social and religious life of the time in the psalm texts is pushed aside and declared to be unimportant.

## A Socio-historical Interpretation of the Psalms

I would like to counterpose the concept of the canonical interpretation of the Psalms (and the Bible) with my idea of a socio-historical interpretation of the Psalms, which distinguishes the different stages of the tradition and, including the final editing, also appreciates them theologically.

The Psalter is not a "book" in our sense, certainly not a theological textbook with progressively unfolding statements about God; according to its nature, it cannot be. It has been proven that it consists of sub-collections and individual items that can no longer be clearly defined. They must have grown over the centuries and are intertwined in a variety of ways. The successive editorial interventions are limited to the proemium,[20] concluding text (Ps 150), superscriptions, some communal doxologies (e.g., Ps 72:18–20), a few text changes in the individual psalms, occasional regrouping of surviving texts (e.g., Ps 9/10; 108 = from Ps 57:8–12 + 60:7–14?), etc. A "book" consciousness cannot be determined.

What was the purpose of this very disparate collection of texts? The question of the *Sitz im Leben* of the later stages should be decisive for the assessment of the text corpus. Hermann Gunkel and Sigmund Mowinckel and their successors discovered essential things about the original genres. Songs of complaint and thanksgiving as well as hymns are rooted in different worship services of different communities from clans to the state cult. In the case of the so-called Wisdom Psalms, the Jewish community of the exilic and post-exilic period can be recognized as the main group

---

18. Cf. Lohfink, "Psalmengebet," 21; Lohfink, "Psalter."

19. Croatto (*Exodus*) considers such an exegesis necessary; it activates (according to Paul Ricoeur) the "surplus of meaning."

20. Ps 1: The claim of Childs (cf. Wilson, *Editing*, 206) that the Psalter becomes a Torah-like meditation text through Ps 1 is incomprehensible to me.

of origin.[21] Since the exile and the restructuring into a town, temple, and diaspora community, believers in Yahweh have also had prayer texts from various streams of tradition collected and employed in their own services—perhaps also for private devotional life? The models discussed so far (temple services, schools, domestic devotions[22]) may be correct in certain respects. The more I think about it, the more synagogal gatherings I have in mind in which psalms were sung by the choir and/or congregation in response to the reading of the Torah or on special occasions and emergencies. In the first part of my commentary (covering Pss 1–60) I referred in particular to the paraenetic and instructive psalms (cf. Ps 32; 39; 50; etc.) as community formation. Special interests of scribes, messianic monarchists, perhaps also priests can be recognized in individual texts.

However we may imagine the Psalter to have been used, it seems to me that the collection has never served as a coherent whole, possibly even in a complete reversal of the "directions of speech" as the word of God to the congregation. Rather, it seems to me that the individual use of individual texts has always been normal, no matter how much the reference groups have changed. The congregation received complaints and thanks, requests and praise and offered them to their God Yahweh. A certain "communalization" of the individual (better: small group) prayers took place; Gerald Wilson is right about that.[23] But the individual member of the community, of course, related the I-statements to themselves, just as in our hymns the first person means the individual, not the collective "I" of the community. The individual in the worship community sings and prays a completed psalm, perhaps a second or third, just as we sing several verses of a song. But each unit is understood to be complete in itself, not part of a book. The meaning of the psalm does not lie outside of its text, but within it. The theologically conscious reading progression from one psalm to the next is, in my opinion, only to be understood as a reflected, academic further development of the monastic tradition of a *lectio continua*. The normal worshiper can only use and consider the predetermined parts of the Psalter for his and the group-specific worship service, but not the whole book. Some prayer scenes in Old Testament narrative contexts give us the right understanding (Jonah 2; 1 Sam 2; Isa 38). The limited selection of a few psalm passages in a worship service is reflected in 1 Chr 16 with its praise of God composed of three scattered psalms (Pss 105:1–15; 96;

---

21. The investigations of Perdue, *Wisdom*; and Stolz, *Psalmen*, lead—even unintentionally—to the assumption of a worship *Sitz im Leben*.

22. On the last, cf. Lohfink, "Psalmengebet"; and Lohfink, "Psalter."

23. Wilson, "Shape," 139. In his dissertation, the emphasis is on the "privatization" of the Psalter (403)!

106:1, 47–48). There is no biblical record of the continuous, meditative use of the Psalter in the manner of rosary prayers.

From what we know from collections of prayers and hymns from the ancient Near East, they too were veritable liturgical handbooks intended for use in worship and were by no means intended as holistic guides and textbooks. Wilson discovers little trace of editorial activity in two Sumerian catalogs of hymns. In one case, the collection of the forty-one temple hymns ends with a special text (doxology + colophon), in the second case—in various incipit lists of religious texts—tendencies towards grouping genres and songs of the same form can be seen. There is no trace of cross-connections among them or of an integral theological system. (There are other collections of ancient Near Eastern prayers and incantations to compare.)

This latter point deserves emphasis: As nice as it sounds when a transparent ordering principle of the Psalter is presented, there is a great danger precisely in the theological uniformity it claims. One can see that at the beginning of the Psalter the complaints and after Ps 90 the hymns occur relatively frequently. To conclude from this that the editors of the Psalter wanted to lead the praying congregation through the book of Psalms from lamentation to praise[24] is an abstract, leveling, universal judgment. Equally precarious is the Davidic–New Testament interpretation of the Psalter, which up to Ps 89 states the failure of the Davidic dynasty as the main theme and from Ps 90 onwards Israel's opening up to the world of nations and the eschatological (i.e. Christian) future. The unity, and especially the theological uniformity, of the Psalter is a wish on our part that cannot be brought into line with the reality of the texts. Because the individual psalms come from very different streams of tradition and surprisingly are theologically harmonized very little. Names of God and concepts of God appear in such abundance, variety, and contradiction that an unbiased reader of the Bible can become afraid. The weather god of Ps 29 has little to do with the personal god of the individual complaint songs, or the national god of Israel, or the ruler of a pantheon (Ps 82). The worshipers of the individual psalms are by no means always the same group. There we find primary groups who fear for their sick; armies celebrating a military victory; monarchists standing up for their dynast; sages who philosophize about impermanence and injustice; doubters who feel persecuted and betrayed, etc. All of this cannot be brought down to a common denominator by any concatenation and totalizing interpretation. I would like to illustrate all this with a few sentences from my Psalms commentary.

---

24. Cf. Gottwald, *Hebrew Bible*; Childs, *Introduction*; Brueggemann, *Message*.

What was the worship service like that prompted the compilation of the Psalter? And who were after all, those singers entrusted with the responsibility of carrying out cultic ceremonies in late OT times? Judging from postexilic situations in general, we know that cult centralization in Jerusalem was a lofty theological ideal. In reality, downtrodden, dependent, dispersed Israel needed religious rituals of various types that were not physically linked with the temple. That is, Jewish communities in many countries had to develop their own rites and prayers, perhaps in some correspondence with the Jerusalem authorities.[25]

All in all, we have to read the Psalter as a whole in the light of Jewish community organization in Persian and Hellenistic times to understand its significance at this latest stage of liturgical use. The psalms then, were read and prayed in local assemblies and, at least primarily, not in the temple community of Jerusalem. Zion for the most part seems far away (see Pss 42:7 [NRSV 6]; 87; 137:5). Worship without traditional sacrifice is all-important and must be defended against those who doubt its justification (Psalms 40; 50–51). In short, at this latest stage the Psalter is not exactly a hymnbook of the second temple but more precisely a hymnbook of the many synagogal communities..."[26]

## Conclusion

The Psalter is not a book, but a collection of extraordinarily rich, theologically and anthropologically profound, and insightful prayers and songs from different life situations. It is a storehouse of essential texts that can be used again and again in all sorts of ways, which must also be imitated in the new song among all the peoples of the earth. The Psalter is a wonderful basket of the choicest, wholesome, and nutritious fruits that must be savored individually, unless you renounce originality and specificity and prefer a juicy mash or mixed jam to the fresh crops.

---

25. Gerstenberger, *Psalms, Part 1*, 27–28.
26. Gerstenberger, *Psalms, Part 1*, 28.

# Bibliography

Ahlström, Gösta W. *Psalm 89: Eine Liturgie aus dem Ritual des leidenden Königs*. Lund: Ohlssons, 1959.
Aistleitner, Joseph. *Die mythologischen und kultischen Texte aus Ras Schamra*. Bibliotheca orientalis hungarica 8. Budapest: Akadémiai Kiadó, 1959. 2nd ed., 1964.
Albertz, Rainer. *Die Exilszeit*. Biblische Enzyklopädie 7. Stuttgart: Kohlhammer, 2001.
———. *Israel in Exile: The History and Literature of the Sixth Century*. Studies in Biblical Literature 3. Atlanta: SBL, 2003.
———. *Persönliche Frömmigkeit und offizielle Religion*. Calwer theologische Monographien. Reihe A, Bibelwissenschaft 9. Stuttgart: Calwer, 1978.
Albrektson, Bertil. *Studies in the Text and Theology of the Book of Lamentations*. Studia theologica Lundensia 21. Lund: Gleerup, 1963.
Albright, W. F. "A Catalogue of Early Hebrew Lyric Poems (Ps 68)." *HUCA* 23 (1950/51) 1–39.
———. *Yahweh and the Gods of Canaan*. Garden City, NY: Doubleday, 1968.
Alonso Schökel, Luis. *Estudios de poetica hébrea*. Barcelona: Juan Flors, 1963.
———. *A Manual of Hebrew Poetics*. Subsidia Biblica 11. Rome: Pontifical Biblical Institute, 1988.
———. "The Poetic Structure of Psalms 42–43." *JSOT* 2 (1976) 4–11.
Alt, Albrecht. "The God of the Fathers." In *Essays on Old Testament History and Religion*, 3–77. Translated by R. A. Wilson. Oxford: Blackwell, 1966. Reprint, Sheffield: JSOT Press, 1989.
———. *Der Gott der Väter: Ein Beitrag zur Vorgeschichte der israelitischen Religion*. BWANT 48. Stuttgart: Kohlhammer, 1929. Reprinted in *Kleine Schriften zur Geschichte des Volkes Israels*, vol. 1, 1–78. Munich: Beck, 1953.
———. "Die Wallfahrt von Sichern nach Bethel." In *In piam memoriam Alexander von Bulmerincq*, edited by Rudolf Abramowski, 218–30. Abhandlungen der Herder-Gesellschaft und des Herder-Instituts zu Riga 6/3. Riga: Ernest Plates, 1938. Reprinted in *Kleine Schriften zur Geschichte des Volkes Israel*, 1:79–88. Munich: Beck, 1953.
Anderson, Bernhard W. *Out of the Depths: The Psalms Speak for Us Today*. Philadelphia: Westminster, 1974.
Anderson, G. W. "Enemies and Evildoers in the Book of Psalms." *Bulletin of the John Rylands Library* 48 (1965) 16–29.

Ap-Thomas, D. R. "An Appreciation of Sigmund Mowinckel's Contribution to Biblical Studies." *JBL* 85 (1966) 315–25.
Arens, Anton. *Die Psalmen im Gottesdienst des Alten Bundes*. Trier: Paulinus, 1961.
Asensio, Felix. "El Yahweh Malak de los 'Salmos del Reino' en la historia de la 'Salvacion.'" *Estudios Biblicos* 25 (1966) 299–315.
Audet, Jean-Paul. "Le sens du Cantique des Cantiques." *RB* 62 (1955) 197–221.
Austin, J. L. *How to Do Things with Words*. William James Lectures Delivered at Harvard University in 1955. Cambridge: Harvard University Press, 1962.
Balla, Emil. *Das Ich der Psalmen*. FRLANT 16, Göttingen: Vandenhoeck & Ruprecht, 1912.
Bardtke, Hans. *Liber Psalmorum*. Biblia Hebraica Stuttgartensis 11. Stuttgart: Württembergische Bibelanstalt, 1969.
Barth, Christoph. "Concatenatio im ersten Buch des Psalters." In *Wort und Wirklichkeit, Studien zur Afrikanistik und Orientalistik: Eugen Ludwig Rapp zum 70. Geburtstag*, edited by Brigitta Benzing et al., 30–40. Meisenheim: Hein, 1976.
———. *Einführung in die Psalmen*. Biblische Studien 32. Neukirchen-Vluyn: Neukirchener, 1961.
———. *Die Errettung vom Tode in den individuellen Klage- und Dankliedern des Alten Testaments*. Zollikon: Evangelischer, 1947.
———. *Introduction to the Psalms*. Translated by R. A. Wilson. New York: Scribner, 1966.
Barth, Karl. *Church Dogmatics* I/1. Edited by T. F. Torrance and G. W. Bromiley. Translated by G. T. Thomson and Harold Knight. Edinburgh: T. & T. Clark, 1956.
Bastide, Roger. *O Candomblé da Bahia*. Paris: Plon, 2001.
Bauks, Michaela. *Die Feinde des Psalmisten und die Freunde Ijobs: Untersuchungen zur Freund-Klage im Alten Testament am Beispiel von Ps 22*. SBS 203. Stuttgart: Katholisches Bibelwerk, 2004.
Baumann, Eberhard. "Strukturuntersuchungen im Psalter." *ZAW* 61 (1949) 114–76; 62 (1950) 115–52.
Baumgarten, A. I. et al., eds. *Self, Soul, and Body in Religious Experience*. Studies in the History of Religion 78. Leiden: Brill, 1995.
Baumgartner, Walter. *Die Klagegedichte des Jeremia*. BZAW 32. Giessen: Töpelmann, 1917.
———. "Zum 100. Geburtstag von Hermann Gunkel." In *Congress Volume, Bonn*, 1–18. VTSup 9. Leiden: Brill, 1963.
Becker, Joachim. *Israel deutet seine Psalmen: Urform und Neuinterpretation in den Psalmen*. SBS 18. Stuttgart: Katholisches Bibelwerk, 1966.
———. *Wege der Psalmenexegese*. SBS 78. Stuttgart: Katholisches Bibelwerk, 1975.
Begrich, Joachim. "Das priesterliche Heilsorakel." *ZAW* 52 (1934) 81–92. Reprinted in *Gesammelte Studien zum Alten Testament*, 217–31. TB 21. Munich: Kaiser, 1964.
———. "Die Vertrauensäusserungen im israelitischen Klagelied des Einzelnen und in seinem babylonischen Gegenstück." *ZAW* 46 (1928) 221–60. Reprinted in *Gesammelte Studien zum Alten Testament*, edited by Walther Zimmerli, 168–216. Theologische Bucherei 21. Munich: Kaiser, 1964.
Bell, Catherine. *Ritual Theory, Ritual Practice*. New York: Oxford University Press, 1992.
Bentzen, Aage. *King and Messiah*. Translated by the author. London: Lutterworth, 1955.

———. *Messias, Moses redivivus, Menschensohn: Skizzen zum Thema Weissagung und Erfüllung*. Abhandlungen zur Theologie des Alten und Neuen Testaments 17. Zurich: Zwingli, 1948.

Bergler, Siegfried. "Threni V." *VT* 27 (1977) 304–20.

Berkenbrock, Volney J. *A experiência dos Orixás: Um estudo sobre a experiência religiosa no Candomblé*. 2nd ed. Coleção Religião e pesquisa 2. Petrópolis, Brazil: Vozes, 1999.

Bernhardt, Karl-Heinz. *Das Problem der altorientalischen Königsideologie im Alten Testament, unter besonderer Berücksichtigung der Geschichte der Psalmenexegese dargestellt und kritisch gewürdigt*. VTSup 8. Leiden: Brill, 1961.

Berridge, John M. *Prophet, People and the Word of Yahweh: An Examination of Form and Content in the Proclamation of the Prophet Jeremiah*. Basel Studies of Theology 4. Zurich: EVZ, 1970.

Bertalanffy, Ludwig von. *General Systems Theory: Foundations, Developments, Applications*. New York: Braziller, 1968. Rev. ed., 1980.

Beyerlin, Walter. *Die Rettung der Bedrängten in den Feindpsalmen der Einzelnen auf institutionelle Zusammenhänge untersucht*. FRLANT 99. Göttingen: Vandenhoeck & Ruprecht, 1970.

———. "Die *toda* der Heilsvergegenwärtigung in den Klageliedern des Einzelnen." *ZAW* 79 (1967) 208–24.

———. *Werden und Wesen des 107. Psalms*. BZAW 153. Berlin: de Gruyter, 1979.

Birkeland, Harris. *The Evildoers in the Book of Psalms*. ANVAO II/2. Oslo: Dybwad, 1955.

Blenkinsopp, Joseph. "Ballad Style and Psalm Style in the Song of Deborah." *Bib* 42 (1961) 61–76.

———. *Sage, Priest, Prophet*. LAI. Louisville: Westminster John Knox, 1995.

Boas, Franz. *The Mind of Primitive Man*. New York: Macmillan, 1911.

Boling, Robert G. "'Synonymous' Parallelism in the Psalms." *JSS* 5 (1960) 221–55.

Boström, Gustav. *Paronomasi i den äldre hebreiska maschal-literaturen*. Lund: Gleerup, 1928.

Boyce, Mary. *A History of Zoroastrianism*. 2 vols. Handbook of Oriental Studies: Section 1: The Near and Middle East 8/3. Leiden: Brill, 1975–82.

Brettler, Marc Zvi. "Jewish Theology of the Psalms." In *The Oxford Handbook of the Psalms*, edited by William P. Brown, 485–98. Oxford Handbooks. Oxford: Oxford University Press, 2014.

Bright, John. "Jeremiah's Complaints—Liturgy or Expressions of Personal Distress?" In *Proclamation and Presence: Old Testament Essays in Honor of Gwynne Henton Davies*, edited by J. I. Durham and J. R. Porter, 189–214. Richmond: John Knox, 1970.

Brown, William P. *Psalms*. Interpreting Biblical Texts. Nashville: Abingdon, 2010.

———. "The Psalms and 'I': The Dialogical Self and the Disappearing Psalmist." In *Diachronic and Synchronic: Reading the Psalms in Real Time. Proceedings of the Baylor Symposium on the Book of Psalms*, edited by Joel S. Burnett et al., 26–44. LHBOTS 488. New York: T. & T. Clark, 2007.

Brueggemann, Walter. *Israel's Praise: Doxology against Idolatry and Ideology*. Philadelphia: Fortress, 1988.

———. *The Message of the Psalms: A Theological Commentary*. Minneapolis: Augsburg, 1984.

———. *The Psalms and the Life of Faith*. Edited by Patrick D. Miller. Minneapolis: Fortress, 1995.

———. *Theology of the Old Testament: Testimony, Dispute, Advocacy*. Minneapolis: Fortress, 1997.

———. *Worship in Ancient Israel: An Essential Guide*. Nashville: Abingdon, 2005.

Buber, Martin, and Franz Rosenzweig. *Die Schrift*. 4 vols. 8th ed. Heidelberg: Schneider, 1975.

Budde, Karl. "Ein althebräisches Klagelied." *ZAW* 3 (1883) 299–306.

———. "Das hebräische Klagelied." *ZAW* 2 (1882) 1–52.

———. "Die hebräische Leichenklage." *Zeitschrift des deutschen Palästina-Vereins* 6 (1883) 180–94.

———. "Zum hebräischen Klagelied." *ZAW* 12 (1892) 31–37; 261–75.

Buss, Martin J. *Biblical Form-Criticism in Its Context*. JSOTSup 274. Sheffield: Sheffield Academic, 1999.

———. "The Psalms of Asaph and Korah." *JBL* 82 (1963) 382–92.

Caplice, R. L. "Namburbi Texts in the British Museum." *Or* 34 (1965) 105–31; 36 (1967) 1–38, 273–98; 39 (1970) 1–32; 40 (1971) 133–83.

———. "Participants in the Namburbi-Rituals." *CBQ* 29 (1967) 346–52.

Capone, Stefania. *Searching for Africa in Brazil: Power and Tradition in Candomblé*. Durham: Duke University Press, 2010.

Cardenal, Ernesto. *Zerschneide den Stacheldraht: Lateinamerikanische Psalmen*. Wuppertal: Jugenddienst 1967.

Casetti, Pierre. *Gibt es ein Leben vor dem Tod? Eine Auslegung von Psalm 49*. OBO 44. Göttingen: Vandenhoeck & Ruprecht, 1992.

Castillino, G. R. *Le lamentazioni individuali e gli inni in Babilonia e in Israele: Raffrontati riguardo alla forma e al contenuto*. Turin: Societa Editrice Internazionale, 1939.

Childs, Brevard S. *Introduction to the Old Testament as Scripture*. Philadelphia: Fortress, 1979.

Christian, Viktor. *Untersuchungen zur Laut- und Formenlehre des Hebräischen*. Vienna: Böhlau, 1953.

Clines, David J. A. "Psalm Research since 1955." *Tyndale Bulletin* 18 (1967) 103–26; 20 (1969) 105–25.

Cohen, Gerson D. "The Song of Songs and the Jewish Religious Mentality." In *The Canon and Masorah of the Hebrew Bible: An Introductory Reader*, edited by Sid Z. Leiman, 262–82. 1962. Reprint, Libary of Biblical Studies. New York: Ktav, 1974.

Coppens, Joseph. "La royaute de Yahve dans le Psautier." *Ephemerides theologicae Lovanienses* 53 (1977) 297–362; 54 (1978) 1–59.

Crenshaw, James L. *Hymnic Affirmation of Divine Justice: The Doxologies of Amos and Related Texts in the Old Testament*. SBLDS 24. Missoula, MT: Scholars, 1975.

———. *Old Testament Wisdom: An Introduction*. 3rd ed. Louisville: Westminster John Knox, 2010.

Crim, Keith R. *The Royal Psalms*. Richmond: John Knox, 1962.

Croatto, J. Severino. *Exodus: A Hermeneutics of Freedom*. Translated by Salvator Attanasio. Maryknoll, NY: Orbis, 1981. Reprint, Eugene, OR: Wipf & Stock, 2021.

Cross, Frank M. "Prose and Poetry in the Mythic and Epic Texts from Ugarit." *HTR* 67 (1974) 1–15.

Cross, Frank M., Jr., and David N. Freedman. *Studies in Ancient Yahwistic Poetry*. SBLDS 21. Missoula, MT: Scholars, 1975.

Crüsemann, Frank. *Studien zur Formgeschichte von Hymnus und Danklied in Israel.* WMANT 32. Neukirchen-Vluyn: Neukirchener, 1969.
Culley, Robert C. *Oral Formulaic Language in the Biblical Psalms.* Near and Middle East Series 4. Toronto: University of Toronto Press, 1967.
Cunningham, Graham. *Deliver Me from Evil: Mesopotamian Incantations 2500–1500 BC.* Studia Pohl: Series Maior 17. Rome: Pontifical Biblical Institute, 1997.
Dahood, Mitchell. "The Breakup of Stereotyped Phrases." *Journal of Ancient Near Eastern Studies of Columbia University* 5 (1973) 83–89.
———. "New Readings in Lamentations." *Bib* 59 (1978) 174–97.
———. *Psalms.* 3 vols. AB 16, 17, 17A. Garden City, NY: Doubleday, 1965, 1968, 1970.
Dalglish, Edward R. *Psalm Fifty-One: In the Light of Ancient Near Eastern Patternism.* Leiden: Brill, 1962.
Davies, Philip R. *Scribes and Schools: The Canonization of the Hebrew Scriptures.* LAI. Louisville: Westminster John Knox, 1998.
Deissler, Alfons. *Psalm 119 (118) und seine Theologie: Ein Beitrag zur Erforschung der anthologischen Stilgattung im Alten Testament.* Munich: Zink, 1955.
———. "Zur Datierung und Situierung der 'kosmischen' Hymnen Pss 8; 19; 29." In *Lex tua veritas: Feschrift für Hubert Junker zur vollendung des siebzigsten Lebensjahres am 8. August 1961, dargeboten von Kollegen, Freunden und Schülern*, edited by Heinrich Gross and Franz Mussner, 47–58. Trier: Paulinus, 1961
Delekat, Lienhard. *Asylie und Schutzorakel am Zionheiligtum.* Leiden: Brill, 1967.
———. "Probleme der Psalmenüberschriften." *ZAW* 76 (1964) 280–97.
———. "Zum hebräischen Wörterbuch." *VT* 14 (1964) 7–66.
Dell, Katharine. "A Cultic Setting for Wisdom Psalms?" *VT* 54 (2004) 445–58.
Diebner, Bernd-Jörg. 1985. "Gottesdienst II: Altes Testament." In *Theologische Realenzyklopädie*, edited by Claus-Jürgen Thornton, 14:5–28. Berlin: de Gruyter, 1985.
Díez Macho, Alejandro. "La homonimia o Paronomasia." *Sefarad* 8 (1948) 293–321; 9 (1949) 269–309.
Dommershausen, Werner. "כנף *kanap*." In *ThWAT* 4 (1984) 243–46. = *TDOT* 7 (1995).
Draffkorn-Kilmer, Anne. "The Cult Song with Music from Ancient Ugarit." *Revue archéologique* 68 (1974) 69–82.
Drijvers, Pius. *Over de Psalmen.* Utrecht: Spectrum, 1956.
———. *The Psalms: Their Structure and Meaning.* New York: Herder & Herder, 1965.
Driver, G. R. *Canaanite Myths and Legends.* Old Testament Studies 3. Edinburgh: T. & T. Clark, 1956.
———. "The Psalms in the Light of Babylonian Research." In *The Psalmists*, edited by D. C. Simpson, 109–75. London: Oxford University Press, 1926.
Dryburgh, Bob. *Lessons for Lovers in the Song of Solomon.* New Canaan, CT: Keats, 1975.
Dubarle, André M. "L'amour humain dans le Cantique des Cantiques." *RB* 61 (1954) 67–86.
Duhm, Bernhard. *Die Psalmen.* 2nd ed. Kurzer Hand-commentar zum Alten Testament 14. Tübingen: Mohr Siebeck, 1922.
Durkheim, Émile. *The Elementary Forms of the Religious Life.* Translated by J. W. Swain. New York: Macmillan, 1915.
———. *Les formes elementaries de la vie religieuse.* Paris: Alcan, 1912.

Ebeling, Erich. *Die akkadische Gebetsserie "Handerhebung."* Veröffentlichung Deutsche Akademie der Wissenschaften zu Berlin. Institut für Orientforschung 20. Berlin: Akademie, 1953.

Edsman, Carl-Martin. "Zum sakralen Königtum in der Forschung der letzten hundert Jahre." In *The Sacral Kingship / La Regalita Sacra: Contributions to the Central Theme of the VIIIth International Congress for the History of Religions (Rome, April 1955)*, 3–17. Numen Book Series 4. Leiden: Brill, 1959.

Eibl-Eibesfeldt, Irenäus. *Grundriss der vergleichenden Verhaltensforschung: Ethologie.* Munich: Piper, 1967. 7th ed., 1987.

Eichrodt, Walther. *Theologie des Alten Testaments.* 3 vols. 1933–1939. 6th ed. Leipzig: Hinrichs, 1959.

———. *Theology of the Old Testament.* 3 vols. in 2. Translated by J. A. Baker. Old Testament Library. Philadelphia: Westminster, 1961–1967.

Eliade, Mircea. *The Myth of the Eternal Return.* Translated by W. R. Trask. New York: Pantheon, 1954. Reprinted as *Cosmos and History.* New York: Harper Torchbooks, 1959.

———. *Le Mythe de l'éternel retour.* Paris: Gallimard, 1949.

Engnell, Ivan. *Studies in Divine Kingship in the Ancient Near East.* Uppsala: Almqvist & Wiksell, 1943. 2nd ed. Oxford: Blackwell, 1967.

Evans-Pritchard, E. E. *Nuer Religion.* Oxford: Clarendon, 1956.

———. *Social Anthropology.* 2nd ed. New York: Free Press, 1966.

Falkenstein, Adam, and Wolfram von Soden. *Sumerische und akkadische Hymnen und Gebete.* Die Bibliothek der alten Welt: Der alte Orient. Zurich: Artemis, 1953.

Fensham, F. C. "Psalm 21—A Covenant Song?" *ZAW* 77 (1965) 193–205.

Feuillet, Andre. *Le Cantique des Cantiques.* Paris: Cerf, 1953.

Fischer, Balthasar. "Christliches Psalmenverständnis im 2. Jahrhundert." *BibLeb* 3 (1962) 111–19.

Fohrer, Georg. *Introduction to the Old Testament.* Initiated by Ernst Sellin. Translated by David Green. Nashville: Abingdon, 1968.

———. "Über den Kurzvers." *ZAW* 66 (1954) 199–236.

Fortune, R. F. *Sorcerers of Dobu: The Social Anthropology of the Dobu Islanders of the Western Pacific.* New York: Dutton, 1932.

Frankfort, Henri, ed. *Kingship and the Gods: A Study of Ancient Near Eastern Religion as the Integration of Society & Nature.* Chicago: University of Chicago Press, 1948.

Frazer, James George. *The Golden Bough: A Study in Magic and Religion.* 3rd ed. 12 vols. New York: Macmillan, 1911–1915.

Frechette, Christopher G. *Mesopotamian Ritual-Prayers of "Hand-lifting" (Akkadian Šuillas): An Investigation of Function in the Light of the Idiomatic Meaning of the Rubric.* AOAT 379. Münster: Ugarit-Verlag, 2012.

Freedman, David N. "Acrostics and Metrics in Hebrew Poetry." *HTR* 65 (1972) 367–92.

———. "Pottery, Poetry and Prophecy." *JBL* 96 (1972) 5–26.

Fretheim, Terence E. "Psalm 132: A Form-Critical Study." *JBL* 86 (1967) 289–300.

Gaster, T. H. "Psalm 45." *JBL* 74 (1955) 239–51.

———. *Thespis: Ritual, Myth, and Drama in the Ancient Near East.* New York: Schuman, 1950; 2nd ed., Garden City, NY: Doubleday, 1961.

Gemser, Berend. "Gesinnungsethik im Psalter." *Oudtestamentische Studiën* 13 (1963) 1–20.

Gennep, Arnold van. *Rites de passage.* Paris: Nourry, 1909.

———. *Rites of Passage.* Translated by Monika B. Vizedom and Gabrielle L. Caffee. Introduction by Solon T. Kimball. Chicago: University of Chicago Press, 1960.

Gerstenberger, Erhard S. "Der bittende Mensch." Habil. diss., University of Heidelberg, 1971.

———. *Der bittende Mensch: Bittritual und Klagelied des Einzelnen im Alten Testament.* WMANT 51. Neukirchen-Vluyn: Neukirchener, 1980. Reprint, Eugene, OR: Wipf & Stock, 2010.

———. "Canon Criticism and the Meaning of 'Sitz im Leben.'" In *Canon, Theology, and Old Testament Interpretation: Essays in Honor of Brevard S. Childs,* edited by Gene M. Tucker et al., 20–31. Philadelphia: Fortress, 1988.

———. "Conflicting Theologies in the Old Testament." *Horizons in Biblical Theology* 22 (2000) 120–34.

———. "Covenant and Commandment." *JBL* 84 (1965) 38–51.

———. "Enemies and Evildoers in the Psalms." *Horizons in Biblical Theology* 4 (1982) 61–77.

———. "'Höre, mein Volk, lass mich reden!' (Ps 50,7)." *Bibel und Kirche* 56 (2001) 21–25.

———. *Israel in der Perserzeit: 5. und 4. Jahrhundert v. Chr.* Biblische Enzyklopädie 8. Stuttgart: Kohlhammer, 2005.

———. *Israel in the Persian Period: The Fifth and Fourth Centuries B.C.E.* Translated by Siegfried S. Schatzmann. Biblical Encyclopedia 8. Atlanta: Society of Biblical Literature, 2011.

———. *Jahwe: Ein patriarchaler Gott? Traditionelles Gottesbild und feministische Theologie.* Stuttgart: Kohlhammer, 1988.

———. "Jeremiah's Complaints. Observations on Jer 14:10–21." *JBL* 82 (1963) 393–408.

———. "Literatur zu den Psalmen." *VuF* 17 (1972) 82–99.

———. "The Lyrical Literature." In *The Hebrew Bible and Its Modern Interpreters,* edited by Douglas A. Knight and Gene M. Tucker, 409–44. The Bible and Its Modern Interpreters 1. Philadelphia: Fortress, 1985. [**Chapter 1 in this volume.**]

———. "Modes of Communication with the Divine in the Hebrew Psalter." In *Mediating between Heaven and Earth: Communication with the Divine in the Ancient Near East,* edited by C. L. Crouch et al., 93–113. LHBOTS 566. London: T. & T. Clark, 2012. [**Chapter 5 in this volume.**]

———. "Non-Temple Psalms: Their Cultic Setting Revisited." In *The Oxford Handbook of the Psalms,* edited by William P. Brown, 338–49. Oxford Handbooks. Oxford: Oxford University Press, 2014. [**Chapter 7 in this volume.**]

———. "Praise in the Realm of Death: The Dynamics of Hymn-Singing in Ancient Near Eastern Lament Ceremonies." In *Lamentations in Ancient and Contemporary Cultural Contexts,* edited by Nancy C. Lee and Carleen Mandolfo, 115–24. SBL Symposium Series 43. Atlanta: Society of Biblical Literature, 2008.

———. "Psalm 12: Gott hilft den Unterdrückten." In *Anwalt des Menschen: Beiträge aus Theologie und Religionspädagogik: Zum Gedenken an Prof. Dr. Friedrich Hahn,* edited by Bernhard Jenndorff and Gerhard Schmalenberg, 82–104. Giessener Schriften zur Theologie und Religionspädagogik des Fachbereichs Religionswissenschaften der Justus-Liebig Universität 2. Giessen: Religionswissenschaften der Justus-Liebig Universität, 1983.

———. "Psalmen und Ritualpraxis." In *Ritual und Poesie: Formen und Orte religiöser Dichtung im Alten Orient, im Judentum und im Christentum*, edited by Erich Zenger et al., 73–90. Freiburg: Herder 2003. [**Translated as Chapter 6 in this volume.**]

———. "Psalms." In *Old Testament Form 0Criticism*, edited by John H. Hayes, 179–223. Trinity University Monograph Series in Relgion 2. San Antonio: Trinity University Press, 1974. [**Chapter 2 in this volume.**]

———. "The Psalms: Genres, Life Situations, and Theologies—Towards a Hermeneutics of Social Stratification." In *Diachronic and Synchronic: Reading the Psalms in Real Time. Proceedings of the Baylor Symposium on the Book of Psalms*, edited by Joel S. Burnett et al., 81–92. LHBOTS 488. New York: T. & T. Clark, 2007. [**Chapter 3 in this volume.**]

———. *Psalms, Part 1: With an Introduction to Cultic Poetry*. FOTL 14. Grand Rapids: Eerdmans, 1988.

———. *Psalms, Part 2, and Lamentations*. FOTL 15. Grand Rapids: Eerdmans, 2001.

———. "The Psalter." In *The Blackwell Companion to the Hebrew Bible*, edited by Leo G. Perdue, 402–17. Blackwell Companions to Religion 3. Oxford: Blackwell, 2001.

———. "Der Psalter als Buch und als Sammlung." In *Neue Wege der Psalmenforschung: Für Walter Beyerlin*, edited by Klaus Seybold and Erich Zenger, 2–12. Herders Biblische Studien 1. 2nd ed. Freiburg: Herder, 1994. [**Translated as Chapter 8 in this volume.**]

———. "Singing a New Song: On Old Testament and Latin American Psalmody." *Word & World* 5 (1985) 155–67.

———. "Social Sciences and Form-Criticism: Towards the Generative Force of Life-Settings."' In *Relating to the Text: Interdisciplinary and Form-Critical Insights on the Bible*, edited by Timothy J. Sandoval and Carleen Mandolfo, 84–99. JSOTSup 384. London: T. & T. Clark, 2003.

———. *Theologie des Lobens in sumerischen Hymnen: Zur Ideengeschichte der Eulogie*. Orientalische Religionen in der Antike: Ägypten, Israel, Alter Orient 28. Tübingen: Mohr Siebeck, 2018.

———. *Theologien im Alten Testament: Pluralität und Synkretismus alttestamentlichen Gottesglaubens*. Stuttgart: Kohlhammer, 2001.

———. "Theologies in the Book of Psalms." In *The Book of Psalms: Composition and Reception*, edited by Peter W. Flint and Patrick D. Miller Jr., 603–25. VTSup 99. Leiden: Brill, 2005. [**Chapter 4 in this volume.**]

———. *Theologies in the Old Testament*. Translated by John Bowden. Minneapolis: Fortress, 2002.

———. "Topographie des Betens." *Zeitschrift für Gottesdienst und Predigt* 19.3 (2001) 3–6.

———. "Weibliche Spiritualität in Psalmen und Hauskult." In *Ein Gott allein? JHWH-Verehrung und biblischer Monotheismus im Kontext der israelitischen und altorientalischen Religionsgeschichte*, edited by Walter Dietrich and Martin A. Klopfenstein, 349–63. OBO 139. Göttingen: Vandenhoeck & Ruprecht, 1994.

———. *Yahweh the Patriarch: Ancient Images of God and Feminist Theology*. Translated by Frederick J. Gaiser. Minneapolis: Fortress, 1996. Reprint, Eugene, OR: Wipf & Stock, 2021.

———. "Zur alttestamentlichen Weisheit." *VuF* 14 (1969) 28–44.

———. "Zur Interpretation der Psalmen." *VuF* 19 (1974) 22–45.

Gerstenberger, Erhard S., and Ulrich Schoenborn, eds. *Hermeneutik—sozialgeschichtlich: Kontextuälitat in den Bibelwissenschaften aus der Sicht (latein)amerikanischer und europäischer Exegetinnen und Exegeten.* Exegese in unserer Zeit 1. Münster: Lit-Verlag, 1999.

Gese, Hartmut. "Die Entstehung der Büchereinleitung des Psalters." In *Wort, Lied, und Gottesspruch: Festschrift für Joseph Ziegler,* edited by J. Schreiner, 57–64. Forschung zum Bibel 1–2. Würzburg: Echter, 1972. Reprinted in *Vom Sinai zum Zion,* 159–67.

———. "Zur Geschichte der Kultsänger am zweiten Temple." In *Abraham unser Vater: Juden und Christen im Gespräch über die Bibel. Festschrift für Otto Michel zum 60. Geburtstag,* edited by O. Betz et al., 222–34. Leiden: Brill, 1963. Reprinted in *Vom Sinai zum Zion,* 147–58.

———. "Psalm 22 und das Neue Testament." *ZTK* n.F. 65 (1968) 1–22. Reprinted in *Vom Sinai zum Zion,* 180–201.

———. *Vom Sinai zum Zion: Alttestamentliche Beiträge zur biblischen Theologie.* Beiträge zur Evangelischen Theologie 64. Munich: Kaiser, 1974.

Gevirtz, Stanley. *Patterns in the Early Poetry of Israel.* Studies in Ancient Oriental Civilization 32. Chicago: University of Chicago Press, 1963. 2nd ed. 1973.

Gill, Sam. *Native American Religious Action: A Performance Approach to Religion.* Studies in Comparative Religion. Columbia: University of South Carolina Press, 1987.

———. "No Place to Stand: Jonathan Z. Smith as *Homo Ludens.* The Academic Study of Religion *Sub Specie Ludi.*" *Journal of the American Academy of Religion* 66 (1998) 283–312.

Ginsberg, H. L. "A Phoenician Hymn in the Psalter." In *Atti del XIX. Congresso Internazionale degli Orientalisti Roma-1935,* 472–76. Rome: Bardi, 1938.

———. "Some Emendations in Psalms." *HUCA* 23 (1950–51) 97–104.

Globe, Alexander. "The Literary Structure and Unity of the Song of Deborah." *JBL* 93 (1974) 493–512.

Goldingay, John. "Repetition and Variation in the Psalms." *Jewish Quarterly Review* 68 (1977–78) 146–51.

Good, E. M. Review of *Formula Criticism and the Poetry of the Old Testament* by William R. Walters. *JBL* 97 (1978) 274–75.

Goodenough, Erwin R. *Jewish Symbols in the Greco-Roman Period.* 13 vols. Princeton: Princeton University Press, 1953–1968.

Gottlieb, Hans. *A Study on the Text of Lamentations.* Acta Jutlandica 48. Aarhus: Aarhus University Press, 1978.

Gottwald, Norman K. *The Hebrew Bible: A Socio-Literary Introduction.* Philadelphia: Fortress, 1985.

———. "Poetry, Hebrew." In *IDB* 3:829–38.

———. *Studies in the Book of Lamentations.* 2nd ed. SBT 1/37. London: SCM, 1962.

Gray, George Buchanan. *The Forms of Hebrew Poetry.* 2nd ed. New York: Ktav, 1972.

Gray, John. "A Cantata of the Autumn Festival: Psalm LXVIII." *JSS* 22 (1977) 2–26.

———. "The Kingship of God in the Prophets and Psalms." *VT* 11 (1961) 1–29.

Griffin, Emory A. *A First Look at Communication Theory.* 7th ed. New York: McGraw Hill, 2009. 10th ed., 2019.

Griffin-Pierce, Trudy. 1992. *Earth Is My Mother, Sky is My Father: Space, Time, and Astronomy in Navajo Sandpainting*. Albuquerque: University of New Mexico Press, 1992.

Grimes, Ronald L. *Beginnings in Ritual Studies*. Washington, DC: University Press of America, 1982. Rev. ed., Studies in Comparative Religion. Columbia: University of South Carolina Press, 1995.

———. "Ritual Studies." In *Encyclopedia of Religion*, edited by Mircea Eliade, 12:422–25. New York: Macmillan, 1987.

Gunkel, Hermann. *Die Psalmen*. 4th ed. HKAT II/2. Göttingen: Vandenhoeck & Ruprecht, 1926.

Gunkel, Hermann, and Joachim Begrich. *Einleitung in die Psalmen: Die Gattungen der religiösen Lyrik Israels*. HKATErg. Göttingen: Vandenhoeck & Ruprecht, 1933.

———. *Introduction to Psalms: The Genres of the Religious Lyric of Israel*. Translated by James D. Nogalski. Macon, GA: Mercer University Press, 1998. Reprint, Eugene, OR: Wipf & Stock, 2020.

Haïk Vantoura, Suzanne H. *La musique de la bible revelee: une notation millénaire décryptée*. 2nd ed. Paris: Dessain et Tolra, 1978.

Halbe, Jörn. "Passa-Massot im deuteronomischen Festkalender." *ZAW* 87 (1975) 147–68.

Hallo, W. W. "Individual Prayer in Sumerian." *JAOS* 88 (1968) 71–89.

Haran, Menahem. *Temple and Temple Service in Ancient Israel: An Inquiry into Biblical Cult*. Oxford: Clarendon, 1978. Reprint, Winona Lake, IN: Eisenbrauns, 1995.

Hartenstein, Friedhelm. *Das Angesicht JHWHs: Studien zu seinem höfischen und kultischen Bedeutungshintergrund in den Psalmen und in Exodus 32–34*. Forschungen zum Alten Testament 55. Tübingen: Mohr Siebeck, 2008.

Heeßel, Nils P. *Babylonisch-assyrische Diagnostik*. AOAT 43 Münster: Ugarit-Verlag, 2000.

Heiler, Friedrich. *Das Gebet: Eine religionsgeschichtliche und religionspsychologische Untersuchung*. Munich: Reinhardt, 1923.

———. *Prayer: A Study in the History and Psychology of Religion*. Edited and translated by Samuel McComb. London: Oxford University Press, 1932.

Hengel, Martin. *Judaism and Hellenism: Studies in Their Encounter in Palestine during the Early Hellenistic Period*. 2 vols. Translated by John Bowden. Philadelphia: Fortress, 1974. Reprint, Eugene, OR: Wipf & Stock, 2003.

———. *Judentum und Hellenismus: Studien zu ihrer Begegnung unter besonderer Berücksichtigung Palästinas bis zur Mitte des 2. Jh.s v. Chr.* WUNT 10. Tübingen: Mohr Siebeck, 1969.

Herkenne, Heinrich. *Das Buch der Psalmen*. Bonn: Hanstein, 1936.

Hermisson, Hans-Jürgen. *Sprache und Ritus im altisraelitischen Kult*. WMANT 19. Neukirchen: Neukirchener, 1965.

———. *Studien zur israelitischen Spruchweisheit*. WMANT 28. Neukirchen-Vluyn: Neukirchener, 1968.

Hillers, Delbert R. *Lamentations*. AB 7A. Garden City, NY: Doubleday, 1972.

Holladay, William L. *Jeremiah: Spokesman out of Time*. Philadelphia: United Church, 1974.

Homan, M. J. "A Comparative Study of the Psalter in the Light of 11 QPsa." *Westminster Theological Journal* 40 (1977–78) 116–29.

Hooke, S. H., ed. *The Labyrinth*. London: Oxford University Press, 1935.

———, ed. *Myth and Ritual*. London: Oxford University Press, 1933.

———, ed. *Myth, Ritual, and Kingship*. London: Oxford University Press, 1958.

Horst, Friedrich. "Die Kennzeichen der hebräischen Poesie." *TRu* 21 (1953) 97–121.

Hossfeld, Frank-Lothar, and Erich Zenger. *Psalmen 1–50*. Neue Echter Bibel: Altes Testament 29. Würzburg: Echter, 1993.

———. *Psalmen 51–100*. 2nd ed. Herders Theologischer Kommentar zum Alten Testament. Freiburg: Herder, 2001.

———. *Psalms 2: A Commentary on Psalms 51–100*. Translated by Linda M. Maloney. Hermeneia. Minneapolis: Fortress, 2005.

———. *Psalms 3: A Commentary on Psalms 101–150*. Translated by Linda M. Maloney. Hermeneia. Minneapolis: Fortress, 2011.

———. "'Selig, wer auf die Armen achtet' (Ps 41,2): Beobachtungen zur Gottesvolk-Theologie des ersten Davidpsalters." *Jahrbuch für Bibel und Theologie* 7 (1992) 21–50.

Iser, Wolfgang. *How to Do Theory*. How to Study Literature. Malden, MA: Blackwell, 2006.

Jacobson, Diane. "Wisdom Language in the Psalms." In *The Oxford Handbook of the Psalms*, edited by William P. Brown, 147–60. Oxford Handbooks. Oxford: Oxford University Press, 2014.

Jahnow, Hedwig. *Das hebräische Leichenlied im Rahmen der Völkerdichtung*. BZAW 36. Giessen: Töpelmann, 1923.

Jennings, Theodore W. "On Ritual Knowledge." *Journal of Religion* 62 (1982) 111–27.

Jeremias, Jörg. *Theophanie: Die Geschichte einer alttestamentlichen Gattung*. WMANT 10. Neukirchen-Vluyn: Neukirchener, 1965. 2nd ed., 1977.

Johnson, Aubrey R. *The Cultic Prophet and Israel's Psalmody*. Cardiff: University of Wales Press, 1979.

———. "Divine Kingship and the Old Testament." *Expository Times* 62 (1950/51) 36–42.

———. "The Psalms." In *The Old Testament and Modern Study*, edited by H. H. Rowley, 162–209. London: Oxford University Press, 1951.

———. *Sacral Kingship in Ancient Israel*. Cardiff: University of Wales Press, 1955. 2nd ed., 1967.

Kant, Immanuel. *Critique of Pure Reason*. Edited and translated by Marcus Weigelt. Rev. ed. Penguin Classics. London: Penguin, 2008.

———. *Kritik der reinen Vernunft*. Edited by Raymund Schmidt. Leipzig: Reclam, 1924.

Kapelrud, A. S. "Scandinavian Research in the Psalms after Mowinckel." *Annual of the Swedish Theological Institute* 4 (1965) 74–90.

———. "Die skandinavische Einleitungswissenschaft zu den Psalmen." *VuF* 11 (1966) 62–93

Kayser, Wolfgang. *Das sprachliche Kunstwerk*. 6th ed. Bonn: Franche, 1960.

Kedar-Kopfstein, Benjamin. "קרן *qrn*." In *ThWAT* 7 (1993) 181–89 = *TDOT* 13 (2004).

Keel, Othmar. *Feinde und Gottesleugner: Studien zum Image der Widersacher in den Individualpsalmen*. Stuttgarter biblische Monographien 7. Stuttgart: Katholisches Bibelwerk, 1969.

———. *The Symbolism of the Biblical World: Ancient Near Eastern Iconography and the Books of Psalms*. Translated by Timothy J. Hallett. New York: Seabury, 1978. Reprint, Winona Lake, IN: Eisenbrauns, 1997.

———. *Die Welt der altorientalischen Bildsymbolik und das Alte Testament, am Beispiel der Psalmen*. Neukirchen-Vluyn: Neukirchener, 1972.

Keet, C. C. *A Study of the Psalms of Ascent*. London: Mitre, 1969.
Kippenberg, Hans G. *Religion und Klassenbildung im antiken Judäa: Eine religionssoziologische Studie zum Verhältnis von Tradition und gesellschaftlicher Entwicklung*. Studien zur Umwelt des Neuen Testaments 14. Göttingen: Vandenhoeck & Ruprecht, 1978.
Kittel, Rudolf. *Die Psalmen*. 5–6th ed. Kommentar zum Alten Testament 13. Leipzig: Scholl, 1929.
Klatt, Werner. *Hermann Gunkel: Zu seiner Theologie der Religionageschichte und zur Entstehung der formgeschichtlichen Methode*. FRLANT 100. Göttingen: Vandenhoeck & Ruprecht, 1969.
Kluckhohn, Clyde. "Myths and Rituals: A General Theory." *HTR* 3 (1942) 45–79.
Knuth, Hans Christian. *Zur Auslegungsgeschichte von Psalm 6*. Beiträge zur Geschichte der Biblischen Exegese 11. Tübingen: Mohr Siebeck, 1971.
Koch, Klaus. "Denn seine Güte währet ewiglich." *Evangelische Theologie* 21 (1961) 531–44.
———. "Tempeleinlassliturgien und Dekaloge." In *Studien zur Theologie der alttestamentlichen Überlieferungen*, edited by Rolf Rendtorff, 45–60. Neukirchen-Vluyn: Neukirchener, 1961.
Kolari, E. *Musikinstrumente und ihre Verwendung im Alten Testament*. Helsinki: Suomalaisen Kirjallisuuden Seuran Kirjapainon Oy, 1947.
Kosmala, Hans. "Form and Structure in Ancient Hebrew Poetry." *VT* 14 (1964) 423–45; 16 (1966) 152–80.
Kramer, Samuel N. *The Sacred Marriage Rite*. Bloomington: Indiana University Press, 1969.
———. "Sumerian Literature." In *The Bible and the Ancient Near East: Essays in Honor of William Foxwell Albright*, edited by G. Ernest Wright, 249–66. Garden City, NY: Doubleday, 1961.
Kraus, Hans-Joachim. *Gottesdienst in Israel*. 2nd ed. Munich: Kaiser, 1962.
———. *Klagelieder*. BKAT 20. Neukirchen-Vluyn: Neukirchener, 1956.
———. *Die Königsherrschaft Gottes im Alten Testament*. Beiträge zur historischen Theologie 13. Tübingen: Mohr Siebeck, 1951.
———. *Psalmen*. 2 vols. BKAT 15/1–2. 5th ed. Neukirchen-Vluyn: Neukirchener, 1978.
———. *Psalms 1–59: A Commentary*. Translated by Hilton C. Oswald. Continental Commentaries. Minneapolis: Augsburg, 1988.
———. *Psalms 60–150: A Commentary*. Translated by Hilton C. Oswald. Continental Commentaries. Minneapolis: Augsburg, 1989.
———. *Theologie der Psalmen*. BKAT 15/3. Neukirchen-Vluyn: Neukirchener, 1979.
———. *Theology of the Psalms*. Translated by Keith Crim. Continental Commentaries. Minneapolis: Augsburg, 1986.
———. *Worship in Israel*. Translated by G. Buswell. Richmond: John Knox, 1966.
Krecher, J. *Sumerische Kultlyrik*. Wiesbaden: Harrassowitz, 1966.
Krinetzki, L. "Zur Poetik und Exegese von Psalm 48." *Biblische Zeitschrift* 4 (1960) 70–97.
Kunz, L. "Zur Liedgestalt der ersten fünf Psalmen." *Biblische Zeitschrift* 7 (1963) 261–70.
Kurz, Paul K., ed. *Psalmen vom Expressionismus bis zur Gegenwart*. Freiburg: Herder, 1978.

Kutsch, Ernst. "Erwägungen zur Geschichte der Passahfeier und des Massotfestes." *ZTK* 55 (1958) 1–35.

Lambert, W. G. *Babylonian Creation Myths*. Mesopotamian Civilizations 16. Winona Lake, IN: Eisenbrauns, 2014.

———. *Babylonian Wisdom Literature*. Oxford: Clarendon, 1960.

Lambert, W. G., and S. B. Parker. *Enuma eliš: The Babylonian Epic of Creation. The Cuneiform Text*. Oxford: Clarendon, 1966.

Lanczkowski, G. "Iranische Religionen." In *Theologische Realenzyklopädie*, edited by Claus-Jürgen Thornton, 16:249–50. Berlin: de Gruyter, 1987.

Lang, Bernhard, ed. *Der einzige Gott? Die Geburt des biblischen Monotheismus*. Munich: Kösel, 1981.

———. "Ritual/Ritus." In *Handbuch religionswissenschaftlicher Grundbegriffe*, edited by Hubert Cancik et al., 4:442–58. Stuttgart: Kohlhammer, 1998.

Leslie, Elmer A. *The Psalms: Translated and Interpreted in the Light of Hebrew Life and Worship*. Nashville: Abingdon, 1949.

Leveen, Jacob. "Textual Problems in the Psalms." *VT* 21 (1971) 48–58.

Levy-Bruhl, Lucien. *Les fonctions mentales dans les sociétés inférieurs*. Paris: Alcan, 1910.

———. *How Natives Think*. Translated by Lilian A. Clare. Human Relations Collection. London: Allen & Unwin, 1926.

Ley, Julius. *Grundzüge des Rhythmus: Des Vers- und Strophenbaues in der hebräischen Poesie. nebst Analyse einer Auswahl von Psalmen und anderen strophischen Dichtungen der verschiedenen Vers- und Strophenarten mit vorangehendem Abriss der Metrik der hebräischen Poesie*. Halle: Waisenhauses, 1885.

Liebreich, Leon J. "Psalm 34 and 145 in the Light of Their Key Words." *HUCA* 27 (1956) 181–92.

Lipinski, Edouard. *La liturgie penitentielle dans la Bible*. Lectio Divina 52. Paris: Cerf, 1969.

———. *Le Poeme royal du Psaume LXXXIX, 1–5, 20–38*. Cahiers de la Revue biblique 6. Paris: Gabalda, 1967.

———. *La royaute de Yahwe dans la poesie et le cult de l'ancien Israel*. Verhandelingen van de Koninklijke Vlaamse Academie voor Wetenschappen, Letteren en Schone Kunsten van België, Klasse der Letteren, jaarg. 27, nr. 55. Brussels: Paleis der Academien, 1965.

Littmann, Enno. *Abessinische Klagelieder: Alte Weisen in neuer Gewandung*. Tübingen: Mohr Siebeck, 1949.

Lohfink, Norbert. "Psalmengebet und Psalterredaktion." *Archiv für Liturgiewissenschaft* 34 (1992) 1–22.

———. "Der Psalter und die christliche Meditation: Die Bedeutung der Endredaktion für das Verständnis des Psalters." *Bibel und Kirche* 47 (1992) 195–200.

———. "Was wird anders bei kanonischer Schriftauslegung?" *Jahrbuch für biblische Theologie* 3 (1988) 29–53.

Long, Burke O. "The Divine Funeral Lament." *JBL* 85 (1966) 85–86.

Loretz, Oswald. "Nekromantie und Totenevokation in Mesopotamien, Ugarit und Israel." In *Religionsgeschichtliche Beziehungen zwischen Kleinasien, Nordsyrien und dem Alten Testament*, edited by Bernd Janowski et al., 285–315. OBO 129. Göttingen: Vandenhoeck & Ruprecht, 1993.

———. *Die Psalmen*. Vol. 2: *Beiträge der Ugarit-Texte zum Verständnis von Kolometrie und Textologie der Psalmen: Psalm 90–150*. AOAT 207/2. Neukirchen-Vluyn: Neukirchener, 1979.

———. "Die Teraphim als 'Ahnen- Götter-Figur(in)en.'" *Ugarit-Forschungen* 24 (1993) 133–78.

Lys, Daniel. "Une histoire d'amour." *Foi et Vie* 75 (1976) 48–61.

Mand, Fritzlothar. "Die Eigenständigkeit des Danklieder des Psalters als Bekenntnislieder." *ZAW* 70 (1958) 185–99.

Mansoor, Menahem. *The Thanksgiving Hymns. Studies in the Texts of the Desert of Judah* 3. Leiden: Brill, 1961.

Maul, Stefan M. *Zukunftsbewältigung: Eine Untersuchung altorientalischen Denkens anhand der babylonisch-assyrischen Löserituale (Namburbi)*. Baghdader Forschungen 18. Mainz: von Zabern, 1994.

Mauss, Marcel. "Essai sur le don: Forme et raison de l'echange dans les societies archaiques." *L'Annee Sociologique* 1 (1923–24) 30–186.

———. *The Gift: The Form and Reason for Exchange in Archaic Societies*. Translated by W. D. Halls. Routledge Classics. New York: Routledge, 2002.

Mayer, Werner R. *Untersuchung zur Formensprache der babylonischen "Gebetsbeschwörungen."* Studia Pohl: Series Maior 5. Rome: Pontifical Biblical Institute, 1976.

McCarthy, Dennis J. *Treaty and Covenant: A Study in Form in the Ancient Oriental Documents and in the Old Testament*. Analecta biblica 21. Rome: Pontifical Biblical Institute, 1963. 2nd ed., 1978.

Melamed, Ezra Z. "Break-up of Stereotype Phrases as an Artistic Device in Biblical Poetry." In *Studies in the Bible*, edited by Chaim Rabin, 115–53. Scripta Hierosolymitana 8. Jerusalem: Magnes, 1961.

Mendenhall, George E. "Ancient Oriental and Biblical Law." *Biblical Archaeologist* 17 (1954) 26–46; and "Covenant Forms in Israelite Tradition." *Biblical Archaeologist* 17 (1954) 50–76. Reprinted in *The Biblical Archaeologist Reader III*, edited by Edward F. Campbell and David Noel Freedman, 3–53. Garden City, NY: Doubleday, 1970.

Michel, Diethelm. "Studien zu den sogenannten Thronbesteigungspsalmen." *VT* 6 (1956) 40–68.

———. *Tempora und Satzstellung in den Psalmen*. Abhandlungen zur evangelischen Theologie. Bonn: Bouvier, 1960.

Miller, Patrick D. *The Divine Warrior in Early Israel*. Harvard Semitic Monographs 5. Cambridge: Harvard University Press, 1973.

———. "Kingship, Torah Obedience, and Prayer: The Theology of Psalms 15–24." In *Neue Wege der Psalmenforschung: Für Walter Beyerlin*, edited by Klaus Seybold and Erich Zenger, 127–42. Herders Biblische Studien 1. 2nd ed. Freiburg: Herder, 1994.

———. *They Cried to the Lord: The Form and Theology of Biblical Prayer*. Minneapolis: Fortress, 1994.

Montgomery, James A. "Stanza Formation in Hebrew Poetry." *JBL* 64 (1945) 379–84.

Moor, Johannes C. de. *New Year with Canaanites and Israelites*. 2 vols. Serie Kamper Cahiers 21–22. Kampen: Kok, 1972.

Morgenstern, J. "The Cultic Setting of the Enthronement Psalms." *HUCA* 25 (1964) 1–42.

Mowinckel, Sigmund. *Der achtundsechzigste Psalm*. ANVAO II/1. Oslo: Dybwad, 1953.

———. *Le Decalogue*. Paris: Alcan, 1927.

———. *Han som kommer*. Copenhagen: Gad, 1951.

———. *He That Cometh: The Messiah Concept in the Old Testament and Later Judaism*. Translated by G. W. Anderson. Nashville: Abingdon, 1956. Reprint, with foreword by John J. Collins. Biblical Resource Series. Grand Rapids: Eerdmans, 2005.

———. *Offersang og sangoffer: Salmediktningen i Bibelen*. Oslo: Aschehoug, 1951.

———. *Psalmenstudien*. 6 vols. Kristiania: Dybwad, 1921–1924. Reprinted, Amsterdam: Schippers, 1961.

———. *Psalm Studies*. 2 vols. Translated by Mark E. Biddle. SBL History of Biblical Studies 2, 3. Atlanta: SBL Press, 2014.

———. "Psalms and Wisdom." In *Wisdom in Israel and in the Ancient Near East: Presented to Professor Harold Henry Rowley by the Society for Old Testament Study in Association with the Editorial Board of Vetus Testamentum, in Celebration of His Sixty-fifth Birthday, 24 March 1955*, 205–24. VTSup 3. Leiden: Brill, 1955.

———. *The Psalms in Israel' s Worship*. 2 vols. Translated by D. R. Ap-Thomas. Nashville: Abingdon, 1962. Reprint, with foreword by James L. Crenshaw. Grand Rapids: Eerdmans, 2004.

———. *Real and Apparent Tricola in Hebrew Psalm Poetry*. Oslo: Norske Videnskaps Akademi, 1957. Reprint, Eugene, OR: Wipf & Stock, 2012.

———. *Religion and Cult: The Old Testament and the Phenomenology of Religion*. Edited by K. C. Hanson. Translated by John Sheehan. Eugene, OR: Cascade Books, 2012.

———. *Religion und Kultus*. Göttingen: Vandenhoeck & Ruprecht, 1953.

Muilenburg, James. "A Study in Hebrew Rhetoric." In *Congress Volume: Copenhagen, 1953*, 97–111. VTSup 1. Leiden: Brill, 1953.

Müller, Hans-Peter. "Formgeschichte/Formenkritik I." In *Theologische Realenzyklopädie*, edited by Claus-Jürgen Thornton, 11:271–85. Berlin: de Gruyter, 1983.

———. "Die lyrische Reproduktion des Mythischen im Hohenlied." *ZTK* 73 (1976) 23–41.

Muntingh, Lukas M. "A Few Social Concepts in the Psalms and Their Relation to the Canaanite Residential Area." *Die Outestamentiese Werkgemeenskap in Suid-Afrika* 6 (1963) 48–57.

Murphy, Roland E. "A Consideration of the Classification of Wisdom Psalms." In *Congress Volume: Bonn, 1962*, 156–67. VTSup 9. Leiden: Brill, 1963.

———. "The Interpretation of Old Testament Wisdom Literature." *Interpretation* 23 (1969) 289–301.

———. "Towards a Commentary on the Song of Songs." *CBQ* 39 (1977) 482–96.

Niditch, Susan. *Oral World and Written Word: Ancient Israelite Literature*. LAI. Louisville: Westminster John Knox, 1996.

Niehr, Herbert. "שפט *šapaṭ*." In *ThWAT* 8 (1995) 408–28 = *TDOT* 15 (2006).

Nielsen, Eduard. *Shechem: A Traditio-Historical Investigation*. Copenhagen: Gad, 1955.

Noth, Martin. "God, King, People in the Old Testament." In *The Laws in the Pentateuch and Other Essays*, Translated by D. R. Ap-Thomas, 145–78. Edinburgh: Oliver & Boyd, 1966.

———. "Gott, König, Volk im Alten Testament." *ZTK* 47 (1950) 157–91. Reprinted in *Gesammelte Studien zum Alten Testament*, 188–229. TB 6. Munich: Kaiser, 1957.

Nötscher, Friedrich. *Die Psalmen*. Echterbibel 4. Würzburg: Echter, 1947.

Oesterley, W. O. E. *The Sacred Dance*. London: Cambridge University Press, 1923.

Ortlund, Eric Nels. *Theophany and Chaoskampf: The Interpretation of Theophanic Imagery in the Baal Epic, Isaiah, and the Twelve*. Gorgias Ugaritic Studies 5. Piscataway, NJ: Gorgias, 2010.

Otto, Eckart. *Theologische Ethik des Alten Testament*. Theologische Wissenschaft 3/2. Stuttgart: Kohlhammer, 1994.

Patterson, John. *The Praises of Israel: Studies Literary and Religious in the Psalms*. New York: Scribner, 1950.

Perdue, Leo G., ed. *Families in Ancient Israel*. Family, Religion, and Culture. Louisville: Westminster John Knox, 1997.

———. *Wisdom and Cult: A Critical Analysis of the Views of Cult in the Wisdom Literature of Israel and the Ancient Near East*. SBLDS 30. Missoula, MT: Scholars, 1977.

Perlitt, Lothar. *Bundestheologie im Alten Testament*. WMANT 36. Neukirchen-Vluyn: Neukirchener, 1969.

Piatti, P. T. "I carmi alfabetici della Bibbia: chiave della metrica ebraica?" *Bib* 31 (1950) 281–315, 427–58.

Ploeg, J. P. M. van der. *Psalmen*. 2 vols. Boeken van het Oude Testament 7. Roermond: Romen & Zonen, 1971–75.

Podechard, E. *Le Psautier*. 2 vols. in 3. Lyon: Facultes Catholiques, 1949–54.

Pope, Marvin H. *Song of Songs*. AB 7C. Garden City, NY: Doubleday, 1977.

Porten, Bezalel. *The Elephantine Papyri in English: Three Millennia of Cross-Cultural Continuity and Change*. Documenta et Monumenta Orientis Antiqui 22. Leiden: Brill, 1996.

Posner, Ernst. *Archives in the Ancient World*. Cambridge: Harvard University Press, 1972. Reprint, 2014.

Pröschild, Sibylle. *Das Heilige in der Umbanda: Geschichte, Merkmale und Anziehungskraft einer afro-brasilianischen Religion*. Kontexte 39. Göttingen: Ruprecht, 2009.

Quell, Gottfried. *Das kultische Problem der Psalmen*. Beiträge zur Wissenschaft vom Alten Testament 32. Berlin: Kohlhammer, 1926.

Rad, Gerhard von. "The Form-Critical Problem of the Hexateuch." In *The Problem of the Hexateuch and Other Essays*, 1–78. Translated by E. W. T. Dicken. New York: McGraw-Hill, 1966.

———. *Das formgeschichtliche Problem des Hexateuch*. BWANT IV/26. Stuttgart: Kohlhammer, 1938. Reprinted in *Gesammelte Studien zum Alten Testament*, 9–86. TB 6. Munich: Kaiser, 1958.

———. "'Gerechtigkeit' und 'Leben' in der Kultsprache der Psalmen." 1950. Reprinted in *Gesammelte Studien zum Alten Testament*, 225–47. TB 6. Munich: Kaiser, 1958.

———. *Gesammelte Studien zum Alten Testament*. TB 6. Munich: Kaiser, 1958.

———. "Israel vor Jahwe (Die Antwort Israels)." In *Theologie des Alten Testaments*, 1:352–415. Munich: Kaiser, 1957. ET = "Israel before Yahweh (Israel's Answer)." In *Old Testament Theology*, 1:355–418. Translated by D. M. G. Stalker. New York: Harper, 1962.

———. "The Judean Royal Ritual." In *The Problem of the Hexateuch and Other Essays*, 222–31. Translated by E. W. T. Dicken. New York: McGraw-Hill, 1966.

———. "Das jüdische Königsritual." *Theologische Literaturzeitung* 72 (1947) 211–16. Reprinted, in *Gesammelte Studien*, 205–13.

———. *Old Testament Theology*. Vol. 1: *The Theology of Israel's Historical Traditions*. Translated by D. M. G. Stalker. New York: Harper, 1962. Reprint, with a foreword by Walter Brueggemann. Old Testament Library. Louisville: Westminster John Knox, 2001.

———. *Old Testament Theology*. Vol. 2: *The Theology of Israel's Prophetic Traditions*. Translated by D. M. G. Stalker. New York: Harper, 1965. Reprint, with a foreword by Walter Brueggemann. Old Testament Library. Louisville: Westminster John Knox, 2001.

———. "'Righteousness' and 'Life' in the Cultic Language of the Psalms." In *The Problem of the Hexateuch and Other Essays*, 243–66. Translated by E. W. T. Dicken. New York: McGraw-Hill, 1966.

———. *Theologie des Alten Testament*. Vol. 1: *Die Theologie der geschichtlichen Überlieferungen Israels*. Munich: Kaiser, 1960.

———. *Theologie des Alten Testament*. Vol. 2: *Die Theologie der prophetischen Überlieferungen Israels*, Munich: Kaiser, 1960.

———. *Weisheit in Israel*. Neukirchen-Vluyn: Neukirchener, 1970.

———. *Wisdom in Israel*. Translated by James Martin. Nashville: Abingdon, 1972.

Reichard, Gladys A. *Navajo Religion: A Study of Symbolism*. New York: Pantheon, 1950. 2nd ed., 1963. Reprint, Bollingen Series 18. Princeton: Princeton University Press, 1990.

———. *Prayer: The Compulsive Word*. Monographs of the American Ethnological Society. New York: Augustin, 1944.

Reinelt, Heinz. "Die altorientalische und biblische Weisheit und ihr Einfluss auf den Psalter." PhD diss., University of Freiburg, 1966.

Reventlow, Henning Graf. *Gebet im Alten Testament*. Stuttgart: Kohlhammer, 1986.

———. *Liturgie und prophetisches Ich bei Jeremia*. Gütersloh: Gütersloher, 1963.

———. "Der Psalm 8." *Poetica* 1 (1967) 304–32.

Reynolds, Kent A. *Torah as Teacher: The Exemplary Torah Student in Psalm 119*. VTSup 137. Leiden: Brill, 2010.

Ribeiro, Darcy. *The Civilization Process*. Translated by Betty J. Meggers. Smithsonian Publication 4749. Washington, DC: Smithsonian Institution Press, 1968.

———. *O Processo Civilisatório: Etapas da Evolução Sócio-Cultural*. Estudios de Antropologia da Civilizacao 1. 5th ed. Petropolis: Vozes, 1979.

Ridderbos, Nicolaus H. *Die Psalmen: Stilistische Verfahren und Aufbau mit besonderer Berücksichtigung von Ps 1-41*. Translated by Karl E. Mittring. BZAW 117. Berlin: de Gruyter, 1972.

———. "Psalmen und Kult." In *Zur neueren Psalmenforschung*, edited by Peter H. A. Neumann, 234–79. Darmstadt: Wissenschaftliche Buchgesellschaft, 1976. Dutch original, 1950.

Riede, Peter. *Im Netz des Jägers: Studien zur Feindmetaphorik der Individualpsalmen*. WMANT 85. Neukirchen-Vluyn: Neukirchener, 2000.

Ringgren, Helmer. "Einige Bemerkungen zum LXXIII. Psalm." *VT* 3 (1953) 265–72.

———. *The Faith of the Psalmists*. Translated by the author. Philadelphia: Fortress, 1963. Swedish original, 1957.

Ringgren, Helmer, and B. Johnson. "צדק ṣedeq." In *ThWAT* 6 (1989) 898–924 = *TDOT* 12 (2004).

Ritter, E. K. "Magical-Expert (= ašipu) and Physician (= asû): Notes on Two Complementary Professions in Babylonian Medicine." In *Studies in Honor of Benno Landsberger on His Seventy-fifth Birthday, April 21, 1965*, 299–321. Assyriological Studies 16. Chicago: University of Chicago Press, 1965.

Robertson, David A. *Linguistic Evidence in Dating Early Hebrew Poetry*. SBLDS 3. Missoula, MT: Scholars, 1972.
Robinson, Theodore H. "Hebrew Poetic Form." In *Congress Volume: Copenhagen, 1953*, 128–49. VTSup 1. Leiden: Brill, 1953.
———. *The Poetry of the Old Testament*. London: Duckworth, 1947.
Rowley, H. H. "The Text and Structure of Psalm 2." *JTS* 42 (1941) 143–54.
———. *Worship in Ancient Israel: Its Forms and Meaning*. London: SPCK, 1967. Reprint Eugene, OR: Wipf & Stock, 2010.
Rudolph, Kurt. "Mandäer/Mandäismus." In *Theologische Realenzyklopädie*, edited by Claus-Jürgen Thornton, 22:19–25. Berlin: de Gruyter, 1992.
Rudolph, Wilhelm. *Das Buch Ruth. Das Hohelied. Die Klagelieder*. Kommentar zum Alten Testament 16. Gütersloh: Gütersloher, 1962.
Sabourin, Leopold. *The Psalms: Their Origin and Meaning*. Staten Island, NY: Alba, 1969.
Sanders, James A. *The Dead Sea Psalms Scroll*. Ithaca, NY: Cornell University Press, 1967.
———. "Variorum in the Psalms Scroll (11QPsa)." *HTR* 59 (1966) 83–94.
Säve-Söderbergh, Torgny. *Studies in the Coptic Manichean Psalm-book: Prosody and Mandaean Parallels*. Arbeten utgivna med understöd av Vilhelm Ekmans universitetsfond, Uppsala 55. Uppsala: Almqvist & Wiksell, 1949.
Saydon, Pierre P. "Assonance in Hebrew as a Means of Expressing Emphasis." *Bib* 36 (1955) 36–50, 287–304.
Scharbert, Josef. "Das 'Wir' in den Psalmen auf dem Hintergrund altorientalischen Betens." In *Freude an der Weisung des Herrn: Beiträge zur Theologie der Psalmen: Festgabe zum 70. Geburtstag von Heinrich Gross*, edited by Ernst Haag and Frank-Lothar Hossfeld, 297–325. Stuttgarter biblische Beiträge 13. Stuttgart: Katholisches Bibelwerk, 1986.
Schmid, Hans Heinrich. *Gerechtigkeit als Weltordnung: Hintergrund und Geschichte des alttestamentlichen Gerechtigkeitsbegriffes*. Beiträge zur historischen Theologie 40. Tübingen: Mohr Siebeck, 1968.
Schmid, Herbert. "Jahwe und die Kulttraditionen von Jerusalem." *ZAW* 67 (1955) 168–97.
Schmidt, Hans. *Das Gebet der Angeklagten im Alten Testament*. BZAW 49. Giessen: Töpelmann, 1929.
———. *Die Psalmen*. Handbuch zum Alten Testament 1/15. Tübingen: Mohr Siebeck, 1934.
———. *Die Thronfahrt Jahves am Fest der Jahreswende im alten Israel*. Sammlung gemeinverständlicher Vorträge und Schriften aus dem Gebiet der Theologie und Religionsgeschichte 122. Tübingen: Mohr Siebeck, 1927.
Schmidt, Uta. *Zentrale Randfiguren: Strukturen der Darstellung von Frauen in den Erzählungen der Königebücher*. Gütersloh: Gütersloher, 2003.
Schmidt, Werner Hans. *Königtum Gottes in Ugarit und Israel*. BZAW 80. Berlin: Töpelmann, 1961. 2nd ed., 1966.
Schmökel, Hartmut. *Heilige Hochzeit und Hoheslied*. Abhandlungen für die Kunde des Morgenlandes. Wiesbaden: Steiner, 1956.
Schmuttermayr, Georg. *Psalm 18 und II Sam 22: Studien zu einem Doppeltext. Probleme der Textkritik und Übersetzung und das Palterium Pianum*. Studien zum Alten und Neuen Testament 25. Munich: Kösel, 1971.

Schneekloth, Larry Gilbert. "The Targum of the Song of Songs." PhD diss., University of Wisconsin–Madison, 1977.
Schroer, Silvia. *In Israel gab es Bilder: Nachrichten von darstellender Kunst im Alten Testament*. OBO 74. Göttingen: Vandenhoeck & Ruprecht, 1987.
Sciadini, Patricio. *Salmos do homem contemporaneo*. Rio de Janeiro: Civilizaqao Brasileira, 1978.
Searle, John R. *Speech Acts: An Essay in the Philosophy of Language*. London: Cambridge University Press, 1969.
Segal, Moses H. "The Song of Songs." *VT* 12 (1962) 470–90.
Segert, Stanislav. "Problems of Hebrew Prosody." In *Congress Volume: Oxford, 1959*, 283–91. VTSup 7. Leiden: Brill.
Seux, M.-J. *Hymnes et prieres aux dieux de Babylonie et d' Assyrie*. Littératures anciennes du Proche-Orient 8. Paris: Cerf, 1976.
Seybold, Klaus. *Das Gebet des Kranken im Alten Testament: Untersuchungen zur Bestimmung und Zuordnung der Krankheits- und Heilungspsalmen*. BWANT 99. Stuttgart: Kohlhammer, 1973.
———. "Thesen zur Entstehung der Lieder vom Gottesknecht." *Biblische Notizen* 3 (1977) 33–34.
———. "Das 'Wir' in den Asaph-Psalmen." In *Neue Wege der Psalmenforschung: für Walter Beyerlin*, edited by Klaus Seybold and Erich Zenger, 143–55. Herders biblische Studien 1. Freiburg: Herder, 1994.
Seybold, Klaus, and Erich Zenger, eds. *Neue Wege der Psalmenexegese*. 2nd ed. Herders biblische Studien 1. Freiburg: Herder, 1994.
Shehata, Dahlia. *Musiker und ihr vokales Repertoire: Untersuchungen zu Inhalt und Organisation von Musikerberufen und Liedgattungen in altbabylonischer Zeit*. Göttingener Beiträge zum Alten Orient 3. Göttingen: Göttingen Universitäts-Verlag, 2009.
Sievers, Eduard. *Metrische Studien*. 7 vols. Abhandlungen der Philologisch-historischen klasse der Königl. sächsischen Gesellschaft der Wissenschaften. Leipzig: Teubner, 1901–1919.
Skehan, Patrick W. "Again the Syriac Apocryphal Psalms." *CBQ* 38 (1976) 143–58.
———. "Borrowings from the Psalms in the Book of Wisdom." *CBQ* 10 (1948) 384–97.
———. "Strophic Structure in Ps 72 (71)." *Bib* 40 (1959) 302–8.
———. *Studies in Israelite Poetry and Wisdom*. CBQ Monograph Series 1. Washington, DC: Catholic Biblical Association, 1971.
Smith, Jonathan Z. *To Take Place: Toward Theory in Ritual*. Chicago Studies in the History of Judaism. Chicago: University of Chicago Press, 1987.
Snaith, Norman. *Hymns of the Temple*. London: SCM, 1951.
Soggin, J. A. "Il canto di Debora." *Rendiconto dell' Academia nazionale die Lincei* 8/32 (1977) 97–112.
Spencer, Katherine. *Mythology and Values: An Analysis of Navaho Chantway Myths*. Memoirs of the American Folklore Society 48. Philadelphia: American Folklore Society, 1957.
Staerk, Willi. *Lyrik: Psalmen, Hoheslied und Verwandtes*. 2nd ed. Die Schriften des Alten Testaments III/1, Göttingen: Vandenhoeck & Ruprecht, 1920.
Staiger, Emil. *Grundbegriffe der Poetik*. 2nd ed. Zurich: Atlantis, 1951.
Stamm, J. J. "Ein Vierteljahrhundert Psalmenforschung." *TRu* 23 (1955) 1–68.

Stauder, Wilhelm. *Die Harfen und Leiern Vorderasiens in babylonischer und assyrischer Zeit*. Frankfurt: Bildstelle d. J. W. Goethe-Universität, 1961.
Stegemann, Hartmut. *Die Essener, Qumran, Johannes der Täufer und Jesus: Ein Sachbuch*. Herder Spektrum. Freiburg: Herder, 1993. 4th ed., 1994.
Stolz, Fritz. *Psalmen im nachkultischen Raum*. Theologische Studien 129. Zurich: Theologischer Verlag, 1975.
Sukenik, Eleazer L. *The Dead Sea Scrolls of the Hebrew University*. Oxford: Oxford University Press, 1955.
Talayesva, Don C. *Sun Chief: The Autobiography of a Hopi Indian*. Edited by Leo W. Simmons. New Haven: Yale University Press, 1942. 2nd ed., 2013.
Thieberger, Frederic. *King Solomon*. Oxford: East and West Library, 1947.
Thureau-Dangin, F. *Rituels accadiens*. Paris: Leroux, 1921. Reprint, 1975.
Toorn, Karel van der. *Family Religion in Babylonia, Syria and Israel: Continuity and Change in the Forms of Religious Life*. Studies in the History and Culture of the Ancient Near East 7. Leiden: Brill, 1996.
Towner, W. Sibley. "'Blessed be YHWH' and 'Blessed art thou, YHWH': The Modulation of a Biblical Formula." *CBQ* 30 (1968) 386–99.
Trible, Phyllis. *God and the Rhetoric of Sexuality*. Overtures to Biblical Theology. Philadelphia: Fortress, 1978.
———. "Wisdom Builds a Poem." *JBL* 94 (1975) 509–18.
Tröger, K.-W. "Hermetica." In *Theologische Realenzyklopädie*, edited by Claus-Jürgen Thornton, 18:749–52. Berlin: de Gruyter, 1989.
Tropper, Josef. *Nekromantie: Totenbefragung im Alten Orient und im Alten Testament*. AOAT 223. Neukirchen-Vluyn: Neukirchener, 1989.
Turner, Victor. *The Ritual Process: Structure and Anti-structure*. Lewis Henry Morgan Lecture 1966. Chicago: Aldine, 1969.
Tur-Sinai, Naftali H. "Zum literarischen Charakter des Psalmen." In *Zur neueren Psalmenforschung*, edited by Peter H. A. Neumann, 217–33. Darmstadt: Wissenschaftliche Buchgesellschaft, 1976.
Tylor, Edward B. *Primitive Culture: Researches into the Development of Mythology, Philosophy, Religion, Language, Art, and Custom*. 2 vols. New York: Holt, 1871. 4th ed., 1903.
VanGemeren, W. A. "Oracles of Salvation." In *Cracking Old Testament Codes: A Guide to Interpreting the Literary Genres of the Old Testament*, edited by D. Brent Sandy and Ronald L. Giese, 135–77. Nashville: Broadman & Holman, 1995.
Vaux, Roland de. *Ancient Israel: Its Life and Institutions*. 2 vols. Translated by J. McHugh. New York: McGraw-Hill, 1961.
———. *Les institutions de l'Ancien Testament*. 2 vols. Paris: Cerf, 1960.
Velden, Frank van der. *Psalm 109 und die Aussagen zur Feindschädigung in den Psalmen*. Stuttgarter biblische Beiträge 37. Stuttgart: Katholisches Bibelwerk, 1997.
Volz, Paul. *Das Neujahrsfest Jahwes: Laubhüttenfest*. Sammlung gemeinveständlicher Vorträge und Schriften aus dem Gebiet der Theologie und Religionsgeschichte 67. Tübingen: Mohr Siebeck, 1912.
Vorländer, Hermann. *Mein Gott: Die Vorstellungen vom persönlichen Gott im Alten Orient und im Alten Testament*. AOAT 23. Neukirchen-Vluyn: Neukirchener, 1975.
Wanke, Gunther. *Die Zionstheologie der Korachiten in ihrem traditionsgeschichtlichen Zusammenhang*. BZAW 97. Berlin: Töpelmann, 1966.

Watson, Rebecca Sally. *Chaos Uncreated: A Reassessment of the Theme of Chaos in the Hebrew Bible*. BZAW 341; Berlin: de Gruyter, 2005.
Watters, William R. *Formula Criticism and the Poetry of the Old Testament*. BZAW 138. Berlin: de Gruyter, 1976.
Weir, Cecil J. Mullo. *A Lexicon of Accadian Prayers in the Ritual of Expiation*. London: Oxford University Press, 1934.
Weiser, Artur. "Die Darstellung der Theophanie in den Psalmen und im Festkult." In *Festschrift für Alfred Bertholet zum 80. Geburtstag*, edited by Walter Baumgartner, 513–31. Tübingen: Mohr Siebeck, 1950.
———. *Die Psalmen*. 2 vols. Das Alte Testament Deutsch 14, 15. Göttingen: Vandenhoeck & Ruprecht, 1950.
———. *The Psalms: A Commentary*. Translated by Herbert Hartwell. Old Testament Library. Philadelphia: Westminster, 1962.
Weiss, Meir. "Wege der neuen Dichtungswissenschaft in ihrer Anwendung auf die Psalmenforschung." *Bib* 42 (1961) 255–302. Reprinted in *Zur neueren Psalmenforschung*, edited by Peter H. A. Neumann, 400–451. Darmstadt: Wissenschaftliche Buchgesellschaft, 1976.
Welke-Holtmann, Sigrun. *Die Kommunikation zwischen Frau und Mann: Dialogstrukturen in den Erzähltexten der Hebräischen Bibel*. Exegese in unserer Zeit 13. Münster: Lit-Verlag, 2004.
Wellek, Rene, and Austin Warren. *Theory of Literature*. 3rd ed. New York: Harcourt Brace Jovanovich, 1975.
Werner, Eric. "Music" and "Musical Instruments." In *IDB* 3:457–76.
Westermann, Claus. *Das Loben Gottes in den Psalmen*. 2nd ed. Göttingen: Vandenhoeck & Ruprecht, 1961.
———. *Praise and Lament in the Psalms*. Translated by Keith R. Crim and Richard N. Soulen. Atlanta: John Knox, 1981.
———. *The Praise of God in the Psalms*. Translated by Keith R. Crim. Richmond: John Knox, 1965.
———. *The Psalms: Structure, Content and Message*. Translated by Ralph D. Gehrke. Minneapolis: Augsburg, 1980.
———. *Der Psalter*. 2nd ed. Stuttgart: Calwer, 1967.
———. "Struktur und Geschichte der Klage im Alten Testament." *ZAW* 66 (1954) 44–80.
Wevers, J. W. "A Study in the Form-Criticism of Individual Complaint Psalms." *VT* 6 (1956) 80–96.
Whallon, William. *Formula, Character, and Context: Studies in Homeric, Old English, and Old Testament Poetry*. Publications of the Center for Hellenic Studies. Washington, DC: Center for Hellenic Studies, 1969.
White, John B. *A Study of the Language of Love in the Song of Songs and Ancient Egyptian Poetry*. SBLDS 38. Missoula, MT: Scholars, 1978.
Widengren, Geo. *The Accadian and Hebrew Psalms of Lamentation as Religious Documents: A Comparative Study*. Stockholm: Almqvist & Wiksell, 1936.
———. "Hieros gamos och underjordsvistelse." *Religion och Bibel* 7 (1948) 17–46.
———. *Sakrales Königtum im Alten Testament und im Judentum*. Franz Delitzsch Vorlesung 1952. Stuttgart: Kohlhammer, 1955.
Williams, Neal D. *A Lexicon for the Poetical Books*. Irving, TX: Williams & Watrous, 1977.

Willis, John T. "The Genre of Isaiah 5:1–7." *JBL* 96 (1977) 337–62.

———. "I. Engnell's Contribution to Old Testament Scholarship." *Theologische Zeitschrift* 26 (1970) 385–94.

Wilson, Gerald Henry. *The Editing of the Hebrew Psalter*. SBLDS 76. Chico, CA: Scholars, 1985.

———. "The Shape of the Book of Psalms." *Interpretation* 46 (1992) 129–42.

Winter, Urs. *Frau und Göttin: Exegetische und ikonographische Studien zum weiblichen Gottesbild im alten Israel und in dessen Umwelt*. OBO 53. Göttingen: Vandenhoeck & Ruprecht, 1983.

Wolff, Hans Walter. "Der Aufruf zur Volksklage." *ZAW* 76 (1964) 48–56. Reprinted in *Gesammelte Studien zum Alten Testament*, 392–401. 2nd ed. Theologische Bücherei 22. Munich: Kaiser, 1973.

Würthwein, Ernst. "Erwägungen zu Psalm 73." In *Festschrift für Alfred Bertholet zum 80. Geburtstag*, edited by Walter Baumgartner, 532–49. Tübingen: Mohr Siebeck, 1950. Reprinted in *Wort und Existenz: Studien zum Alten Testament*, 161–78. Göttingen: Vandenhoeck & Ruprecht, 1970.

———. "Zum Verständnis des Hohenliedes." *TRu* 32 (1967) 177–212.

Wyman, Leland C. *Beautyway: A Navajo Ceremonial*. Told by Singer Man. Bollingen Series 53. New York: Pantheon, 1957.

———. *Blessingway*. With Three Versions of the Myth Recorded and Translated from the Navaho by Father Benard Haile O.F.M. Tucson: University of Arizona Press, 1970. Reprint, 2017.

Zenger, Erich. "Die Provokation des 149. Psalms." In *"Ihr Völker alle, klatscht in die Hände!": Festschrift für Erhard S. Gerstenberger zum 65. Geburtstag*, edited by Rainer Kessler et al., 181–94. Exegese in Unserer Zeit 3. Münster: Lit-Verlag, 1997.

———. "Was wird anders bei kanonischer Psalmenauslegung?" In *Ein Gott, eine Offenbarung: Beiträge zur biblischen Exegese, Theologie und Spiritualität: Festschrift für Notker Füglister, OSB, zum 60. Geburtstag*, edited by Friedrich V. Reiterer, 397–413. Würzburg: Echter, 1991.

———. "Zur redaktionsgeschichtlichen Bedeutung der Korachpsalmen." In *Neue Wege der Psalmenforschung: Für Walter Beyerlin*, edited by Klaus Seybold and Erich Zenger, 175–98. Herders Biblische Studien 1. 2nd ed. Freiburg: Herder, 1994.

Zgoll, Annette. "Audienz—Ein Modell zum Verständnis mesopotamischer Handerhebungsrituale: Mit einer Deutung der Novelle vom Armen Mann von Nippur." *Baghdader Mitteilungen* 34 (2005) 181–203.

Zimmerli, Walther. "Zwillingspsalmen." In *Studien zur alttestamentlichen Theologie und Prophetie*, 261–71. TB 51. Munich: Kaiser, 1974.

Zimmern, Heinrich. *Beiträge zur Kenntnis der babylonischen Religion: Die Beschwörungstafeln Šurpu, Ritualtafeln für den Wahrsager, Beschwörer und Sänger*. Assyriologische Bibliothek 12. Leipzig: Hinrichs, 1901. Reprint, Leipzig: Zentralantiquariat der Deutschen Demokratischen Republik, 1975.

Zuesse, Evan M. "Ritual." In *The Encyclopedia of Religion*, edited by Mircea Eliade, 12:405–22. New York: Macmillan, 1987.

# Author Index

Ahlström, Gösta W., 49, 167
Aistleitner, Joseph, 39, 43, 64, 167
Albertz, Rainer, 21, 29–30, 94, 110, 139, 167
Albrektson, Bertil, 4, 14, 167
Albright, W. F., 3, 12, 17, 19, 29, 58, 167
Alonso Schökel, Luis, 5–6, 8–10, 16, 20, 167
Alt, Albrecht, xi, 92
Anderson, Bernhard W., 29, 167
Anderson, G. W., 49, 167
Ap-Thomas, D. R., 31, 168
Arens, Anton, 30, 44, 168
Asensio, Felix, 26, 168
Audet, Jean-Paul, 14, 168
Austin, J. L., 125, 168

Balla, Emil, 35–36, 168
Bardtke, Hans, 3, 168
Barth, Christoph, 35, 38–39, 49, 56, 111, 157–58, 168
Barth, Karl, 26, 39, 45, 168
Bastide, Roger, 147, 168
Bauks, Michaela, 110, 168
Baumann, Eberhard, 7, 168
Baumgarten, A. I., 124, 168
Baumgartner, Walter, 35–36, 168
Becker, Joachim, 25, 158, 168
Begrich, Joachim, x, 11, 31, 33, 36–37, 50–53, 56–57, 59–60, 62, 67, 69–71, 88, 109–11, 113–14, 121, 127, 130, 144–45, 168, 176

Bell, Catherine, 138, 168
Bentzen, Aage, 14, 25–26, 39, 43, 168–69
Bergler, Siegfried, 4, 17, 169
Berkenbrock, Volney J., 147, 169
Bernhardt, Karl-Heinz, 26, 40, 43, 66, 169
Berridge, John M., 15, 169
Bertalanffy, Ludwig von, 107, 125, 169
Beyerlin, Walter, 14, 22, 25, 37, 49, 52, 55, 60, 161, 169
Birkeland, Harris, 26, 49, 50, 169
Blenkinsopp, Joseph, 58, 169
Boas, Franz, 41, 169
Boling, Robert G., 5, 169
Boström, Gustav, 9, 169
Bousset, Wilhelm, 32
Boyce, Mary, 90, 142, 169
Brettler, Marc Zvi, 154, 169
Briggs, C. A., 32
Bright, John, 15, 169
Brown, William P., 112, 124, 155, 169
Brueggemann, Walter, 108, 118, 120, 124, 155, 164, 169–70
Buber, Martin, 16–17, 170
Budde, Karl, 24, 170
Buhl, Frants, 31
Buss, Martin J., 26, 88, 170

Caplice, R. L., 49, 71, 170
Capone, Stefania, 147, 170
Cardenal, Ernesto, 2, 30, 170

# AUTHOR INDEX

Casetti, Pierre, 121, 170
Cassuto, Umberto, 3
Castillino, G. R., 49, 170
Cheyne, T. K., 32
Childs, Brevard S., 162, 164, 170
Christian, Viktor, 9, 170
Clines, David J. A., 35, 170
Cohen, Gerson D., 30, 170
Coppens, Joseph, 26, 170
Crenshaw, James L., 27, 121, 149, 170, 181
Crim, Keith, 56, 170
Croatto, J. Severino, 162, 170
Cross, Frank Moore, 3, 7, 9, 20, 29, 170
Crüsemann, Frank, 25-26, 37, 50, 52-54, 58, 61, 64, 171
Culley, Robert C., 7-8, 52, 171
Cunningham, Graham, 109, 111, 145-46, 171

Dahood, Mitchell, 3-4, 8, 12, 18, 64, 171
Dalglish, Edward R., 49, 171
Davies, Philip R., 129, 140, 171
Deissler, Alfons, 39, 44, 52, 56, 58, 68, 171
Delekat, Lienhard, 3, 13-14, 25, 37, 49, 55, 62, 171
Dell, Katharine, 149, 171
de Wette, W. M. L., 31
Diebner, Bernd-Jörg, 143, 171
Díez Macho, Alejandro, 9, 171
Dommershausen, Werner, 95, 171
Draffkorn-Kilmer, Anne, 22, 171
Drijvers, Pius, 35, 171
Driver, G. R., 3, 40, 43, 64, 171
Driver, S. R., 31
Dryburgh, Bob, 24, 171
Dubarle, André M., 14, 24, 171
Duhm, Bernhard, 19, 29, 32, 171
Durkheim, Émile, 41, 171
Dussaud, René, 3

Ebeling, Erich, 134, 172
Edsman, Carl-Martin, 40, 172
Eibl-Eibesfeldt, Irenäus, 128, 172
Eichhorn, Albert, 32
Eichrodt, Walther, 45, 172
Eliade, Mircea, 40, 172

Engnell, Ivan, 25-26, 40, 43, 172
Evans-Pritchard, E. E., 40, 134, 172
Ewald, Heinrich, 31

Falkenstein, Adam, 28, 172
Fensham, F. C., 44, 172
Feuillet, André, 5, 14, 172
Fischer, Balthasar, 30, 172
Fisher, Loren R., 3
Fohrer, Georg, 6, 24, 172
Fortune, R. F., 55, 172
Frankfort, Henri, 40, 172
Frazer, James George, 41, 172
Frechette, Christopher G., 111, 172
Freedman, David Noel, 6-7, 9-11, 17, 20, 29, 170, 172
Fretheim, Terence E. 58, 172

Gaster, T. H., 40, 58, 172
Gemser, Berend, 27, 172
Gennep, Arnold van, 28, 172
Gerstenberger, Erhard S., ix-x, 4, 15, 19, 21-25, 29, 46, 49, 69, 74, 80, 85, 87, 89, 91-93, 95, 102-3, 105-6, 108-11, 113-14, 117-19, 121, 123-24, 129-32, 134-35, 137, 139, 141, 143, 145-46, 149-50, 152, 154, 165, 173-75
Gese, Hartmut, 3, 25-26, 29, 37, 175
Gevirtz, Stanley, 8, 24, 175
Gill, Sam, 138, 175
Ginsberg, H. L., 7, 58, 64, 175
Globe, Alexander, 26, 175
Goldingay, John, 175
Good, E. M., 7, 175
Goodenough, Erwin R., 11, 175
Gordon, Cyrus H., 3, 43, 64
Gottlieb, Hans, 4, 175
Gottwald, Norman K., 5, 17, 21, 25, 29, 164, 175
Gray, George Buchanan, 5, 17, 175
Gray, John, 3, 26, 58, 175
Gressmann, Hugo, 32
Griffin, Emory A., 107, 175
Griffin-Pierce, Trudy, 147, 176
Grimes, Ronald L., 128, 138, 176

Gunkel, Hermann, x, 19, 25–26, 28–29, 31–39, 43, 47–48, 50–54, 56–57, 59–60, 62, 64, 67–74, 88, 108

Haïk Vantoura, Suzanne H., 22, 176
Halbe, Jörn, 27, 176
Hallo, W. W., 49, 176
Haran, Menahem, 143, 176
Hartenstein, Friedhelm, 109, 176
Heeßel, Nils P., 110–11, 146, 176
Heiler, Friedrich, 31, 176
Hengel, Martin, 129, 176
Herder, J. G., 33, 40
Herkenne, Heinrich, 160, 176
Hermisson, Hans-Jürgen, 54, 69–70, 176
Hillers, Delbert R., 4, 14, 25, 176
Holladay, William L., 15, 176
Homan, M. J., 3, 176
Hooke, S. H., 40, 43, 176–77
Horst, Friedrich, 5, 36, 177
Hossfeld, Frank-Lothar, 141, 160, 177

Iser, Wolfgang, 107, 125, 177

Jacobson, Diane, 149, 177
Jahnow, Hedwig, 24, 35–36, 177
Jennings, Theodore W., 177
Jeremias, Alfred, 41
Jeremias, Jörg, 45, 99, 177
Johnson, Aubrey R., 15, 31, 40, 43, 66, 177
Johnson, B., 117, 183

Kant, Immanuel, 70, 125, 177
Kapelrud, A. S., 3, 31, 35, 177
Kayser, Wolfgang, 20, 177
Kedar-Kopfstein, Benjamin, 117, 177
Keel, Othmar, 11, 15, 110, 118, 177
Keet, C. C., 62, 178
Kippenberg, Hans G., 135, 178
Kittel, Rudolf, 32, 36, 178
Klatt, Werner, 31–32, 37, 178
Kluckhohn, Clyde, 147, 178
Knierim, Rolf, xi
Knuth, Hans Christian, 30, 178
Koch, Klaus, 37, 44, 58, 178
Kolari, E., 21, 178
Kosmala, Hans, 5, 17, 178

Kramer, Samuel N., 12, 14, 23–24, 178
Kraus, Hans-Joachim, 5, 14, 25–27, 30, 35–36, 39, 52, 56, 58, 60, 62–63, 67, 72, 143, 178
Krecher, J., 49, 178
Krinetzki, L., 59, 68, 178
Kuenen, Abraham, 31
Kunz, L., 7, 178
Kurz, Paul K., 2, 30, 178
Kutsch, Ernst, 37, 63–64, 179

Lambert, W. G., 42, 68, 71, 179
Lanczkowski, G., 142, 179
Lang, Bernhard, 128, 139, 179
Leslie, Elmer A., 27, 35, 56, 179
Leveen, Jacob, 4, 179
Lévy-Bruhl, Lucien, 41, 179
Ley, Julius, 6, 179
Liebreich, Leon J., 18, 179
Lipinski, Edouard, 26, 59, 179
Littmann, Enno, 24, 179
Lods, Adolphe, 31, 179
Loewenstamm, S. E., 3
Lohfink, Norbert, 141, 157–59 162–63, 179
Long, Burke O., 24, 179
Loretz, Oswald, 3–4, 92, 179–80
Lowth, Robert, 5, 33
Lys, Daniel, 24, 180

Mand, Fritzlothar, 25, 180
Mansoor, Menahem, 3, 180
Maul, Stefan M., 109, 111, 113, 129, 131, 134, 142, 146, 180
Mauss, Marcel, 120, 180
Mayer, Werner R., 28, 111, 134, 180
McCarthy, Dennis J., 45, 180
Melamed, Ezra Z., 18, 180
Mendenhall, George E., 44–45, 180
Michel, Diethelm, 11–12, 37, 65, 180
Miller, Patrick D., v, 93, 99, 108–10, 113–14, 120, 124, 145, 157–58, 180
Montgomery, James A., 7, 180
Moor, Johannes C. de, 3, 26, 180
Moore, G. F., 31
Morgenstern, J., 59, 180

Mowinckel, Sigmund, x, 5–7, 13, 15, 19,
    22, 25–27, 31, 33–35, 40, 42–43,
    47–50, 52, 54, 56–60, 62–74, 88,
    108, 110–11, 121, 127, 130, 133,
    149, 154, 162, 180–81
Muilenburg, James, 16, 181
Müller, Hans-Peter, 24, 88, 181
Muntingh, Lukas M., 29, 181
Murphy, Roland E., 24, 27, 69, 71, 181

Niditch, Susan, 140, 181
Niehr, Herbert, 117, 181
Nielsen, Eduard, 44, 181
Noth, Martin, xi, 40, 43, 181
Nötscher, Friedrich, 39, 181

Oesterley, W. O. E., 63, 181
Ortlund, Eric Nels, 118, 182
Otto, Eckart, 97, 182

Parker, S. B., 42, 179
Patterson, John, 59, 182
Perdue, Leo G., 27, 92, 149, 163, 182
Perlitt, Lothar, 45, 182
Piatti, P. T., 6, 182
Ploeg, J. P. M. van der, 27, 182
Podechard, E., 27, 182
Pope, Marvin H., 3–4, 14, 24, 64, 182
Porten Bezalel, 153, 182
Posner, Ernest, 140, 182
Pröschild, Sibylle, 147, 182

Quell, Gottfried, 44, 182

Rad, Gerhard von, 30, 36, 38, 44–45, 54,
    58, 67, 69–70, 120, 182–83
Reichard, Gladys A., 134, 147, 183
Reinelt, Heinz, 69, 183
Reventlow, Henning Graf, 15, 59, 88,
    183
Reynolds, Kent A., 150, 183
Ribeiro, Darcy, 97, 130, 183
Ridderbos, Nicolaus H., 5–7, 15–18,
    25, 183
Riede, Peter, 110, 183
Ringgren, Helmer, 15, 30, 69, 117, 183
Ritter, E. K., 49, 183
Robertson, David A., 11, 184

Robinson, Theodore H., 5, 184
Rosenzweig, Franz, 16, 170
Rowley, H. H., 59, 72, 143
Rudolph, Kurt, 184
Rudolph, Wilhelm, 6, 24, 184

Sabourin, Leopold, 14, 35, 52, 56, 58,
    60, 67, 184
Sanders, James A., 3, 159, 184
Säve-Söderbergh, Torgny, 184
Saydon, Pierre P., 9, 184
Scharbert, Josef, 81, 135, 184
Schmid, Hans Heinrich, 184
Schmid, Herbert, 184
Schmidt, Hans, 35–37, 49, 55–56, 184
Schmidt, Uta, 107, 184
Schmidt, Werner Hans, 66, 184
Schmökel, Hartmut, 14, 23, 24, 184
Schmuttermayr, Georg, 4, 184
Schneekloth, Larry Gilbert, 4, 30, 185
Schoenborn, Ulrich, 87, 175
Schroer, Silvia, 94, 185
Sciadini, Patricio, 30, 185
Searle, John R., 125, 185
Segal, Moses H., 24, 185
Segert, Stanislav, 6, 185
Seux, M.-J., 28, 185
Seybold, Klaus, v, 15, 22, 25, 81, 185
Shehata, Dahlia, 154, 185
Sievers, Eduard, 6, 185
Skehan, Patrick W., 7, 27, 69, 185
Smith, Jonathan Z., 185
Snaith, Norman H., 59, 185
Soden, Wolfram von, 28, 172
Soggin, J. A., 25–26, 185
Spencer, Katherine, 147, 185
Staerk, Willi, 35–36, 185
Staiger, Emil, 10, 185
Stamm, J. J., 35, 185
Stauder, Wilhelm, 21, 186
Stegemann, Hartmut, 142, 186
Stolz, Fritz, 127, 163, 186
Sukenik, Eleazer L., 3, 186

Talayesva, Don C., 134, 186
Thieberger, Frederic, 14, 186
Thureau-Dangin, F., 42, 186

Toorn, Karel van der, 92, 94, 113, 130, 143, 186
Towner, W. Sibley, 59, 186
Trible, Phyllis, 27, 29, 186
Troeltsch, Ernst, 32
Tröger, K.-W., 142, 186
Tropper, Josef, 92, 186
Turner, Victor, 29, 134, 186
Tur-Sinai, Naftali H., 25, 186
Tylor, Edward B., 41, 186

VanGemeren, W. A., 113, 186
Vaux, Roland de, 63, 72, 186
Velden, Frank van der, 110, 186
Virolleaud, Charles, 3
Volz, Paul, 40, 42, 186
Vorländer, Hermann, 30, 110, 186

Wanke, Gunther, 26, 37, 68, 186
Warren, Austin, 20, 187
Watson, Rebecca Sally, 118, 187
Watters, William R., 7, 187
Weir, Cecil J. Mullo, 13, 187
Weiser, Artur, 22, 25, 27, 36, 44–47, 56, 187
Weiss, Meir, 10, 14, 17, 20, 187
Welke-Holtmann, Sigrun, 107, 187
Wellek, Rene, 20, 187

Wellhausen, Julius, 29, 31–32, 98
Werner, Eric, 21–22, 187
Westermann, Claus, 25–26, 29–30, 35–36, 38, 49, 52–53, 58–59, 61, 65, 124, 187
Wevers, J. W., 49, 52, 56, 187
Whallon, William, 8, 187
White, John B., 24, 47, 187
Widengren, Geo, 14, 25–26, 40, 43, 49, 52, 114, 134, 187
Williams, Neal D., 13, 187
Willis, John T., 7, 40, 188
Wilson, Gerald Henry, 141, 158, 160–64, 188
Winckler, Hugo, 41, 188
Winter, Urs, 94, 188
Wolff, Hans Walter, xi, 25, 49, 188
Wrede, William, 32
Wünsch, G., 33
Würthwein, Ernst, 69, 188
Wyman, Leland C., 134, 188

Zenger, Erich, v, 141, 158, 160, 185, 188
Zgoll, Annette, 109, 188
Zimmerli, Walther, 159–60, 188
Zimmern, Heinrich, 41, 142, 188
Zuesse, Evan M., 138, 188

# Scripture Index

## Old Testament

### Genesis

| | |
|---|---:|
| 1:1–5 | 118 |
| 4:23–24 | 15 |
| 12:7 | 129 |
| 14:18 | 68 |
| 24 | 24 |
| 28:20–21 | 92 |
| 31:34 | 93 |
| 32:23–33 | 111 |
| 49 | 15 |

### Exodus

| | |
|---|---:|
| 5–15 | 153 |
| 13:14 | 153 |
| 13:8–9 | 153 |
| 14–15 | 100 |
| 15:1–19 | 61 |
| 15:20 | 21, 61 |
| 15:21 | 15, 26, 61, 89 |
| 17:8–16 | 100 |
| 21:6 | 93 |
| 23 | 114, 150 |
| 23:3 | 98 |
| 23:14–17 | 60, 63 |
| 24:7 | 140 |
| 32:18 | 22 |
| 34 | 114, 150 |
| 34:12 | 42 |
| 34:22–23 | 60 |

### Leviticus

| | |
|---|---:|
| 1–7 | 129 |
| 8–9 | 129 |
| 11–15 | 129 |
| 13:2–8 | 145 |
| 16 | 123, 129 |
| 16:19 | 98 |
| 23 | 60, 114, 150 |
| 23:34–44 | 42 |
| 25 | 150 |

### Numbers

| | |
|---|---:|
| 5:11–31 | 21, 55, 110, 129, 145 |
| 10:1ff. | 21 |
| 21:13–14 | 23 |
| 21:14 | 16 |
| 23:7–10 | 15 |

### Deuteronomy

| | |
|---|---:|
| 1:17 | 98 |
| 5:1 | 152 |
| 6:4–9 | 152 |
| 6:20 | 153 |
| 11:18–21 | 153 |
| 12 | 144 |
| 16 | 114, 150 |
| 16:1–7 | 60 |
| 16:19 | 98 |

## Deuteronomy (continued)

| | |
|---|---:|
| 17:18–19 | 152 |
| 18:15 | 153 |
| 19:1–13 | 55 |
| 20 | 100 |
| 29–31 | 82, 139, 150 |
| 29 | 140 |
| 31:19–22 | 151, 152 |
| 31:24–27 | 151 |
| 31:30 | 142, 151 |
| 32 | 15, 23, 150 |
| 32:44–47 | 142 |
| 34:10 | 153 |

## Joshua

| | |
|---|---:|
| 1:8 | 152 |
| 4:6 | 153 |
| 4:21 | 153 |
| 24 | 139, 152 |
| 24:14–18 | 150 |

## Judges

| | |
|---|---:|
| 4–5 | 100 |
| 5 | 1, 15, 26, 61, 78, 135 |
| 5:2–31 | 61 |
| 6:25–32 | 78 |
| 8:22–23 | 149 |
| 9 | 90 |
| 9:8–15 | 149 |
| 11:34 | 61 |
| 14 | 24 |
| 16 | 24 |
| 16:23–24 | 61 |
| 17:1–5 | 93 |
| 17:5 | 78 |
| 17:10 | 78 |
| 20:26–28 | 57 |
| 21:2–3 | 57 |
| 21:11 | 23 |
| 21:19–21 | 77 |

## 1 Samuel

| | |
|---|---:|
| 1–2 | 76 |
| 1 | 25, 47, 96 |
| 1:10–13 | 132 |
| 1:15 | 133 |
| 1:24—2:10 | 52–53 |
| 2 | 163 |
| 2:1–10 | 132, 145 |
| 7–12 | 90 |
| 8:1–18 | 149 |
| 9 | 78 |
| 9:12 | 23, 135 |
| 9:13 | 93 |
| 9:16 | 93 |
| 9:19–20 | 23 |
| 19:13 | 93 |
| 19:16 | 93 |
| 20:6 | 135 |
| 20:29 | 135 |

## 2 Samuel

| | |
|---|---:|
| 1:18 | 16 |
| 1:19–27 | 24 |
| 1:19–24 | 15 |
| 2:1–10 | 15 |
| 3:33–34 | 24 |
| 6 | 62 |
| 6:14–15 | 119 |
| 6:14 | 22 |
| 7 | 79 |
| 7:14 | 66 |
| 12:15–23 | 131 |
| 15:7 | 148 |
| 18:7 | 22 |
| 18:10 | 22 |
| 22 | 15, 79, 108, 132 |

## 1 Kings

| | |
|---|---:|
| 8:23–53 | 144 |
| 8:30–32 | 55 |
| 8:31–53 | 148 |
| 8:41–43 | 148 |
| 14:1–3 | 110 |
| 14:3 | 131 |
| 17:24 | 145 |
| 18:21–40 | 152 |

## 2 Kings

| | |
|---|---:|
| 1:1–2 | 110 |
| 1:2 | 131 |

## SCRIPTURE INDEX

| | | | |
|---|---|---|---|
| 4 | 76 | 5:3 | 112, 150 |
| 4:13 | 76 | 5:4 | 132 |
| 4:18–37 | 145 | 5:5–7 | 51 |
| 4:32–35 | 131 | 5::8 | 132 |
| 5 | 145 | 6:2 | 51 |
| 22:8–23 | 140 | 6:9 | 54 |
| 23:21 | 129 | 6:10 | 51 |
| | | 7 | 55 |
| | | 7:11 | 93 |
| **1 Chronicles** | | 7:18 | 51, 131, 158 |
| 15:16 | 118 | 8 | 18, 64, 78, 80, 96, |
| 16 | 15, 33, 139, 163 | | 118, 150, 158 |
| 16:7–36 | 153 | 8:2 | 81, 118 |
| | | 8:10 | 81, 118 |
| **2 Chronicles** | | 9/10 | 69, 80, 91, 121, |
| 6 | 82 | | 149, 151, 158 |
| 17:9 | 140 | 9:2 | 158 |
| 20:19 | 118 | 9:12–15 | 17 |
| 29–30 | 82 | 9:12 | 17, 23 |
| 34:29–33 | 140 | 9:13 | 17 |
| 35 | 82 | 9:14 | 17 |
| | | 9:15 | 17 |
| | | 9:19–20 | 23 |
| **Job** | | 11 | 93, 132 |
| | 107, 112 | 11:4 | 18 |
| 28 | 117 | 12 | 18, 80, 96, 148 |
| 30 | 1 | 13:2–3 | 17 |
| 33:23–28 | 145 | 13:6 | 51 |
| 33:23–24 | 131 | 14 | 80, 122 |
| 38–42 | 119 | 15–24 | 160 |
| 38–41 | 117 | 15 | 62, 80 |
| | | 16 | 80, 93, 148 |
| | | 17 | 55 |
| **Psalms** | | 17:8 | 95 |
| | | 18 | 45, 56, 57, 79, 90, |
| 1–60 | 163 | | 101, 119 |
| 1 | 17, 27, 80, 82, 90, | 18:2–4 | 53 |
| | 104, 121, 122, | 18:5–20 | 53 |
| | 123, 137, 149, | 18:8–16 | 99, 118 |
| | 150, 158, 160 | 18:33–49 | 61 |
| 1:1 | 69 | 18:47–49 | 53 |
| 1:2 | 121, 140, 151 | 19 | 80, 82, 90, 115, |
| 2 | 43, 46, 66, 79, 90, | | 121, 122, 123, |
| | 104, 159, 160 | | 137, 149, 150, 160 |
| 2:7 | 66 | 19:1 | 104 |
| 3–14 | 160 | 19:2–5 | 123 |
| 3:8 | 51 | 19:4c | 104 |
| 4 | 93, 132 | 19:5a | 104 |
| 4:6 | 132 | 19:7 | 104 |

## Psalms (continued)

| | |
|---|---|
| 19A | 46, 64 |
| 19B | 27 |
| 20 | 18, 51, 56, 57, 79, 90, 101 |
| 21 | 56, 57, 79, 90, 101 |
| 21:13 | 136 |
| 21:14 | 81 |
| 22 | 96 |
| 22:1–9 | 51 |
| 22:1 | 110, 133 |
| 22:3 | 115 |
| 22:6–7 | 132 |
| 22:10–11 | 51, 92 |
| 22:10 | 95 |
| 22:11 | 93 |
| 22:13–19 | 51 |
| 22:21 | 112 |
| 22:23–32 | 148 |
| 22:30 | 3–4 |
| 23 | 91, 93, 148 |
| 24 | 26, 33, 62, 119 |
| 24:1 | 104 |
| 24:2–4 | 104 |
| 24:7–10 | 104, 129 |
| 25 | 17, 69, 149 |
| 26 | 55 |
| 26:1 | 51 |
| 26:4–6 | 51 |
| 26:6 | 22, 129, 132 |
| 26:11 | 51 |
| 27 | 93 |
| 27:10 | 93 |
| 28 | 80 |
| 29 | 46, 78, 80, 100, 115, 164 |
| 29:1–2 | 17 |
| 29:1 | 100, 115 |
| 29:3–5 | 17 |
| 30:2 | 53 |
| 30:3–4 | 53 |
| 30:5–6 | 53 |
| 30:9–12 | 53 |
| 31:2–6 | 51 |
| 31:15 | 93 |
| 31:20–25 | 51 |
| 32 | 148, 163 |
| 33 | 64, 80, 121, 149 |
| 33:20–22 | 136 |
| 34 | 17, 69, 80, 149 |
| 34:12 | 69 |
| 35–41 | 160 |
| 35:1–8 | 51 |
| 35:3 | 112 |
| 35:11 | 132 |
| 35:13–14 | 129, 131–32 |
| 35:13 | 132 |
| 36:8 | 95 |
| 37 | 17, 27, 69, 80, 91, 121, 122, 149, 150, 151, 158 |
| 37:1–8 | 69 |
| 37:1 | 122 |
| 37:16 | 69 |
| 37:21 | 69 |
| 38 | 95, 96 |
| 38:1–9 | 51 |
| 38:2 | 51 |
| 38:11–15 | 51 |
| 38:18 | 51 |
| 38:20–21 | 51 |
| 39 | 80, 82, 91, 106, 121, 149, 150, 158, 163 |
| 39:2 | 122 |
| 39:5–7 | 123 |
| 39:5 | 122 |
| 40 | 165 |
| 40:3–4 | 53 |
| 40:5 | 53, 110 |
| 40:6 | 53 |
| 41:6–10 | 93 |
| 42–49 | 153, 160 |
| 42/43 | 7 |
| 42:5 | 63 |
| 42:7 | 132, 165 |
| 43:4 | 131 |
| 44 | 46, 57, 58, 80, 81, 91, 96, 98, 136 |
| 45 | 24, 43, 46, 51, 79, 90, 101, 159 |
| 45:7 | 79 |
| 46 | 26, 67, 80, 81, 82, 136, 137, 151 |
| 46:2–8 | 67 |

| | | | |
|---|---|---|---|
| 46:9 | 67 | 60 | 58, 80, 81, 136 |
| 47 | 26, 42, 46, 65, 47, 81, 104, 119, 136, 137 | 60:2 | 133 |
| | | 61 | 80 |
| | | 61:3 | 132 |
| 47:2 | 66, 129 | 62 | 80, 93, 132, 148 |
| 47:3 | 66 | 63:2 | 93 |
| 47:4 | 66 | 63:3 | 132 |
| 47:6 | 65 | 63:5 | 132 |
| 47:7 | 66 | 63:8 | 95 |
| 47:9 | 18 | 64:3–7 | 54 |
| 48 | 26, 33, 63, 67, 48, 81, 82, 119, 136, 137, 151 | 65 | 43, 63, 77, 96 |
| | | 65:2–5 | 78 |
| | | 65:10–14 | 77–78 |
| 48:2 | 67 | 66 | 80, 81, 136 |
| 48:3 | 67 | 66:1–13 | 82 |
| 48:13–14 | 67 | 66:1–12 | 65 |
| 48:13 | 22, 129 | 66:8–12 | 58 |
| 49 | 26, 80, 91, 121, 122, 149, 150, 158 | 66:13–15 | 53 |
| | | 67 | 46, 58, 63, 80 |
| 49:2–5 | 69 | 67:7 | 78 |
| 49:13 | 123 | 68 | 26, 46, 61, 63, 78, 80, 98, 119 |
| 49:21 | 123 | | |
| 50–51 | 165 | 68:8–11 | 99 |
| 50 | 45, 80, 137, 139, 153, 163 | 68:12–15 | 61 |
| | | 68:25–28 | 129 |
| 50:5 | 150 | 68:25–26 | 61, 129 |
| 50:7 | 150 | 68:25 | 61 |
| 50:8–23 | 150 | 68:26 | 22 |
| 51:2 | 133 | 69:2b–5 | 51 |
| 51:5–7 | 51 | 69:8–13 | 51 |
| 51:19 | 132 | 69:11 | 132 |
| 51:21 | 132 | 69:20–22 | 51 |
| 52 | 80 | 69:23–29 | 51 |
| 53 | 80 | 69:33–37 | 51 |
| 54:1 | 133 | 71 | 80, 150, 151 |
| 54:6 | 93 | 71:3–6 | 110 |
| 55 | 96 | 71:3 | 93 |
| 55:15 | 62 | 71:4–6 | 150 |
| 56 | 93 | 71:17–18a | 92–93 |
| 56:1 | 133 | 71:22 | 131 |
| 56:13 | 51 | 72 | 56, 79, 90, 101 |
| 57:1 | 133 | 73–83 | 153 |
| 57:2 | 51, 95 | 73 | 27, 80, 91, 121, 149, 150, 151, 158 |
| 57:8–9 | 131 | | |
| 58 | 58, 80 | 73:13 | 129, 132 |
| 59:1 | 133 | 74 | 57, 58, 80, 81, 136, 151 |
| 59:3 | 54 | | |
| 59:8 | 54 | 74:13–15 | 118 |

## Psalms *(continued)*

| | |
|---|---|
| 75 | 80, 81, 136 |
| 76 | 26, 67, 80 |
| 76:8 | 67 |
| 76:12 | 67 |
| 77 | 42, 46, 65, 80 |
| 77:3 | 132 |
| 77:17–20 | 99, 118 |
| 78 | 11, 23, 65, 80, 98, 101, 118, 122, 149, 150 |
| 78:1–2 | 69 |
| 78:65–66 | 61 |
| 79 | 58, 80, 81, 82, 136, 137 |
| 80 | 58, 80, 81, 82, 136 |
| 81 | 45, 46, 80, 137 |
| 82 | 46, 80, 164 |
| 82:1 | 100 |
| 83 | 58, 80 |
| 84–85 | 153, 160 |
| 84 | 62, 67, 80 |
| 84:2 | 62 |
| 84:3 | 62 |
| 84:4 | 150 |
| 84:5–6 | 62 |
| 84:9 | 132 |
| 84:11 | 62, 132 |
| 85 | 80, 81, 136 |
| 86 | 80 |
| 86:2 | 51 |
| 87–88 | 153, 160 |
| 87 | 26, 67, 80, 151, 165 |
| 88:9 | 93 |
| 88:10 | 132 |
| 88:19 | 93 |
| 89 | 56, 57, 66, 79, 80, 91, 96, 98, 101, 164 |
| 89:7–12 | 118 |
| 89:20–38 | 57 |
| 90 | 80, 81, 82, 91, 121, 123, 136, 149, 150, 158, 164 |
| 90:1 | 122 |
| 90:12 | 123 |
| 91 | 70–71, 80, 95, 129 |
| 91:2–6 | 95 |
| 91:4 | 95 |
| 91:14–16 | 71 |
| 92 | 129 |
| 93 | 26, 42, 65, 80, 104, 115 |
| 93:1–4 | 118 |
| 93:1 | 11, 65 |
| 94 | 80, 118 |
| 95–99 | 100, 104 |
| 95 | 80, 81, 82, 121, 136, 137, 139 |
| 95:6 | 132 |
| 95:7–11 | 101 |
| 96–99 | 26, 65 |
| 96 | 42, 80, 115, 117, 163 |
| 96:1–3 | 66 |
| 96:1 | 115 |
| 96:3 | 115 |
| 96:6 | 66 |
| 96:7–9 | 66 |
| 96:7 | 115 |
| 96:10–13 | 115–16 |
| 96:13 | 117 |
| 97 | 42, 80 |
| 97:1–5 | 118 |
| 97:1 | 65 |
| 97:2–5 | 66, 99 |
| 97:6 | 66 |
| 98 | 80, 119 |
| 98:4–8 | 66 |
| 99 | 42, 80, 99 |
| 99:4 | 66 |
| 99:6–7 | 66 |
| 99:7 | 66 |
| 100 | 80, 81–82, 136, 100 |
| 100:1–5 | 136 |
| 101 | 56, 57, 66, 80 |
| 102 | 129, 148 |
| 103 | 80, 81, 97, 118, 136 |
| 103:1–2 | 118 |
| 103:8–13 | 97 |
| 104 | 42, 46, 64, 78, 80, 100, 118 |

| | | | |
|---|---|---|---|
| 104:1–9 | 118 | 119:9 | 122 |
| 104:1 | 100, 118 | 119:12–13 | 103 |
| 104:2–9 | 100 | 119:147–48 | 103 |
| 104:27–30 | 119 | 119:151–52 | 103 |
| 104:31–35 | 119 | 120–34 | 62, 133, 151 |
| 105 | 11, 65, 80, 98, 122, 150 | 121 | 62, 80 |
| 106 | 46, 80, 81, 84, 91, 98, 101, 122, 136, 150 | 122 | 26, 62, 67, 80, 81, 129, 136 |
| | | 122:1–2 | 129 |
| 106:1 | 164 | 122:1 | 62 |
| 106:47–48 | 164 | 122:3 | 62 |
| 107 | 114 | 122:6–9 | 62 |
| 107:1 | 53 | 123 | 81, 136 |
| 107:4–32 | 148 | 124 | 46, 58, 80, 81, 82, 98, 136 |
| 108 | 80, 81, 136 | | |
| 109 | 96 | 126 | 62, 65, 80 |
| 109:6–20 | 51 | 129 | 46, 58, 80 |
| 109:24 | 132 | 130 | 80 |
| 109:30 | 51 | 130:1 | 110 |
| 110 | 43, 51, 66, 79, 90, 101, 104, 159 | 131 | 80, 93 |
| | | 131:2 | 95 |
| 110:4 | 68 | 132 | 26, 42, 56, 63, 67, 80, 90, 101, 119, 129, 151 |
| 111 | 6, 17, 80, 149 | | |
| 112 | 6, 17, 69, 80, 149 | | |
| 112:1 | 69 | 132:6–7 | 129 |
| 113 | 80 | 132:7 | 132 |
| 114 | 65, 80 | 133 | 95 |
| 114:3–8 | 118 | 134:2 | 132 |
| 115 | 65, 80, 81, 82, 136 | 135 | 65, 80 |
| 115:4–7 | 150 | 135:15–18 | 150 |
| 116 | 148 | 136 | 33, 65, 81, 98, 129, 136, 150 |
| 116:17 | 132 | | |
| 117 | 80 | 136:1–26 | 17, 89 |
| 118 | 80, 81, 96, 136, 148 | 136:1–9 | 64 |
| | | 137 | 80, 91 |
| 118:1–4 | 53 | 137:5 | 165 |
| 118:8–9 | 53 | 138:2 | 53, 132 |
| 118:15–16 | 61 | 138:4–6 | 53 |
| 118:19–20 | 62 | 139 | 80, 91, 121, 149, 150, 158 |
| 118:26 | 53 | | |
| 118:27 | 129 | 139:1–12 | 30 |
| 118:28 | 53, 93 | 139:1–4 | 106 |
| 118:33–49 | 61 | 139:1 | 122 |
| 119 | 17, 27, 69, 80, 82, 90, 103, 121, 122, 123, 137, 149, 150, 158 | 139:19–22 | 119 |
| | | 140:7 | 93 |
| | | 141:2 | 1132 |
| | | 142:2 | 132 |
| | | 142:6 | 51 |

## Psalms (continued)

| | |
|---|---|
| 144 | 56, 80, 81, 90, 101, 136 |
| 144:3–4 | 101 |
| 145 | 17, 69, 80 |
| 146–50 | 160 |
| 146 | 80 |
| 147 | 80, 81, 136, 147 |
| 147:10 | 101 |
| 148 | 80, 98, 115, 116, 117 |
| 148:1–14 | 116–17 |
| 148:14 | 117 |
| 149 | 80 |
| 150 | 160 |
| 150:3–5 | 21, 80 |

## Proverbs

| | |
|---|---|
| 1–9 | 153 |
| 15:16 | 69 |

## Ecclesiastes

| | |
|---|---|
| | 112 |

## Song of Songs

| | |
|---|---|
| | 1, 4, 7, 14, 16, 23, 24 |

## Isaiah

| | |
|---|---|
| | 9, 16, 140 |
| 2:3 | 62 |
| 5:1–7 | 7, 15 |
| 5:11–12 | 23 |
| 6:10 | 17 |
| 11:2 | 18 |
| 12 | 1 |
| 14:4–21 | 24 |
| 17:12 | 9 |
| 18:2 | 9 |
| 19:3 | 18 |
| 21:11–12 | 23 |
| 24:8–9 | 23 |
| 27:13 | 21 |
| 38 | 108, 131, 163 |
| 38:1 | 76, 145 |
| 38:2 | 145 |
| 38:9–20 | 15 |
| 38:21–22 | 131 |
| 38:21 | 76, 145 |
| 56:7 | 144 |
| 63:1–6 | 100 |
| 63:7—64:11 | 21, 82, 150 |
| 63:10 | 6 |
| 63:16 | 82 |
| 64:7 | 82 |

## Jeremiah

| | |
|---|---|
| | 16 |
| 7:34 | 22 |
| 10:17–25 | 132 |
| 11 | 122 |
| 11:1–8 | 153 |
| 11:18—12:6 | 15 |
| 12:1–6 | 132 |
| 14 | 82 |
| 14:1–22 | 21 |
| 14:2 | 57 |
| 15:10–21 | 15, 132 |
| 16:8–9 | 22 |
| 17:12–18 | 15, 132 |
| 18:19–23 | 15, 132 |
| 20:7–18 | 15, 132 |
| 36 | 140 |

## Lamentations

| | |
|---|---|
| | 1, 16 |
| 3 | 17 |

## Ezekiel

| | |
|---|---|
| 33:32 | 22 |

## Hosea

| | |
|---|---|
| | 16 |
| 2:10 | 64 |

## Joel

| | |
|---|---|
| 1–2 | 21, 82 |

| Amos | |
|---|---|
|  | 16 |
| 5:1–3 | 24 |
| 5:21–24 | 82 |

| Jonah | |
|---|---|
| 2 | 108, 132, 163 |
| 2:10 | 53 |

| Habakkuk | |
|---|---|
| 3 | 23, 119 |
| 3:3–15 | 99 |

| Zechariah | |
|---|---|
| 9:14 | 21 |

## New Testament

| Matthew | |
|---|---|
| 23:37 | 95 |

| Acts | |
|---|---|
| 8:28 | 140 |